Classical

Feng Shui

for

Wealth &

Abundance

About the Author

Master Denise Liotta Dennis is one of fewer than one hundred genuine Feng Shui masters in America today. She has studied with four noted Feng Shui masters from China, Malaysia, and Australia, including Grand Master Yap Cheng Hai, and she belongs to his four-hundred-year-old Wu Chang Pai Feng Shui Mastery lineage. Born to an entrepreneurial family, Denise possesses more than thirty years of business ownership experience and is among a rare breed of Feng Shui consultants. Denise divides her time between Scottsdale, Arizona, and her hometown of Houston, Texas.

To Write to the Author

If you wish to contact the author or would like more information about this book, please write to the author in care of Llewellyn Worldwide, and we will forward your request. Both the author and the publisher appreciate hearing from you and learning of your enjoyment of this book and how it has helped you. Llewellyn Worldwide cannot guarantee that every letter written to the author can be answered, but all will be forwarded. Please write to:

Master Denise Liotta Dennis
℅ Llewellyn Worldwide
2143 Wooddale Drive
Woodbury, MN 55125-2989

Please enclose a self-addressed stamped envelope for reply,
or $1.00 to cover costs. If outside the USA, enclose
an international postal reply coupon.

Many of Llewellyn's authors have websites with additional information and resources. For more information, please visit our website at www.llewellyn.com.

Classical
Feng Shui
for
Wealth &
Abundance

Activating Ancient Wisdom
for a Rich & Prosperous Life

MASTER DENISE LIOTTA DENNIS

Llewellyn Publications
Woodbury, Minnesota

FIRST EDITION
First Printing, 2013

Book design by Bob Gaul
Cover art: Background © iStockphoto.com/Yap Siew Hoong
        Border © iStockphoto.com/MeiKIS
        Coins © iStockphoto.com/dibrova
Cover design by Ellen Lawson
All interior art © Llewellyn art department except Figure 13: Chinese Luo Pan/
        Compass © *Guide to the Feng Shui Compass* by Stephen Skinner,
        published 2010 by Golden Hoard Press/Llewellyn Publications.
Editing by Laura Graves

Llewellyn Publications is a registered trademark of Llewellyn Worldwide Ltd.

Library of Congress Cataloging-in-Publication Data (Pending)
978-0-7387-3353-1

Llewellyn Worldwide Ltd. does not participate in, endorse, or have any authority or responsibility concerning private business transactions between our authors and the public.
   All mail addressed to the author is forwarded, but the publisher cannot, unless specifically instructed by the author, give out an address or phone number.
   Any Internet references contained in this work are current at publication time, but the publisher cannot guarantee that a specific location will continue to be maintained. Please refer to the publisher's website for links to authors' websites and other sources.

Llewellyn Publications
A Division of Llewellyn Worldwide Ltd.
2143 Wooddale Drive
Woodbury, MN 55125-2989
www.llewellyn.com

Printed in the United States of America

This book is dedicated to my father,
L. D. Dennis—the Builder

Contents

Acknowledgments

Feng Shui is like a good friendship—it takes time, space, and effort to develop a long-lasting relationship that will stand the test of time. I am deeply grateful for the friends and mentors who brought luck and symmetry to my life.

Without my Feng Shui teachers—Grandmaster Yap Cheng Hai, Kuala Lumpur, Malaysia; Grandmaster Joseph Yu, Ontario, Canada; Master Gayle Atherton, Sydney, Australia; and Nancilee Wydra, Florida, USA—none of this would have come to fruition. I am especially grateful to Grandmaster Yap, my primary teacher and mentor, who taught me the most secretly held knowledge of Feng Shui, much of which is revealed in this book.

I'd like to extend much gratitude to all of my amazing clients, with special thanks to William and Joan Porter. Much love to my dear friend Joanie Sharpe who has always been there for me, and to my extraordinary friend Julia Griffin.

I also want to thank my family for their love, support, and encouragement, including my beloved son, Mark Weightman; my beautiful daughter-in-law, Amanda Weightman; and my gorgeous grandchildren Makenzy, Kaitlyn, and Grayson, who inspire me to bring forth this information to future generations. My dear sister, Linda Dennis, thanks for your love and laughter!

I dedicated this book to the loving memory of my father, L. D. Dennis. He had such an enormous influence on my life's work. As a little girl, I followed and emulated his lead as he buzzed around the building industry, wheeling and dealing. From him I learned passion—something you don't learn in school. I wish to express love and appreciation to my beautiful mother, Rosalie M. Liotta Dennis, who is still missed after all these years. And finally, I'd like to extend my deep appreciation to my former husband, Bud Weightman, for his generous financial support while I attained my world-class Feng Shui education.

Enormous pride and thanks to my personally mentored Master graduates—Katherine Gould and Jennifer Bonetto. I'm equally proud of my soon-to-be masters: Peg Burton, Porcha Frost, Nathalie Ekobo, and Marianne Kulekowskis. I wish to acknowledge my esteemed colleagues whose association I greatly value and whose Feng Shui practice and teachings are a credit to the world: Jennifer Bartle-Smith, Australia; Maria Santilario, Spain; Bridgette O'Sullivan, Ireland; Cynthia Murray, Colorado; Jayne Goodrick; England; Di Grobler and Christine McNair, South Africa; Angle de Para, Florida; Scheherazade "Sherry" Merchant, India; Nathalie Mourier and Helen Weber, France; and Birgit Fischer, Petra Coll-Exposito, Nicole Zoremba, and Eva-Maria Spöetta, Germany.

—Master Denise Liotta Dennis

Introduction

I'm the daughter of a builder, and for my whole life I've been fascinated with buildings, homes, landscaping, and the art of arranging space. With no formal training in interior design, people sought my opinion and taste at a very young age. My life took me on a journey of exploring spirituality and the world of metaphysics, which began in my mid-twenties. I became a true seeker of arcane knowledge.

So, how does a fast-talkin' girl from Texas become a Feng Shui Master? While in a bookstore one day in the mid-1990s, a friend held up a Feng Shui book and said, "Denise, you should study this, you would be great! You're so good at designing interiors, and Feng Shui has an element of the esoteric. Besides, look at all the Chinese objects in your home." Her simple comment and observation set things in motion, turning my life in a totally different direction. I went from barely pronouncing the words "Feng Shui" to learning from one of the world's most respected and famous Grand Masters in Kuala Lumpur, Malaysia. In learning, practicing, and teaching Feng Shui, I discovered myself and my purpose.

Early on, it was readily apparent that most Feng Shui Masters were male and Chinese, and they did not feel compelled to write books revealing their techniques or the "secrets of the universe" as they are often called. I had a very different philosophy—one that included sharing genuine Feng Shui with as many people as would listen.

This book reveals what you didn't know to ask about Feng Shui. Numerous works have been penned about this intriguing subject, but few have spoken of the real-wealth potential locked inside these ancient secrets. Among these pages, you will experience firsthand Classical Feng Shui and its fundamental principles. You will also learn about a little-known discrepancy between traditional or Classical Feng Shui, developed and practiced in Asia for thousands of years, and the new schools or Westernized Feng Shui, which began in the 1970s. Though developing expertise in this practice requires time, effort, and patience, this book will assist you in identifying environmental features that can bring financial success—or economic disaster. You will also discover an abundance of wealth-building wisdom known and practiced almost exclusively by highly-trained Feng Shui Masters around the world.

The first two chapters cover Feng Shui history and some of the basic principles that are also known as the building blocks of Chinese metaphysics. Next, we learn about money-depleting features, since no amount of otherwise good Feng Shui can overcome these obstacles. There are Master's Tips throughout the book; I think you will find them very informative. Don't forget to look at the generous glossary of terms to deepen your understanding of the Feng Shui language used in the book.

Chapters 4 and 5 look at the two main methods of Feng Shui for wealth-building: using your personal Gua (Eight Mansions) and good-luck directions, and using your building's natal chart (Flying Stars). The second one is a complicated method, but do not despair! Chapters 6 and 7 do all the work for you and are the most hands-on for non-masters to work with; just grab a compass and look up your building's natal chart to read the wealth-enhancing tips. This extremely valuable information applies to both the Northern and Southern Hemispheres—so no matter where you are located in the world, the recommendations will work. The most advanced methods of increasing wealth are shared in chapter 8, and these are the most secretly held ones.

Even though these techniques are complex (and do require a professional to properly design one, or even two, specifically for your site), I feel it is very important to introduce you to them and what they can bring to your life. With this in mind, I have given you a sample of most of the formulas so that you can see how they work. Please understand that even *without* some of the extraordinary techniques described in chapter 8, if you follow the recommendations presented in chapters 6 and 7 that apply to your home, you will enjoy excellent Feng Shui and increase your riches! However, if you feel you are destined to be a millionaire or billionaire, you may want to avail yourself of the techniques in chapter 8 by hiring a master. At the back of the book, you will find a list of Feng Shui consultants and general guideline for fees.

Some of the exciting, secret techniques discussed in the book are used by the Feng Shui Masters for business moguls Donald Trump and Steve Wynn. Thirty billionaires call Hong Kong home. This Asian financial center ranks fifth on *Forbes* magazine's top ten cities for billionaires. It's not surprising that evidence of Feng Shui-inspired design abounds in every corner of this modern metropolis. But Feng Shui isn't just for the affluent; it's for everyone.

Keep in mind while reading the book that Feng Shui specifically helps improve your luck in the most important aspects of the human experience—money, relationships, and health. But remember, Feng Shui isn't a cure-all. It must work in tandem with solid financial acumen. Even the best applications of these Chinese axioms will not save you from bad investments, shoddy business deals, and the repercussions of misused Feng Shui. While Feng Shui is not the definitive solution—nothing is—it does give you a distinct advantage in life's ups and downs. I hope you find a few jewels in the book and begin increasing your wealth today. Some of the most powerful and influential people in the world use Feng Shui to their advantage. Whatever you think personally of Donald Trump, you cannot deny his incredible success. You may not agree with or subscribe to gambling, but you cannot ignore that Steve Wynn has enjoyed the lion's share of success in the casino world. And there are thousands of other businesses and individuals who continually benefit from the wisdom and practicality of Classical Feng Shui.

Note, I said thousands, not millions, because millions are not aware of authentic Feng Shui. And even fewer have ever been exposed to the level described in this book. You, reader, are among a select few who are the first to hear about the most secret aspects of this ancient knowledge. Once you have, use it. May you always have great wealth in every area of your life!

Enjoy,

Master Denise Liotta Dennis

Scottsdale, Arizona

Note: In this book I have used the Chinese-to-English translations of both the official pinyin and the nonstandard Wade-Giles method. If you're not familiar with these terms, pinyin is the internationally recognized Roman transliteration of Chinese characters. It was officially adopted by the People's Republic of China in 1979. The Wade-Giles system of transcription, developed by sinologists Thomas Wade and Herbert Giles in the late nineteenth century, served as the Chinese-to-English benchmark for most of the twentieth century. For instance, the word chi *(pronounced "chee") is spelled* ch'i *according to Wade-Giles and* qi *in pinyin.*

I use these two translations because until recently more than 95 percent of all Feng Shui books printed in English followed the Wade-Giles method. Newer texts, of course, are increasingly incorporating the pinyin translation, which is now accepted throughout China. Thankfully you don't have to learn Chinese to understand Feng Shui. In some cases, though, three different terms apply to the same idea. Because of this, I've included the most popular version and what I learned from Grand Master Yap Cheng Hai.

One

The Power of Feng Shui: How It Really Works

*If you understand, things are just as they are; if you
do not understand, things are just as they are.*

Zen Proverb

Classical Feng Shui:
The Secrets of an Esoteric Praxis

Classical Feng Shui provides a powerful collection of wealth-building
tools if executed in accordance with ancient principles. That's not, however, the case when it comes to contemporary, popular applications. Like
the shag carpets and the avocado dining sets of the seventies, Feng Shui
is a trend; it's all the rage. But when the amulets, crystals, and candles
fail to bring fame, fortune—even a bit of serenity—consumers are left
spiritually bankrupt and with a houseful of expensive tchotchkes.

To successfully implement Feng Shui as the Eastern world does, Westerners must understand this venerable doctrine as a comprehensive approach to a balanced life. And unless you've traveled the Far East extensively or lived in Hong Kong, Singapore, Taiwan, or Malaysia; or you're a disciple of classical or traditional Feng Shui (either term is correct)—you probably haven't experienced its pure essence.

That is why it is important to grasp what Feng Shui is not. Turn on the television, surf the web, or read any book about this subject and you'll discover plenty of DIY Feng Shui tips and tricks from self-proclaimed digital gurus. These so-called experts have distilled Feng Shui from an all-encompassing science to color and object placement—banish TVs from the bedroom, avoid sofa sets, open the doors, don't open the doors, paint those southern walls red, and so on. Hawkers of modern-style Feng Shui sell it as either an Asian-inspired interior design contrivance or a sustainable, eco-friendly approach to living in harmony with the environment.

Perhaps part of the problem lies in mainstream media's simplistic and uninformed presentation of Feng Shui. Television programs, such as *Dateline*, shows on HGTV (Home & Garden Television), and *Oprah* carve it into delicious pieces of information, easily digested by the viewing audience. And voilà! A hip, new morsel of pop culture for public consumption—a Westernized and diluted version of ancient, scientific principles.

Classical Feng Shui is far more complex. Consider this: mirrors and blue northern walls in an ancient master's tamped-earth hut? Probably not. The point is, past and present masters follow the strict application of these techniques in their living spaces.

As practitioners of true Classical Feng Shui, the masters have sought to resolve this East-versus-West philosophical conundrum. How does one enlighten the public and the design community, replace watered-down interpretations with the true meaning of Classical Feng Shui, and transform oral tradition and into words on a page?

Classical Feng Shui: Past and Present

The English translation of Feng Shui—"wind and water"—aptly describes society's relationship over the eons with this dynastic relic. Wind changes direction; water ebbs and flows. Like most trends, Feng Shui, throughout its four-thousand-year history, has fallen in and out of vogue with the public. But that's only part of it. Political doctrines, too, have suppressed, even endangered, the popularity and the practice of Feng Shui in China.

Communism—in little more than half a century—has thwarted the progress of a metaphysical movement that has evolved over thousands of years. The disintegration of Feng Shui in Chinese culture started in 1966 with the Great Proletarian Cultural Revolution. Communist Party leader Mao Zedong demanded an end to Chinese antiquity, and with the help of the Red Army, launched a zealous massacre of all things created before 1949. He called these edifices of Chinese culture the Four Olds: Old Custom, Old Culture, Old Habits, and Old Ideas.

Many masters fled the People's Republic of China during these dark days of despotic oppression. They found refuge in Taiwan and Hong Kong, then a British colony. Today, this autonomous territory—the unofficial seat of Classical Feng Shui—provides shelter to a thriving hub of the Four Olds. Other members of the Feng Shui community followed the defeated Chinese general Chiang Kai-shek to the island of Taiwan. Some say that the Chinese nationalists who joined the deposed leader smuggled a treasure trove of ancient Feng Shui books from the Forbidden City in Beijing.

Taiwan also defines its bustling business culture through the power of Feng Shui. There, the discipline flourishes as an integral aspect of design and construction, transforming this once agrarian society into an international financial powerhouse. In his early twenties, Grand Master Yap Cheng Hai traveled there to study Feng Shui with several learned scholars.

Though the Cultural Revolution eased up after Chairman Mao's death in 1976, the practice of Feng Shui is still illegal in the People's Republic of China, and it has suffered greatly; its nonpractice disrespecting the natural environment with the "Iron Man" mentality[1]. Restrictions against Feng Shui, however, continue to relax as Communist tenets fail to meet the demands of a financially sophisticated and environmentally savvy younger generation (Spencer 2008). Case in point: Beijing Capital International Airport. Designers incorporated Classical Feng Shui elements into this ultra-modern, Olympic-friendly hub to greet the global sporting community for the 2008 Summer Games (*Seattle Times*, 2008).

But even the Chinese want in on the action, if it means a promotion or not losing a job. Some members of the Iron Rice Bowl—mostly civil servants and military personnel who once enjoyed airtight job security—are paying consultants top dollar to reconfigure their offices with the prosperity-enhancing energy of Feng Shui (Reuters, 2007).

Thus, West meets East. As the Orient gains financial momentum in the global market, you can bet your bottom dollar that Asian investors will want some of that good chi. Chinese, Taiwanese, and other Far Eastern financiers are increasingly nudging their overseas business partners—including plenty of U. S. megafirms—to espouse Classical Feng Shui in the architecture of their buildings. Even as far back as the early nineties, this mixing of Eastern capital with American moxie has been reported by the media. Everyone, from local real estate brokers to major celebrities such as Donald Trump, is receiving the Asian treatment: no Feng Shui, no money (Dunn, 1994).

---

1. The Iron Man mindset—man against nature—started with Mao and continued with Iron Man Wang. Refer to the book *China Shakes the World* by James Kynge.

Feng Shui Meets the Metropolitan Tycoon

He said it to John Larson on *Dateline*; he said it to Bob McKeown on the *CBS Evening News*—he even addressed a younger audience on VH1's *The Fabulous Life*. When it comes to innovation, all-around mogul Donald Trump believes in the power of Feng Shui. He's not afraid to admit it or capitalize on the latest and greatest (or in this case, ancient) trend. And that's exactly what he did beginning in the mid-1990s. Hoping to improve the life force of his projects, the developer-cum-superstar consulted with the world's premier practitioners. They helped Trump transform the not-so-enlightened former Gulf and Western building into the opulent Trump International Hotel and Tower, and it wouldn't have been official without some pre-construction pomp and circumstance. And though Trump may not sprinkle himself with a post-shower dusting of cinnabar powder anytime soon, he's found the Taoist sweet spot, and he's sticking with it. Trump said it best: "We study it, we work on it, we actually hired somebody—an expert. It's important to adhere to the principles of a large group of people who truly believe these principles, and if they believe in them, then that's good enough for me." (Interview with Bob McKeown, January 1995, *CBS Evening News-Eye on America*)

Trump, however, hasn't cornered the Feng Shui market by a long shot. Sheldon Adelson, Stanley Ho? Okay, how about Steve Wynn? This trio of casino barons are to the gaming industry what Marcus Loew, William Fox, and Adolph Zukor were to the entertainment business: money, brawn, and genius. They are bitter rivals when it comes to who builds the biggest, best casino. Adelson, Ho, and Wynn, however, agree on one thing: Feng Shui.

Las Vegas? Passé. Víva Macau! VIP gamblers with the money, the time, and the resources flock to Sin City East: Macau and the Cotai Strip. The CIA, yes, the Central Intelligence Agency, reports that Macau is the world's largest and most lucrative gaming center. Fortune-savvy casino denizens of Asia expect plenty of good Feng Shui to maximize their luck, wealth, and prosperity. No surprise there. That's why Adelson, Ho, and Wynn seek the wisdom of the masters when it comes to developing their ultra-modern resorts.

With the exception of huge projects like Disneyland, major banks and large corporations in Hong Kong, a few master-planned communities scattered throughout southeast Asia, and some of Trump's buildings, *casinos* are using the most sophisticated forms of Classical Feng Shui. I say hurrah for Wynn, Ho, Adelson and others; their empires grow daily, which demonstrates the wealth-building potential of Classical Feng Shui's potent formulas. What a pity that the news is not filled with large Feng Shui projects throughout the world that involve living and working spaces for everyday life, not just gambling.

Western Feng Shui:
Popular, Recognized, and Mainstream

Feng Shui is often mistaken as a religion; it is not. That is why it is so important that the brazen pioneers of industry, such as Trump, Wynn, and Adelson, publicly embrace it. Their enthusiasm has energized the resurgence of Feng Shui among practitioners and the public.

In the mid-1980s, internationally renowned professor Thomas Lin Yun, a Tibetan Buddhist monk, founded Tibetan Black Hat Tantric Feng Shui (TBHT) and introduced it to the Western world. Like most monks (or nuns), Lin Yun possesses a working knowledge of Chinese medicine, martial arts, and Feng Shui. TBHT focuses specifically on the Ba Gua, one of the basic tenets of Feng Shui (see the glossary for more information on the Ba Gua). Lin Yun relied on his extensive teachings in the healing arts and Eastern philosophy to simplify the Ba Gua—a diagram that identifies the profound mysteries of energy in the eight directions—for a Western palate. Stephen Skinner, author of the *Keep It Simple* series, described Lin Yun's American debut in his book *K.I.S.S. Guide to Feng Shui*:

The arrival of Professor Lin Yun in the United States from Taiwan via Hong Kong in the 1980s, and the work of his pupil Sarah Rossbach, put Feng Shui on the map in the U. S. Initially, Lin Yun taught a fairly traditional style of Feng Shui, but soon found, at that early stage, that a simpler form of Feng Shui was required. Accordingly, he modified the Ba Gua and launched it in the 1985 as Tibetan Black Hat Tantric Buddhist (TBHT) Feng Shui. *(73)*

By allying Feng Shui with Buddhism, he gave Feng Shui a cloak of spiritual respectability, and by adding in the mystery of the Black Hat Tibetan Lamaism, he distanced it from its Chinese roots. "Tantric" was the final seductive addition that made Feng Shui far more popular in the United States than it would have been otherwise.[2]

Lin Yun called his revision of the Ba Gua the Eight Life Stations or the Eight Life Aspirations (easily recognized by terms such as the "wealth corner," "marriage corner," "fame sector," and so forth.) It served as the mainstay of Feng Shui in America for many years and is perhaps the reason behind the widely held perception of Feng Shui as a religious practice. When words such as "holiness," "sect," and "temple" are tossed in the popular vernacular, all sorts of assumptions take place. Furthermore, most of Lin Yun's students are also trained in Buddhist invocations and chanting as part of a consultation. Though these rituals can be wonderful experiences, they are not a part of the study or practice of Classical Feng Shui. Regardless of the unorthodox nature of TBHT, Feng Shui in general may not have been as well known if it hadn't been for Lin Yun's work.

---

2. The TBHT and Western styles of Feng Shui were also the most practiced and recognized in Europe, Australia, New Zealand, Mexico, and Canada.

Over the years, variations of Lin Yun's newfangled Feng Shui, though not considered TBHT, have cropped up everywhere and are Westernized versions. Western Feng Shui achieved mainstream status in the late 1990s, when it was featured extensively in books and on popular television programs. Feng Shui even found its way into commercials.[3] Western schools of practice, including TBHT, employ similar Feng Shui ideas and cures—Lin Yun's Eight Life Stations, symbols of fortune, coin-choked frogs, clever lighting arrangements, unique colors and wall hangings, live plants and animals, and aesthetically pleasing furniture arrangement. Western Feng Shui reminds me of a favorite Texas saying: "all hat, no cattle." That is, Western Feng Shui has lots of style but no meat.

Feng Shui is not a spiritual pursuit; it does not spawn miracles, create magic, or bring overnight results. Its true purpose will help attract success, protect against misfortune, generate opportunities, enhance the quality of life, create a supportive space, and maximize potential. Be careful of experts, books, and other resources that make outlandish claims or promises. Feng Shui is not by any means a quick fix. Rather, good Feng Shui evolves over time to generate deep, lasting results. The outcomes will depend on the quality of energy near and around your home or property.

MASTER'S TIP

Mainstream Western Feng Shui, or TBHT Feng Shui, is not authentic Feng Shui—the kind that has been practiced for thousands of years. If you have used Western Feng Shui and experienced results, wonderful. Most likely your home design falls in line with some basic precepts of Classical Feng Shui. Or perhaps your site holds energy well. Classical Feng Shui comprises hundreds of layers, and that's what makes it so effective, even in modern times.

---

3. The latest is Red Robin's (hamburger restaurant chain) promise on a Houston, Texas, billboard which states "Tummy Feng Shui."

Eastern and Classical Chinese Feng Shui

Many schools, textbooks, and manuscripts have documented Eastern or Classical Feng Shui—the metaphysical science of energy in relationship to the environment. Basically, Classical Feng Shui has three main functions—corrective, to remedy existing problems; constructive, to enhance wealth or health or create specific outcomes; and predictive, to expose the past, accurately describe the present, and foretell the future. Outcomes are infinite because people are complex, and so are the structures we live in. The scholars of old China embraced this secret school of knowledge and developed it into a sustainable, scientific, and practical cultural canon. The genesis of this ancient form of Feng Shui dates back at least 4,000 years. Its present-day incarnation of complexity, however, includes the past 1,500 years. Many cultures have something akin to Feng Shui. For instance, the Hindus follow Vastu Shastra, a set of metaphysical design principles that maximize the flow of energy. Though Feng Shui is also widely practiced in Tibet, Vietnam, and Korea, the Chinese took it to unparalleled heights of sophistication. In ancient times, Feng Shui was considered too potent for the common citizenry, so it was reserved for royalty, the powerful, and the privileged. Later, thanks to the charitable work of Master Yang Yun Song, everyone had access to this information and could help themselves. Yang, known as the savior of the poor, developed his own school of Feng Shui during the Tang Dynasty, which lasted from 618 to 907 AD.

Modern-day masters and pioneers, such as Grand Master Yap Cheng Hai, Grand Master Joseph Yu, Master Larry Sang, Master Peter Leung, Master Raymond Lo, Master Eva Wong, Stephen Skinner, and the prolific author Lillian Too, introduced authentic Classical Feng Shui to the Western world, particularly North America, which was still attached to Black Hat and Western Feng Shui.

In essence, Feng Shui was born out of the observation of the environment. Some people experienced fantastic success, while others faced great difficulty, depending on where they lived. The ancients deduced that the energy of a location had something to do with it, so they posed questions. Would living near water or close to mountains affect people's luck and life events? The Chinese were tenacious in documenting the results of their studies. Over thousands of years they formulated the sophisticated body of knowledge that is the Feng Shui of today. Part of it involved the development of schematics and the organization of systems and techniques to assess environs, which included designing layouts, predicting outcomes, and altering the energy of a site. Feng Shui eventually came to address the following three areas of life: wealth, relationships, and health. Thus, all techniques were formulated to encompass and amplify these fundamentals of the human experience. The environment, man-made or natural, can either support life or destroy it.

Directional energy—the flow of energy to your home or building— dictates the quality of a site. Therefore, Classical Feng Shui relies on a compass known as a Luo Pan to determine physical orientation. The Luo Pan is the main and most essential instrument of a Feng Shui Master or practitioner. Once a compass direction of a property is ascertained, a wealth of information is revealed. Western styles of Feng Shui do not use the Luo Pan. Its deliberate exclusion is what author Stephen Skinner likes to call the "dumbing down" of Feng Shui.

These two different approaches cannot be mixed together in assessing or designing a site. Classical Feng Shui, including all its various techniques, is a living science, deeply rooted in the traditional texts and practices based on thousands of years of empirical observation and knowledge. Tossing a few amulets and colored walls into the mix only cheapens the experience.

MASTER'S TIP

If your Feng Shui Master or practitioner does not show up with a Chinese compass or Luo Pan, you are not experiencing genuine Feng Shui.

The External Environment: How Energy Works

Energy is everywhere; it is the foundation of the practice of Classical Feng Shui. We humans are pure energy, our entire universe is energy, and all things around us emit an energy field. Even the chair you are sitting on to read this book will look like Swiss cheese under a microscope. All things actually comprise more space than we realize. Quantum physics tells us this and more.

In Elizabeth Moran's book *The Complete Idiot's Guide to Feng Shui*, authors Masters Joseph Yu and Val Biktashev describe energy this way:

> Chi moves. It is in perpetual process of change. Chi accumulates, disperses, expands, and condenses. It moves fast, slow, in, out, up, and down. Chi meanders and spirals. It flows along straight, angular, and curved pathways. It rides with the wind (feng) and is retained by water (shui). There's no escaping chi's influence. We are all products of and subject to the enormous power of chi. (Moran, 43)

Rhonda Byrne's groundbreaking book and popular movie *The Secret* explore the universal law of attraction, which is all about the exchange of positive and negative energy. One of the teachers in the movie was among the luminaries asked to weigh in on the subject. He says he gives the same answer when describing God or energy. "It can never be created or destroyed, it always was, always has been. Everything that ever existed is always moving into form, through form, and out of form." (Byrne, 159)

In the language of Feng Shui, modern contrivances, too, imitate Mother Nature. Roads become powerful, fast-moving rivers of energy. Tall, heavy, and still, high-rise buildings emulate virtual mountains by exuding the power and the stature of the real thing. Throughout this book, keep the concepts of real water and virtual water, and real mountains and virtual mountains in mind. It will deepen your understanding of how energy and Feng Shui work together.

Not only do environmental features release powerful energy, they can also affect luck regarding wealth, health, and relationships. I'm not talking about the weather; I'm talking about natural and man-made landforms. Terrain and structures will maintain a particular energy depending on what is nearby. Think about it. How could living next to a cemetery (dead energy), a police station, a huge mountain, a skyscraper, a river, or a major highway not influence you? These spaces expel energy in different ways; human behavior, health, and money react accordingly.

Energy exists on a continuum—from vibrant to dead. Humans resonate with the environment surrounding their home or workplace. This vibration very much affects behavior too. People who live next to cemeteries often feel depressed, unmotivated, ill, lethargic, and forlorn. But the consequences aren't immediate. The cumulative effects of one's environment manifest over months and years. Thus, Feng Shui is the great Chinese discovery of the workings of energy and how it can influence luck and the events in a lifetime.

People get into unlucky homes because of lack of confidence or lack of luck. Many people do not trust their initial instincts when it comes to making a decision. They either didn't want the home they're living in, they settled for a certain house, or they almost passed up a property before buying it. More than once I've about heard about folks leaving a home they loved and going to one that brought them misfortune—divorce, affairs, illness, and bankruptcy—shortly after they moved in. A most unlucky space, indeed. Remarkable, but this happens every day.

We know it is natural for luck to cycle. Sometimes we are on top of the world and everything seems to go our way; other times we feel picked on and nothing is right.

If you want your environment to support your efforts in life, particularly wealth, the information in the following chapters will open your eyes wide! And remember this: Great Feng Shui increases your luck tremendously, but the rest is left up to the other two categories of luck—heaven luck and man luck, explained later. Having said that, if you feel you're on a down cycle in life, good Feng Shui can lift you up and hold you steady.

MASTER'S TIP

There is a big difference between Westernized and Classical Feng Shui. Read books and attend classes on real Feng Shui; hire practitioners who use Classical Feng Shui principles.

Two

....

Chinese Metaphysics: The Art and Science of Feng Shui

....

Learning is a treasure that will follow its owner everywhere.

Chinese Proverb

The principles and tools of Feng Shui are intricate and beautifully complex; the following information is to introduce you to them. Please note that you do not need to master or fully understand them—just sit back and enjoy these titillating concepts. If you are familiar with them, just skip to the next chapter. However, if you wish to review the basic building blocks of Feng Shui and energy, read on. I've made a brief comment on the purpose of each tool or concept, and hopefully it will deepen your appreciation and understanding of its origin.

The Five Metaphysical Arts (Wu Shu)

The Purpose: Feng Shui is part of Chinese metaphysics

The art of Feng Shui is just one of many disciplines of Chinese metaphysics; the five variations evolved by observing the principles of nature in a very different context. Intrinsic in all five categories are the principles of yin-yang, the five-element theory, the Ba Gua, and the Luo Shu.

Rooted in the I Ching, these philosophical tenets—mountain, medicine, divination, destiny, and physiognomy—define the foundation of Chinese culture and have served for thousands of years as a fundamental guide to living. But because of the complexity involved, mastering all of these disciplines is nearly impossible. These studies are deeply profound, rich in content, and mastering *one* would be a worthwhile life accomplishment.

Mountain (Shan or Xian Xue): This category encompasses philosophy, including the teachings of the fourth-century BC philosophers Lao Zi and Zhuang Zi, Taoism, martial arts, qi gong, tai chi chuan, meditation, healing, and diet. This category also encompasses the study of alchemy—the science of prolonging life through specific rituals and exercises, which are deeply rooted in Taoism.

Medicine (Yi): The Chinese follow an integrated, holistic, and curative approach to medicine: acupuncture, herbal prescriptions, and massage fall into this category.

Divination (Po): The Chinese are well known for their intuitive skills and abilities to read and interpret symbols. The divination techniques of Da Liu Ren, Tai Yi mystical numbers, Qi Men, and Mei Hua Xin Yi (Plum Blossom oracle) employ numbers to predict everything from wars to missing persons, to the details of one's past and future.

Destiny (Ming): Most forms of Chinese augury seek to interpret fate and determine the timing of life events; the ancient sages devoted much time and research to this study. The most popular methods of Chinese fortune-telling include *Zi Wei Dou Shu* (purple star astrology) and *Ba Zi* (literally means "eight characters" but is also commonly known as the Four Pillars of Destiny), both of which examine a person's destiny and potential based on their date and time of birth. A complementary form of Ming is the science of divination, Bu Shi, which is analogous to the mathematics of probability.

Physiognomy (Xiang Xue): Master Yap refers to this category as *Sow*, and it involves making predictions based on the image, form, and features of the landscape, the human face and palms, architecture, and grave sites. Feng Shui is the fortune-telling of a building by rendering an accurate observation of the structure's appearance, shape, direction, and other surrounding environmental features.

The Nature of Chi

The Purpose: energy (chi) permeates our universe;
Feng Shui analyzes the quality of energy at property sites

According to the preceding adage, energy (chi) is everywhere. It is carried by the wind, and when chi encounters water, it pools and gathers; therefore, water is filled with this vital energy. Chi, also spelled *qi* (either spelling is pronounced "chee"), is the life-force energy of the universe, heaven, earth, and man. Chi, also referred to as cosmic breath, is present in every living and non-living entity; it can be auspicious, inauspicious, or benign. It is also identified in cultures around the world: *ki* to the Japanese, *prana* to the Hindus, *pneuma* to the Greeks, *ankh* to the Egyptians, *ruah* to the Hebrews, *tane* to the Hawaiians, and *arunquiltha* to the Australian Aborigine.

Chi is the life-force energy that pervades humankind's existence; it is the unseen momentum that moves through the human body and the environment. The art and practice of Feng Shui is about attracting and harnessing good energy to support people. Energy determines the shape and form of the landscape as well as the vitality of all living things. Chi energy falls into three categories: cosmic, earthly, and human.

The classic Chinese philosophical text, the Huainanzi, written in the second century BC, best chronicles the essence of chi:

> Heaven is seen here as the ultimate source of all beings, falls as the formless. Fleeting, fluttering, penetrating, amorphous it is, and so it is called the Supreme Luminary. The Tao begins in the Void Brightening. The Void Brightening produces the universe. The universe produces qi. Qi has bounds. The clear, yang [qi] was ethereal and so formed heaven. The heavy, turbid [qi] was congealed and impeded and so formed earth. The conjunction of the clear, yang [qi] was fluid and easy. The conjunction of the heavy, turbid [qi] was strained and difficult. So heaven was formed first and earth was made fast later. The pervading essence of heaven and earth becomes yin and yang. The concentrated essences of yin and yang become the four seasons. The dispersed (san) essences of the four seasons become the myriad creatures. The hot qi of yang in accumulating produces fire. The essence of the fire-qi becomes the sun. The cold qi of yin in accumulating produces water. The essence of the water-qi becomes the moon. The essences produced by coitus (yin) of the sun and moon become the stars and celestial mark points (chen, referring to the planets).

The following chart describes the formation of chi according to Taoist tradition and Feng Shui. It begins with Wu Chi, the great void or nothingness—the genesis of all things in our universe. The polarities of yin and yang energy then separate and give rise to the legendary yin-yang symbol. This ancient trademark of Chinese culture, also called the Tai Chi, resembles a pair of interlocking fish with two eyes. After that, an equal mix of yin-yang energy known as the Four Images emerges. The Trigrams or Guas (both terms are correct)—made of three lines each—are then formed with a combination of yin and yang energy. The solid lines are male/yang, while the broken lines are female/yin. There are a total of eight Guas or Trigrams; these form the Ba Gua.

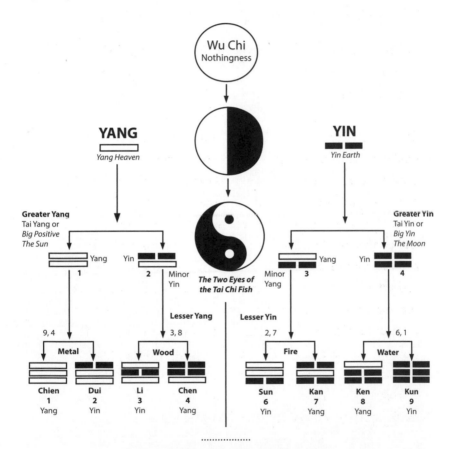

Figure 1: The Evolution of the Eight Trigrams–
This chart shows how chi (energy) grows from nothingness (Wu Chi) then forms Yang and Yin energy, and finally the Trigrams or Guas which represent the eight directions of north, south, east, west, southeast, southwest, northwest and northeast.

The Eight Guas or Trigrams

The Purpose: Feng Shui uses the Guas (Trigrams) to represent the eight directions

The Trigrams, also known as Guas, are about as ancient as it gets regarding Chinese metaphysics—they date back thousands of years. Simply put, the Guas are a global perspective of the universe, and they fully express how the Chinese understand energy. Each Gua has three lines, composed of solid lines (yang energy) or a broken line (yin energy). These three lines also represent the cosmology of heaven, earth and man. The famous Ba Gua is composed of eight Trigrams; *ba* means eight, and *gua* refers to the result of divination.

The eight Trigrams have also been assigned a name describing their energy or essence, such as the gentle, the creative, the arousing, and so forth. These associations to the Trigrams are significant when learning Feng Shui, as they assist in analysing energy more effectively. The Guas contain a goodly amount of information; each one represents yin or yang energy and relates to a family member, an element, a body part, or a possible related illness, a season, a number, human personality types, direction, and natural and human phenomena. Furthermore, they have multiple interpretations and subtle nuances that make understanding them a bit difficult for a novice. Nevertheless, these meanings and interpretations have great importance to Feng Shui and other Chinese metaphysical studies. The eight Guas are Xun, Li, Kun, Dui, Chien, Kan, Gen, and Chen, representing southeast, south, southwest, west, northwest, north, northeast, and east respectively.

The Eight Trigrams (Guas)

Chien Gua

The "Creative" and Heaven
Family Member: Father
Element: Big Metal
Represents the Northwest
Color: Gold, Silver, White
Body Part: Head, Lungs
Luo Shu Number: 6

Kun Gua

The "Receptive"
Family Member: Mother
Element: Earth
Represents the Southwest
Color: Brown, Yellow
Body Part: Stomach, Abdomen
Luo Shu Number: 2

Chen Gua

"Arousing" and Thunder
Family Member: Oldest Son
Element: Big Wood
Represents the East
Color: Jade Green
Body Part: Liver, Feet
Luo Shu Number: 3

Xun Gua

"Gentle" and the Wind
Family Member: Oldest Daughter
Element: Small Wood
Represents the Southeast
Color: Green
Body Part: Liver, Thighs, Buttocks
Luo Shu Number: 4

Kan Gua

The "Abysmal" and Water
Family Member: Middle Son
Element: Water
Represents the North
Color: Black, Blue
Body Part: Kidneys, Blood
Luo Shu Number: 1

Li Gua

"Clinging" and Fire
Family Member: Middle Daughter
Element: Fire
Represents the South
Color: Red, Purple, Orange, Pink
Body Part: Heart, Eyes
Luo Shu Number: 9

Gen Gua

"Stillness" and Earth
Family Member: Youngest Son
Element: Mountain Earth
Represents the Northeast
Color: Brown, Yellow
Body Part: Bones, Hands/Fingers
Luo Shu Number: 8

Dui Gua

"Joyful" and the Marsh
Family Member: Youngest Daughter
Element: Small Metal
Represents the West
Color: Gold, Silver, White
Body Part: Mouth, Throat, Lungs
Luo Shu Number: 7

Figure 2: The Eight Guas in detail.

Principles of Yin-Yang

The Purpose: Feng Shui uses the polarity of energy to seek balance at property sites

The white (yang) and black (yin) half circles look like two fish interlocked at the eyes. This legendary Chinese symbol is known as the Tai Chi (pronounced "tie chee"), and it means "mutually correlated opposites." In Eastern philosophy, yin and yang are general terms that describe the mutual correlations and interaction of energy in the natural world. These forces, while being total opposites, complement and complete each other. Therefore, the Tai Chi represents the exquisite pull of these two energies and the notion of opposites—the yin-yang theory and the foundation of energy. This theory is derived from Taoist tradition, dating back thousands of years. The Taoists understood that the polarity of energy emerged first from Wu Chi—limitlessness, or the great void—yet it contained all things or all possibilities.

Figure 3: The famous Yin-Yang symbol–
Represents the polarity of our Universe.

The Twelve Principles of Yin-Yang given by the Yellow Emperor Huangdi, 2698–2598 BC

1. That which produces and composes the universe is the Tao, the undivided oneness or ultimate nothingness.

2. Tao polarizes itself. Yang becomes the active pole of the cosmos; yin becomes the solidified pole.

3. Yang and yin are opposites, and each accomplishes the other.

4. All beings and things in the universe are complex aggregates of universal energy composed of infinitely varying proportions of yin and yang.

5. All beings and things are in a dynamic state of change and transformation; nothing in the universe is absolutely static or completed; all is in unceasing motion because polarization, the source of being, is without beginning and without end.

6. Yin and yang attract one another.

7. Nothing is entirely yin or yang; all phenomena are composed of both yin and yang.

8. Nothing is neutral. All phenomena are composed of unequal proportions of yin and yang.

9. The force of attraction between yin and yang is greater when the difference between them is greater, and smaller when the difference between them is smaller.

10. Like activities repel one another. The closer the similarity between two entities of the same polarity, the greater the repulsion.

11. At the extremes of development, yin produces yang and yang produces yin.

12. All beings are yang in the center and yin on the surface.[4]

---

4. The original principles of yin and yang were taken from *Tao: The Subtle Universal Law and the Integral Way of Life,* translated by Hua-Ching Ni.

Tien-Di-Ren
(The Three Types of Luck/Opportunities)

The Purpose: To understand that good Feng Shui covers roughly 65–80% of overall luck and opportunities

The Chinese identify three types of luck, not to be confused with the three categories of Feng Shui, which are prosperity, health, and relationships. It is known as tien-di-ren (heaven-earth-human) or the cosmic trinity. Tien-di-ren makes a distinction among heaven luck, man luck, and earth luck as affecting humans differently. Each category of the cosmic trinity accounts for a third of your overall luck. However, with excellent Feng Shui, you may increase that significantly more to give you a real advantage in your residence or business.

Heaven luck refers to the fortune bestowed by the heavens: it is destiny. The Chinese believe this is fixed at birth and cannot be controlled or changed by humans. In fact, the heaven luck a person experiences during his or her lifetime is influenced by the good or bad deeds of past lives—Buddhists and Hindus call this karma.

Man luck is the serendipity created by your own efforts and choices—including education, hard work, morals, and beliefs—and your ability to exploit the opportunities that come your way. The best results will come by using Feng Shui.

Earth luck is the realm of Feng Shui. If you live in harmony with the environment and your natural surroundings, you will reap the rewards of benevolent energy and good fortune. This category counts for one third of your overall luck as well, but many masters believe you can double your overall luck with excellent Feng Shui.

The He Tu and Luo Shu (aka Magic Square)

The Purpose: Feng Shui uses these numerical diagrams to unlock the secrets of universal energy

The He Tu and Luo Shu are two distinct mathematical diagrams that represent the universe and form the foundation of Chinese philosophy. The He Tu in particular takes us back to Feng Shui's origins. The secrets of these divinatory tools—mentioned frequently in ancient Chinese literature—are surrounded by mystery and legend. Both diagrams appear as a series of lines connected to black and white dots. Some scholars say the He Tu chronicles the cycle of birth, while the Luo Shu represents the process of death: yin and yang.

The lore of the He Tu began with the reign of the shaman king Fu Xi, who was born in the twenty-ninth century BC. According to ancient texts, this sage ruler witnessed a mythical dragon-horse—bearing strange, unusually patterned markings on its back—emerge from the mighty Yellow River. This motif became known as the He Tu (pronounced "hur too"). As Fu Xi studied these markings (see illustration on the next page), valuable information pertaining to cosmic laws of the universe was revealed. The dots (black are yin and white are yang) of the He Tu illustrate several concepts, including direction, the five elements of Feng Shui, and the flow of chi.

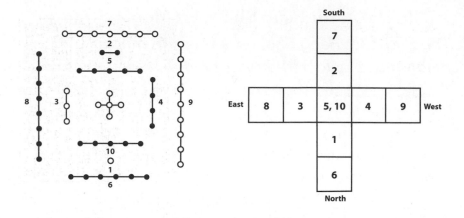

Figure 4: The He Tu River Map–
First represented by "dots" that were discovered on the back of a Dragon-
Horse, then in the "cross" form showing the 4 Cardinal directions.

Subsequent scholars carefully preserved and passed down the wisdom of the He Tu. It is found in written texts and ancient scrolls, and it pervades Eastern ideologies, including traditional Chinese medicine and some of the earliest principles of Feng Shui. The He Tu also forms the basis of the five-elements theory—water, wood, fire, earth, and metal—which identifies, interprets, and predicts natural phenomena. Therefore, it is usually referred to as the Early Heaven He Tu. Later, more advanced symbols—the Guas, or Trigrams—were used to supplement yin and yang and numbers. As a result, these theories gave birth to the first Ba Gua, known as the Early Heaven Ba Gua (Xien Tien Ba Gua).

The Luo Shu is simply a square grid divided into nine sectors, containing nine numbers. The legend of the Luo Shu, also known as the River Book or the Magic Square of 15, dates back to 2100 BC and Emperor Yu of the Xia Dynasty. One day, sitting by the Lo River, a tributary of the Yellow River, Emperor Yu watched a giant turtle amble from the water. He noticed a pattern, a series of dots, lines, and figures emblazoned on its shell (see the left illustration). Each of the Luo Shu's nine grids represents a Trigram, body organ, family member, direction, or element, and is either male or female energy.

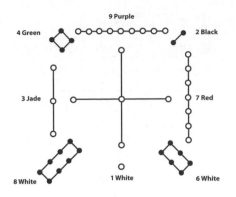

4	9	2
Southeast	South	Southwest
3	5	7
East		West
8	1	6
Northeast	North	Northwest

Figure 5: The Luo Shu River Map–
The Luo Shu aka the "Magic Square of 15" is a wealth of information and a major tool of Classical Feng Shui in assessing energy of a site. Notice that no matter how you add three cells in any direction and you'll get a total of 15. This image also came by way of a giant, mystical turtle from the River Lo in the form of Yin and Yang dots thousands of years ago.

This arrangement of numbers became part of the Later Heaven Ba Gua (LHB). The numbers in any direction add up to fifteen and represent the LHB in its numerical form. The Luo Shu is used extensively in all methods and applications of Classical Feng Shui.

Though the Luo Shu and He Tu are used as "energy" tools to assess land and buildings, these coded maps also represent the cosmology of heaven and earth. The Chinese developed facts about astronomy, geography, Feng Shui, and mathematics based on the He Tu and the Luo Shu. According to historical texts, it is likely that the ancients received this information through meditation or channeling. No matter how they got it, this knowledge is valuable, practical for Feng Shui applications, and helpful in evaluating energy today, as in ancient times.

The He Tu and the Luo Shu date back thousands of years and are ancient oracles considered the backbone of Chinese metaphysics. Learning their mysteries takes many years of study, contemplation, and the assistance of a learned teacher.

The Five Elements: Wu Xing

The Purpose: Feng Shui places energy into five categories

In traditional Chinese philosophy and metaphysics, everything in the natural world can be classified into one of five categories of chi or movements of energy, known as wu xing, the five phases. As is the case with so many brilliant discoveries, nature was the inspiration. The ancients paid close attention to the consistent and predictable cycles of energy—fire burns wood, and metal comes from the earth. By associating this information with the human body and everyday events, the Five Elements theory was born. It offered a feasible solution to evaluating the interaction of energy by placing *all* energy into one of the five categories.

These five elements are metal (jin—literally the word for gold), wood (mu), water (shui), fire (ho), and earth (tu). Each element is a representation of matter and energy as it changes from one form to the next. Wu xing simply illuminates the relationship among these types of energy—and is to be understood as both figurative and literal. It is used extensively in many fields of Eastern thought, such as Feng Shui, Chinese astrology, traditional Chinese medicine, and martial arts. The five elements have three cycles—productive, weakening, and controlling. To master Feng Shui, you must master the Five Elements.

Element	Color	Shape	Physical Objects	Direction	Properties	Number
Fire	Red, purple, pink, bright orange	Triangular, pointed or sharp	Stoves, fireplaces, candles, lamps, computers, microwaves, ovens, outdoor fireplaces/ kitchens, large TVs	South	Heat, radiates and spreads in every direction	9
Earth	Brown, terra-cotta, orange, beige	Square, cubic, flat or broad shapes	Mountains, granite, boulders, crystals, rocks, high ground	Southwest Northeast	Attractive, dense, stables and centered	2, 5, 8
Metal	White, gold, grey, copper	Round and spherical	Swords/ knives, axe, jewelry, gold, silver, copper, bronze, coins, brass, wrought-iron, stainless steel	Northwest West	Sharp, pointing and piercing	6, 7
Water	Black and dark blue	Wavy and indefinite	Ponds, pools, spas, lakes, rivers, streams, oceans, fountains, waterfalls, sidewalks, highways and streets	North	Unfettered, free, runs downhill	1
Wood	Greens	Tall and rectangular	Trees, plants, furniture, bamboo, tall objects	East Southeast	Grows upwards, tall and outwards	3, 4

Figure 6: The Five Categories of Energy (Wu Xing).

The Productive Cycle: Wood feeds fire. Fire produces ash and creates earth. Earth gives birth to metal. Metal melts to a fluid and becomes water, which in turn produces wood.

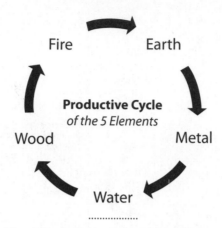

Figure 7: The Productive Cycle of the Five Elements.

The Weakening Cycle: This process is the reverse of the productive cycle, because what we give birth to weakens us. Wood stokes fire; therefore, fire weakens wood. Fire generates ash and creates earth; therefore, earth weakens fire. Earth produces metal; therefore, metal weakens earth. Metal melts to a fluid and produces water; therefore, water weakens metal. Water produces wood; therefore, wood weakens water.

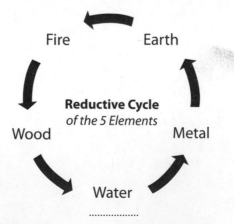

Figure 8: The Reductive Cycle of the Five Elements.

The Controlling Cycle: This process is also known as the destructive cycle. Water extinguishes fire, fire melts metal, and metal cuts wood. Wood, in the form of plants or tree roots, controls the earth by breaking it apart or keeping it together. Earth is big enough to hold water—without earth, water would have no boundary.

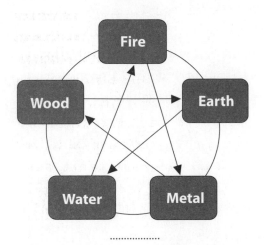

Figure 9: The Controlling Cycle of the Five Elements.

The Two Ba Guas

The Purpose: the arrangement of these two Ba Guas give birth to all Feng Shui formulas/techniques

Any novice to the practice of Feng Shui will recognize the Ba Gua; it appears in many books and discussions on the subject. The Ba Gua is an octagonal map that depicts the eight Trigrams. There are actually two arrangements of the Guas or Trigrams, known as the Early Heaven and Later Heaven Ba Gua.

It is believed that when Fu Xi first drew the Ba Gua, it was a square diagram. As the years passed, the square morphed into a round shape to symbolize the cyclical and contrasting forces of nature. A circle has no beginning and no end; it is most suitable when used to represent the infinite loops of the universe and nature. This first arrangement is known as the Early Heaven Ba Gua—Fu Xi or Xien Tien Ba Gua.

The Early Heaven Ba Gua (EHB), which dates back 6,000 years, depicts the polarities in nature and contains all the principles of Feng Shui. It reflects the ideal world of chi in a constant state of polarization. The Early Heaven sequence represents the pattern of life-force energy in its most polarized form. After all, polarity—the notion of opposites—makes life move. The eight Guas, or symbols, create a conceptual template that tracks changes in energy. Notice the perfect opposites— heaven and earth, fire and water, and so forth. This is the Ba Gua used to deflect sha chi (seen over doors of people's homes), and you can always identify it with the three solid lines at the top.

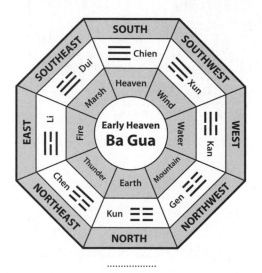

Figure 10: The Early Heaven Ba Gua–
The first arrangement of the 8 Guas, known as the Xien Tien or Fu Xi Ba Gua.

According to lore, the Later Heaven Ba Gua (*Ho Tien* or *Wen Wang Ba Gua)* is the result of the work of King Wen, a Chou Dynasty ruler who elaborated on Fu Xi's earlier diagrams. During his imprisonment in the twelfth century BC, King Wen developed this new sequence of Trigrams to illustrate the cyclical forces of nature. The Later Heaven Ba Gua (Ho Tien Ba Gua), describes the patterns of environmental changes. Unlike Early Heaven Ba Gua, the LHB is dynamic, not static; it represents the ever-changing structure of the universe and the circular nature of life. Many of the Feng Shui applications stem from the understanding of the Later Heaven Ba Gua. For instance, the Luo Shu is the numerical representation of the Later Heaven Ba Gua.

Figure 11: The Later Heaven Ba Gua–
The later arrangement of the 8 Guas, known as the Ho Tien or Wen Wang Ba Gua.

Schools of Classical Feng Shui: San He and San Yuan

The Purpose: Classical Feng Shui is a huge body of knowledge divided into two major schools of study

At its core, Classical Feng Shui is based on the keen observations of the heavens (time), earthly forces (exterior landscapes and interior spaces), and how these elements exchange energy or chi. The origins of Feng Shui date back thousands of years; some sources say it began around 4000 BC. *Kan Yu* is the old term for Feng Shui. In fact, the term *Feng Shui* has only been in use for a little more than a hundred years, since the Ching Dynasty. The golden era of Feng Shui was during the Tang Dynasty between the seventh and tenth centuries AD.

Over time, two main schools of practice emerged, San He and San Yuan. These ideologies form the foundation of Classical Feng Shui. It is important to understand that Feng Shui is highly dynamic and constantly developing, even today. Modern-day Feng Shui Masters combine these schools into one large body of knowledge. But, there are a few who use one or the other exclusively; this is not bad, but rather unusual.

All Feng Shui systems share a common set of principles and theories. For example, all schools refer to the principles of yin-yang, the five elements, the Ba Gua, and the four factors—direction, occupants, time, and location. San He and San Yuan both use a Luo Pan (the Chinese compass) in order to consider the landforms and topography. Many popular Feng Shui books mistakenly describe these two schools as "Form School" and "Compass School," but this would be like an interior designer saying they will incorporate the "color school" and the "shape school" into their design—it is understood that color and shape are integral aspects of design.

The notions of Compass School and Form School came about, no doubt, from the different approaches each theory takes. The San He school places emphasis on examining form, shape, contour, appearance, flow, and confirmation.[5] San Yuan places its focus on time; it considers the influence, qualities, and types of chi and time dimension.[6] Despite the fact that the strategies of these ideologies are slightly different, the objectives are the same—to examine the energy of the site using form, shape, direction, timing, a compass, and the individual themselves who will rent, own, occupy, or develop it.

---

5. This approach to examining the environment is known as Xing Fa or Xing Shi Pai; it places great emphasis on the shape of mountains, the flow and shape of a river, how the land conforms (confirmation), and the contours of the area.

6. This approach, known as Li Chi Pai, has its main focus on direction, timing, and the time dimension of energy. A compass or Luo Pan is used to determine the directional flow of energy.

The San He School

San He, also known as San Hup, means "three harmonies," "three uni-
ties," or "three combinations," depending on the Mandarin or Cantonese translation. It is considered the oldest form of Classical Feng Shui.
The San He school gives great importance and consideration to environmental qualities, such as mountains and topography. The direction,
shape, flow, and appearance of these features were important issues to
evaluate before the construction of a building or when planning a city.
In Neolithic China, Feng Shui was first used to select the ideal location
for a home, a village, or the perfect grave site for an ancestor—known
as the practice of Yin Feng Shui. By the Tang Dynasty, Feng Shui had
blossomed into a science, sophisticated and complex.

Since San He focuses on the environment—mountains, rivers, and
landforms—it strives to understand how the natural landscape shapes
and creates chi. San He techniques are focused on finding the most
advantageous or strategic location in which to extract the chi from the
environment. This school recognizes that chi is dynamic and changes
through time. This notion is based on immutable yin energy, such as
mountains, to counter fluctuating yang energy, such as time cycles. San
He systems do not try to adapt to cycles of chi. Rather, this approach
attempts to insulate against and outlive any unfavorable energy cycles
by selecting or creating superior landforms.

San He also relies on extensive systems and formulas to assess formations for disaster, wealth potential, and good luck. For example, a
Peach Blossom Sha Road formation indicates bad romance and illicit
affairs; an Eight Roads of Destruction (Pa Loo Hwang Chuen) causes
bankruptcy, divorce, and disaster; and an Eight Killing Forces (Pa Sha
Hwang Chuen) suggests bad health, money, and romance. Other formulas—such as the Five Ghost Carry Treasure, a well-guarded secret
from Taiwan, and the Three Harmony Doorways, He Tu Roads, Assistant Star Water Method, Court Official, and Sky Horse—are used to

enhance wealth. Water Dragons fall under this school and are considered the most powerful of the wealth-producing formulas. There are still other techniques such as the 72 Dragons, 120 Gold Divisions, the 60 Dragons, Triple Goat Punishment, and Six Harms—all with various methods in analyzing, enhancing, or adjusting the Feng Shui of a site.

When it comes to large-scale Feng Shui projects, such as master-planned communities, city planning, high-rise buildings, hotels, resorts, airports, hospitals, and so forth, San He is the best approach. Because this system is so highly developed in landforms—natural and manmade—it excels in methodologies that place the structure in relationship to real (and virtual) mountains and water. These macro-level considerations should be addressed prior to attempting the micro-engineering design of any structure. But it is perfectly suited for the average home as well, with numerous techniques that address every area of life.

The San Yuan School

Also known as Three Cycles, San Yuan is the contemporary cousin of San He. In San Yuan, chi is understood as dynamic with the disposition to cycle. Nothing in our universe is stagnating; everything is constantly in motion. Even so, it is possible to identify certain dependable trends. That's why it is necessary to regularly update your Feng Shui to stay current with the time cycles of energy. Both San Yuan and San He take into consideration the factors of time and form. The main difference between the two is that San He gives great credence to forms and San Yuan has an extreme focus on time.

The Flying Stars system (Xuan Kong Fei Xing) and Eight Mansions system (Pa Chai or Ba Zhai) fall under the San Yuan school. These are two of the more popular Feng Shui systems used today, especially for interior Feng Shui. In Flying Stars, an energy map of the property is derived from calculations and used to determine the quality of chi in each sector of the home. Eight Mansions, by contrast, is concerned with harmonizing the occupants with the distinctive energies of the house.

Flying Stars explains why no structure will forever enjoy good or bad Feng Shui as it cycles through time. Every structure has its own unique natal Flying Star chart that gives vital clues to the distinct energy held there. Some Flying Star charts are special and indicate exceptional auspiciousness, including Pearl String Formations (Lin Cu San Poon Gua), Parent String Formations (Fu Mo San Poon Gua), and Combinations of 10. All three are famous for bringing great money or relationship luck. Other techniques, such as the Castle Gate Theory (Sent Mun Kuet), are used to tap the energy of a natural body of water for greater prosperity.

Other Feng Shui techniques that fall under the San Yuan method include Zi Bai (Purple-White Flying Stars); Xuan Kong Da Gua (Big 64 Hexagrams Method), which is excellent for date selection and precision; and Xuan Kong Shui Fa (Time-Space Water Method), used to enhance the site through wealth-producing water features. The Dragon Gate Eight (Long Men Ba Da Ju) method is part of the San Yuan school and is used to attract wealth and enhance career luck.

The San Yuan system also developed and adopted techniques from the San He School, which assess annual visiting negative energies. The Three Killings (Sam Sart), Grand Duke (Tai Sui), and the Year Breaker (Sui Po) can cause disastrous outcomes by disturbing the earth with a digging project such as pool construction or major landscaping. The annual visit of the 5 Yellow Star is also disturbed by digging and construction. The Great Sun Position (Tai Yang Dou San Pan) is a technique devised to counter the effect of these negative energies by selecting a good date to begin your construction or digging project and offers protection from harmful results.

The Robbery Mountain Sha (Chor San Kibb Sart), the calculation of the daily, monthly, and yearly "stars" are other techniques used to assess the Feng Shui, and are part of the San Yuan school. You'll find more information about these negative energies in chapter 3.

The Best School for the Job

Both San Yuan and San He take into consideration the factors of time and form. The main difference between the two systems is that San He gives great credence to forms and San Yuan focuses on time. Neither school is superior to the other except in application or priority of examination. For example, if you are using Feng Shui to design a large, fifty-acre resort, timing is probably not the first priority. When you have a raw piece of land in front of you, the available landforms become the driving force. Therefore, the San He school is best for this situation until you begin designing the structures on the site. At that stage of the project, the San Yuan's Flying Stars will excel in its ability to distribute the chi in the houses and buildings.

At the end of the day, San He and San Yuan have common denominators—they both agree that the factor of time must always be considered and that landforms cannot be ignored. Both systems use the Ba Gua and the Five Elements theory and are intrinsically rooted in the yin-yang principle. Ultimately, San He and San Yuan have one goal: to extract the chi of the environment to support the occupants and enhance the human experience.

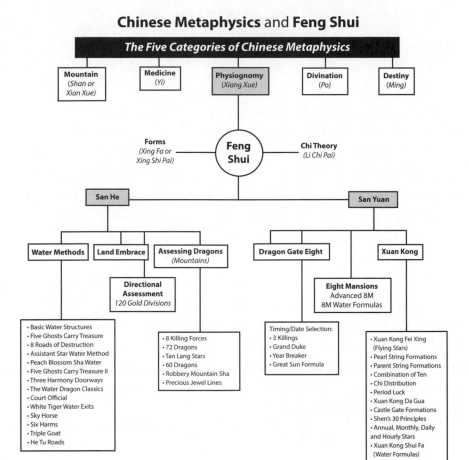

Figure 12: A chart showing the comprehensive studies of Classical Feng Shui.

The Chinese Luo Pan

The Purpose: Feng Shui measures "directional" energy via a compass

The origins of the Chinese magnetic compass, or Luo Pan, date back to the dawn of Chinese civilization. An ancient legend mentions the warrior Goddess of the Nine Heavens presenting the Yellow Emperor Huangdi, the first ruler of a united China, with a compass to defeat his enemies.

Another account of the story chronicles Huangdi's special invention, a compass cart, which forged the path to victory. Either way, the Luo Pan is the quintessential tool of the Feng Shui practitioner.

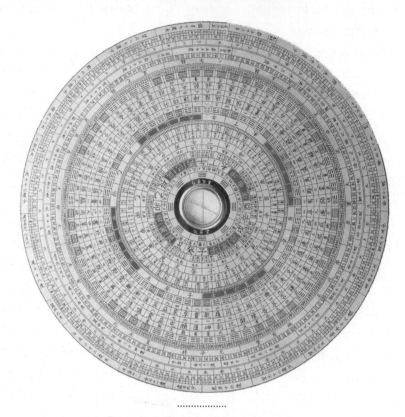

Figure 13: A Chinese Luo Pan or Compass–
A complex, finely crafted compass containing Feng Shui formulas;
the quintessential tool of a Feng Shui Master or Practicioner.

Throughout its illustrious and long history, the Luo Pan has been redesigned, redefined, and refined many times over according to the latest discoveries relating to landforms, techniques, and directional energy. It was and still is a common practice for a Feng Shui Master to design his or her own Luo Pan and embed personal secret formulas reserved for students. Within that framework, however, the basics of Feng Shui fundamentals are always included. There are two standard types of Luo Pans—San He and San Yuan—designed to include formulas of these two major systems of Feng Shui. The third standard Luo Pan is the Chung He, which combines the most important information of the San He and San Yuan Luo Pan.

The purpose of the Luo Pan is the same as a conventional compass—to locate direction. However, the Luo Pan contains some very important differences. A typical compass may display four or eight directions. A Luo Pan divides up the 360 degrees into twenty-four sectors; this is derived by dividing the forty-five degrees of the eight directions into three fifteen-degree increments (3 x 8=24). This is very fundamental in Classical Feng Shui, and this ring on the Luo Pan is known as the 24 mountain ring (not actual mountains, just a term).

Some of the oldest makers and finest craftsmen of Luo Pan are located in Taiwan and Hong Kong. Many newcomers to Feng Shui are awed by the complexity and beauty of the genuine article. The frame is made from fine wood; the rotating metal plate of the Luo Pan is engraved with Chinese characters, compass degrees, and Feng Shui formulas. At the center of the instrument is the heaven's dial or pool: this is the actual compass. In olden days, the compass dial floated in water, but nowadays it is dry-mounted.

Normally, the Luo Pan has between seven and thirty-six rings, depending on the model and to which system it applies. Luo pan vary in size from four to twelve inches—the standard is about ten inches. With so many non-Asians interested in learning Classical Feng Shui, some Luo Pan now include a few rings in English to help the novice. However, learning the Chinese characters associated with Feng Shui and the Luo Pan is preferred by most practitioners, as it establishes a real connection with this ancient knowledge. Either way, it is an impressive and beautiful instrument, truly a work of art and well worth the several hundred dollars it commands.

San Yuan Luo Pan: Used in the Flying Stars and the Xuan Kong systems, the San Yuan Luo Pan is readily identified by the sixty-four hexagrams of the I Ching ring. It has only one 24 mountain ring. The first ring of this Luo Pan is always the Later Heaven Ba Gua arrangement of Trigrams.

San He Luo Pan: The San He Luo Pan, used for San He formulas and methods, is easily identified by its three 24 mountain rings. These rings are used to measure direction, mountains, and water, as each of these elements has distinctly different energy; however, these rings also relate to the three harmonies associated with this school.

Chung He Luo Pan: Also spelled or referred to as Zong He, Zhung He, or Chong He. This Luo Pan is an amalgamation of the San He and San Yuan compasses. This is a great instrument for practitioners who enjoy using both systems. Though some rings have been eliminated for size considerations, all essential rings are in place.

To Feng Shui Masters and practitioners, this extraordinary instrument known as a Luo Pan is "the universe on a plate." For more information on the Luo Pan and its history, refer to Stephen Skinner's book *Guide to the Feng Shui Compass.* It is the most comprehensive book written on the subject.

Three

················

Money-Depleting Buildings, Homes, and Landforms

················

*If you don't change direction, you
may end up where you are heading.*
Lao Tzu

It took thousands of years to discover that where people live and what surrounds them affect their luck and overall ability to thrive, especially regarding wealth. Having great Feng Shui will support your efforts to build assets, but it is not a replacement for good financial acumen. You still must educate yourself on wealth-building strategies. In the book by Donald Trump and Robert Kiyosaki, *Why We Want You to Be Rich*, the authors point out that the vast majority of baby boomers are not financially prepared and will live out their retirement at the poverty level. Make every effort possible to learn about gaining wealth—only live and work in spaces that support you. This chapter may sound a little negative, but I assure you that having this information will empower and insulate you from the bad events described herein.

Many have pondered the question of why some places are good and some are bad, and why some places offer great opportunities and others do not. In his thought-provoking book *The Nature of Things: The Secret Life of Inanimate Objects*, Lyall Watson says:

> It is difficult to describe the difference between "good" and "bad" places in scientific terms. The nearest anyone has yet come to a system of such knowledge is the Chinese practice of *Feng Shui*. This translates literally as "wind" and "water" and embodies an ancient belief that we are linked to our environment by natural forces which make some places more harmonious and auspicious than others. It is part art, part science, combining intuition with a compass, and a set of rules on where and how to build…I know few places where landscaping has been so consistently successful, setting buildings into the environment with what looks like effortless ease. (61)

Essential Topographical Landform Configurations

Gently sloping landforms, rolling hills, and undulating contours are considered excellent Feng Shui. Land that is too steep, completely flat, or severe in any way is regarded as unbalanced and void of vibrant, life-giving energy. Extreme, high, or jagged mountain ranges do not emit benevolent chi either. Not everyone is fortunate enough to find the perfect landforms, so it is often necessary to simulate them. And that's where celestial animals come into play.

To the Chinese, Feng Shui is strongly connected to the celestial animals, namely the Green Dragon, White Tiger, Black Turtle, and Red Phoenix. The celestial animals symbolize important, key land formations that should immediately surround your home site. This is especially important when examining landforms for luck value.

Identifying the needed celestial animals landforms in relation to your house or business is easy. As you look out your front door, the left-hand side is known as the Green Dragon; the right-hand side is called White Tiger. The Black Turtle (or Dark Warrior) resides at the back of your property, while the Red Phoenix (or Vermilion Bird) occupies the front edge of your property. The open space near the front door is called the Ming Tang (bright hall) and is where chi collects.

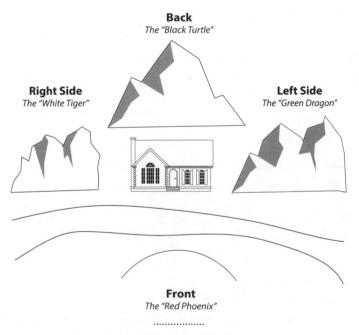

Celestial Animals
(Looking out the front door)

Back
The "Black Turtle"

Right Side
The "White Tiger"

Left Side
The "Green Dragon"

Front
The "Red Phoenix"

Figure 14: The Celestial Animals–
The lyrical names of Black Turtle, Green Dragon, White Tiger and Red Bird simply suggest that energy is contained at a site if it has a subtance (another home, hill, mountain etc.) surrounding it from the back, front, left and right.

Ideally, the celestial animals should be represented by certain landforms. High ground, such as soft rolling hills and ridges, should define the Dragon side—same goes for the Tiger side, but not as pronounced. The Turtle in the back of the property can be a high mountain, but it should not overwhelm the site. The Phoenix, like a low footstool, calls for low ground or a distant mountain. If no ideal landforms surround your living space, or you live in a relatively flat area, other homes can serve as invaluable substitutes. The easiest way to emulate the support needed by landforms is to select a house flanked by other residences. In other words, houses on the left and right sides offer protection. Most modern-day neighborhoods are divided by fences, especially at the back of the property. If your site does not have one, simply create a strong, high backing. You want to be embraced within your home site; this not only protects you but keeps the chi or energy contained. Where energy can collect, pool, or be retained, wealth can accumulate.

For a business to be successful, the left-hand side must be represented; remember this is as you are looking out your front door, not facing the building. If you do not have support on this side, you could experience serious cash flow issues or bankruptcy. People in positions of authority, such as judges, high-powered lawyers, or CEOs, should make sure the right side is higher than the left side, e.g., a two-story home. Without support on the left-hand side, the man of the house could be bullied at work. The celestial animals are Feng Shui Landforms 101—basic but extremely accurate and necessary in building wealth.

Extremely Negative Landforms

In this chapter I will identify the most serious money-eroding formations you will encounter. Some of these are notorious for violating Feng Shui principles and will usually have an immediate effect, while others may take some time to manifest. If you live near two or more of the formations discussed here, your wealth can be depleted in a short amount of time. Pay attention to the following landforms when looking to purchase or lease a home, a building for your business, a parcel of raw land, or office space. These topographical anomalies can, and will, impede your success.

Water, Improperly Placed Water, and Water Exits

Everything is relative, so what constitutes improperly placed water, or water exiting the wrong direction? Both of these considerations factor in the door direction. The proper location of water (such as a pool) on your site is in relationship to the door direction. How water may or may not *exit* is also based on the door direction—generally this means the main, front door (this applies to large, open drains). Although for exits, the back door may also be a considered as well. Once water is introduced to a site, you will have three results regarding your money—a neutral affect, wealth, or bankruptcy or poverty. When real water leaves via an open drain or virtual water (roads or driveways) exits your site which violates Feng Shui principles, money disasters can ensue. The most serious of these formations, such as Eight Roads of Destruction, are addressed in this chapter.

When it comes to manmade water features, the following attributes regarding wealth gain or loss are analyzed: where it is on the site, the direction from which the water flows, and, if it applies, the source and direction of the water's exit. For instance, did your landscape architect design a cool stream, just like the one you saw on a popular television program? Did he also design a drain or water exit somewhere? If any of the basic water principles are not correct, it is possible that wealth could be depleted.

The placement of indoor water features, such as indoor pools, streams, water walls, fish tanks, and fountains, need to follow the same principles as outdoor features. Every home will accept water differently, which is why Classical Feng Shui does not provide a one-size-fits-all solution when it comes to water placement. So watch out for the Western Feng Shui recommendation of placing water in the so-called wealth corner, or in the north—this advice can produce a negative result, as water placement is unique and specific for each building.

Once properly located to bring wealth, a swimming pool should be proportional to and not overwhelm the house. Curved shapes, kidney pools, and ovals are preferred to squares or rectangles: sharp edges can attract sha (negative chi) to the house.

A water feature—a fountain, a water wall, or a fish tank—in a bedroom is never recommended; it will disturb your slumber because moving water is yang. Bedrooms should be yin for deep sleep. One exception to the rule is if you live next to the ocean and keep your doors or windows open—this is allowed. The sound of the ocean is primordial and reminiscent of being in the womb, often lulling people into deep, restful sleep. If you live near the sea, it is best to be in a tall building, such as a condominium or a high-rise. If you're in a private residence, it should be large enough to handle the ocean's powerful energy; otherwise, it can bring you bad luck. Many masters believe the sea is too much water and is too powerful to live next to. However, if you are well placed, it can bring big money as well.

MASTER'S TIP

Get an accurate compass direction of your home. Next, refer to chapter 6 or 7 for the proper placement of water according to your home's facing direction. If you own land next to the ocean, consult a Feng Shui Master or practitioner to orient your home or high-rise correctly in order to receive the wealth benefits it can offer.

Extreme Slopes or Sharp Drop-offs

Craggy sites can make your property, money, and life unstable and elusive, because extreme slopes and drop-offs diffuse and scatter energy. Think of the intensity of water running down a steep ravine. The force moves rocks and displaces dirt—the same happens to your wealth. One of the worst-case scenarios is an extreme grade at the back of a property. The sharper the slope, the more serious the situation. A forty-five-degree incline can precipitate a severe siphoning off of assets. A sheer cliff is even worse. Without the protection of retaining walls, your wealth will quickly slip away. People who move into or build a house on a piece of land like this will experience one bad event after another.

I've seen properties where the land drops off on two or more sides. In some cases, the owners can make a great deal of money, but their wealth is eventually depleted by one thing or another, whether it's a tanking stock market, a hellish divorce, or a bankrupt business. I knew a family that lost more than $2 million in stock investments in less than two years after moving in to a particular home. This house was located in rugged Fountain Hills, Arizona, and extreme drop-offs surrounded all sides of the property. Extreme slopes call for extreme measures: stabilization with extensive landscaping, walls, and hardscapes. Otherwise, your wealth could be in jeopardy. Energy must be able to accumulate and endure to bring you money luck. Note that extreme slopes *toward* the house are equally negative, as they will bring an energy too intense and cause a host of problems with money, health, and relationships.

MASTER'S TIP

Secure extreme slopes with retaining walls, solid fencing, hardscapes, extensive landscaping, or a combination of these techniques. You will get immediate, successful results when your site is protected, and you will feel supported in every area of your life. When land is secure and stable, people thrive. Embracing and holding energy at your site will bring you fabulous money luck.

T-junctures or T-roads

T-juncture or T-road formations occur when two streets intersect, forming the shape of the letter T. One of the most toxic formations for a house or garage is when the structure is situated at the top and center of that T. The road that serves as the stalk of the T acts as a direct conduit of energy to the front door, the place of entry. Energy is good, but too much energy is destructive—energy that moves too fast is called killing energy. The overabundance of energy subjugates the building's occupants, causing discord, money loss, divorce, accidents, and other mishaps.

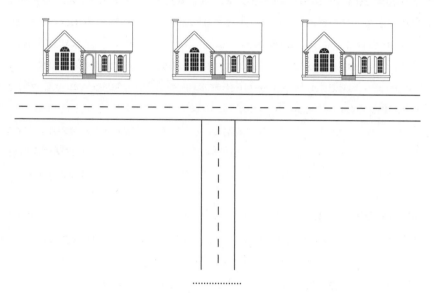

Figure 15: A T-Juncture–
Two roads forming a "T" aimed at the house or door
which can cause a host of money problems.

From an obvious standpoint, a home or a garage at the top and center of the T is a sitting duck, easily hit by cars because of its vulnerable locale. Incidents like these show up in the local news all the time. In Feng Shui, we always prefer to see the main door of a home face the road, but a road coming right to the door is too much and will bring incredibly bad luck. That's why I always advise clients against buying a home on a T-juncture, no matter how great it looks or how good the deal is.

Countermeasures can be applied to slow down the intensity of energy. Primarily, the door must be protected by something with enough substance to stop a car. I have used large landscape boulders, brick walls, and other solid materials. These are necessary for those who have already bought such a home.

I was lecturing for a group of interior designers in Scottsdale, Arizona, at an exclusive furniture store, and we were on the subject of T-junctures. One of the designers told us about a neighbor's home that had been hit three times, even after the owners had installed a protective wall. When I mentioned that these homes are also constantly up for sale, another designer confirmed this. In an eighteen-year period, he knew of a T-juncture house in his neighborhood that changed hands at least six times. You can only take so much bad luck in a house before you finally wake up one morning and say, "We're out of here!"

There are some very rare exceptions when these road formations can benefit the building and occupants, but you will need a skilled Feng Shui Master with experience to properly harness this intense energy.

MASTER'S TIP
Block off a T-juncture with a stucco wall, a solid gate near the front door, boulders, or dense landscaping. Whatever you choose should be enough to stop a car. Protect your door with as much mass as possible. If you're in the market for a home, pass on these residences.

Eight Killing Forces or Eight Mountain Killings
Known in Chinese as Pa Sha Hwang Chuen, this formation is detrimental to your wealth. It happens when the energy of the door direction and the energy of a mountain are in conflict. In urban settings, remember, mountains could be tall buildings.

In Feng Shui, mountains—also known as dragons—are as important as water; they are powerful and will influence your money, health, and relationships. Feng Shui concerns itself with every aspect of a mountain: location, direction, shape, height, color, and even the gaps between mountains. For example, mist hovering over a mountain is called "breath of the dragon," while "blood of the dragon" refers to water flowing down a mountain. A flattop mountain is an earth mountain, and a pointed, triangular-shaped mountain is a fire mountain. The energy from a prominent mountain peak is called "incoming dragon." Each of these mountain features will have an influence on you if you live near one.

Eight Killing Forces is more dangerous than the Eight Roads of Destruction, so it must be remedied. This formation will cause enormously bad luck, such as romance and marriage problems, blood-related accidents, serious injury, disasters, murders, and loss of wealth. What makes this formation particularly harmful is the timing factor, which means the Eight Killing Forces is particularly potent in certain years (year of the Dragon, year of the Dog, and so on) depending on its location.

One example of this detrimental formation is an exterior door facing west (262.6 to 277.5 degrees) and a near mountain located in the southeast direction—here an Eight Killing formation is likely. These formations involve fifteen-degree increments for both the door direction and the mountain. In the above example, the mountain could release its negative force in the year of the Dragon (2012) or the year of the Snake (2013)—or both! This would be devastating to the occupants' wealth and harmony if not remedied. I give all the possible formations in chapters 6 and 7.

MASTER'S TIP

It takes a great deal of practice and skill to determine whether you have the Eight Killing Forces formation because it hinges on such small increments and involves important, exterior doors. Since it is impossible to move a mountain or a building, a Feng Shui Master or practitioner will usually change the degree of the door in question to avoid the "crush of the dragon." They may also modify the driveway degree or move the water, if feasible.

A House Built on Top of a Mountain

Many cultures around the world, including Americans, are addicted to views. After all, who doesn't appreciate a spectacular vista? The problem with a breathtaking panorama, however, is the quality of energy. Sites at higher elevations are vulnerable to all the elements, no matter the area—fierce winds, mud slides, hurricanes, earthquakes, and tornadoes.

This scenario is particularly devastating to businesses and personal relationships. People who occupy these types of homes are exposed to corporate takeovers, infidelity, financial ruin, and underhanded business partners and employees. Think of a giant eagle circling above your home, swooping down, and snatching it and your wealth away with its immense talons.

For these reasons, avoid living in or purchasing a home atop a mountain. Sure, properties with panoramic views are tempting, but the payoff is not worth it. I have heard many horror stories that confirm this basic Feng Shui principle. A generous plateau is better, but it still must be secured because such a site discourages the accumulation of energy. Instead, build your wealth-producing home just below an apex, and use the mountain's girth as support to secure longevity of health, wealth, and relationships.

Many cultures around the world practiced this notion. The cliff-dwelling Anasazi of the western United States built into mountains and cliff faces, using them for fortification and protection. In ancient times, temples, crosses, deities, and public spaces—not homes—were built atop mountains.

That being said, not all mountain homes are bad. If the residence is nestled in the mountain it can be quite auspicious. But seek the advice of an experienced Feng Shui Master or practitioner, because the assessment of mountain energy is quite complex. Though considered yin—still, quiet, and inactive in nature—a mountain exudes vibrant and powerful energy. Therefore, where you place yourself in proximity to one is vital.

MASTER'S TIP
Create a wall around the property of some substance so that the energy can be retained. If you plan to build on such a property, create good support on all sides. Better yet, build so the mountain can be used as backing.

Basement-level Homes and Businesses

In cities all around the world, dwellings—especially townhomes and condominiums—are situated below street level. These spaces are notorious for creating financial misfortune. If you are considering operating a business in a basement-level office, even if the rent is cheap, forget it. This goes for home offices too. You can't succeed if you are below ground, because earth energy is cold, or yin. You need yang energy to make money. People often tell me they experience the presence of ghosts in their basements. Spirits are attracted to dank, yin areas, and that's why businesses should operate elsewhere.

Closed-in, traditional basements in a single-family dwelling, however, are fine for recreation areas, wine cellars, guest and storage rooms, and so on. Just make sure to offset yin energy with yang energy: add a fireplace, a kitchen, or an entertainment center with a television and a stereo. This principle does not apply to walkout basements, which are great since these spaces exude yang energy—lots of sunlight and warmth. These are not true, traditional basements.

A Phoenix-based client of mine, an investor, asked me to take a look at one of his buildings. It was one of his worst performing assets; it had lost money and changed hands many times over the years. After examining the structure, I hardly knew where to begin because its income-producing potential was so compromised. The first floor was below street level, but the building did not have a basement. Rather, it was set on the property in such a way that gave it a basement-like effect. My client installed windows on the cavernous first floor, which did bring in some light, but the view—dirt from the road—was horrible.

My recommendation was to break the lease; this option was available to him and he had been considering this exit strategy. More than 85 percent of the tenants occupied executive office suites. I also told him to encourage the owners to raze the edifice and in its place construct a high-rise building with the main entrance facing the road. The new entrance would receive the vibrant energy of the street and have a view of the famous Camelback Mountain—very auspicious for wealth luck! He took my advice. The owner is currently awaiting city approval for demolition.

Ultimately, it didn't matter how beautiful the interior of this office building was (and it certainly was stunning), the tenants struggled to survive, thus affecting the wealth of the owners. Hanging mirrors or crystals in the windows, as Western Feng Shui sometimes advocates, would not have made one bit of difference to this building or its occupants. In fact, my client had someone "Feng Shui" this space with the usual Western Feng Shui cures to no avail. Remember, trinkets cannot compete, energetically speaking, with powerful landforms. My advice is to pass on buying or leasing a commercial building or an office space with a level that acts as a basement, especially if people will occupy that area. A basement-level garage, however, is fine.

MASTER'S TIP

Do not locate your business on the basement level of an office building. If you want a successful home-based business, do not work out of a traditional, closed-in basement. It will not provide the vibrant, yang energy needed to bring you good wealth luck.

Front Doors That Do Not Face the Street

Front doors in Asian philosophy are key. Consider this popular Chinese saying, "If your door is worth a thousand pieces of gold—your house is only worth four pieces of gold." This means that an excellent door is essential for you to thrive, and a good one is worth more than your entire house. The front door of your home is where the structure absorbs or inhales vibrant energy. So to maximize fortune, your home's front door should face the street, a bustling conduit of energy. In some newer tract communities proper door placement can be an issue. Builders design garages to face the road but position main entrances on the side. Here's the general rule: If the delivery guy can't find your door, that's a problem—and the problem will be with money.

MASTER'S TIP

Relocate the main door to accept the energy of a road. The art of opening a door where one didn't exist before is a big deal in Feng Shui; the house will be "breathing in" energy in a completely different way. To help you determine where to place the door, call a professional practitioner. If this is not possible or practical, and you have experienced bad money luck, consider relocating.

Homes That Back to a Body of Water

Water is the ultimate wealth secret of Feng Shui. But not knowing where to locate your home in proximity to water or where to place water on your property can create money troubles and health issues. The Chinese discovered that water, arguably the most powerful element on the planet, must be respected. Water is dangerous, unpredictable, and unknowable. The ancients believed the perfect setting is a mountain behind you and water in the front.

With that said, don't buy a home near a canal, lake, or river without consulting a Feng Shui Master or practitioner first. Water techniques are the most complex and highly specialized aspects of Feng Shui. Homes that back bodies of water, if not properly handled, will often cause bankruptcy. The direction of the main door in relation to the water is a major factor in determining whether a dwelling will deplete wealth. Water flowing behind a residence can generate missed opportunities, insolvency, illness, drug addiction, sexual misconduct, scandal, and other serious situations. This can be true even if a wall or levee obscures the water.

Ideally, your home should **face** water, that way you can keep an eye on its level. A large, wide wash (a natural and man-made channel that whisks away water from a site) behind your home can also cause money loss, depending on its size and proximity to the structure. These formations are prevalent in cities around the world, so use caution before buying such a property.

MASTER'S TIP

Block the view of the canal with a solid fence or wall. If you live near a lake or river, you should have a Feng Shui Master or practitioner evaluate your site.

Extremely Narrow-Shaped Homes

Extremely narrow homes have what is known as "squeezed chi," which will prevent you from accumulating wealth. Sure, you might be able to earn money, but these types of structures make keeping it difficult.

Here's the general rule to determine whether you have a squeezed-chi building: the length of the structure is about three to four times that of its width. For example, a space that is twenty feet wide and sixty feet long is considered squeezed chi. Townhomes and brownstones are notorious for harboring this design flaw, and people often experience bankruptcy and debt in them. Though not all multifamily dwellings are bad, many do prevent occupants from holding on to their cash. I consulted with a woman in Scottsdale who was leasing a three-story townhome.

She had made a tidy profit from the sale of her previous home and was trying to build a business in her new residence. Instead of succeeding, she lost all of her money in the less than two years she lived there. I convinced her to move out, and we found her a great property with excellent Feng Shui. Many money-making opportunities came to her as a result.

Don't be tempted to buy or rent a home like this, no matter how much beauty and charm it offers. These spaces never bring wealth luck. Many new-home builders are designing and constructing homes with this shape. These buildings have small footprints and require little land, thereby maximizing profit; however, in the long run they are not good for either the developers or homeowners.

MASTER'S TIP

If you have experienced nothing but bad money luck from a narrow-shaped home or business, think seriously about relocating. Mirrors won't increase the width of the space; the building is still narrow and it is still squeezing the energy.

Storm Drains in Front of Your Home or Business

Without a doubt, storm drains serve a practical purpose. In the world of Feng Shui, however, these formations can be a major source of money loss, because water is equivalent to money. Drains are common in all modern cities around the world, varying in size and location to accommodate the local environment. During my studies with Grand Master Yap Cheng Hai, I traveled to several cities in Malaysia with him. He pointed out the complex drainage system in Kuala Lumpur, a region marked by heavy rains and monsoons, and its dangers regarding money loss. These drains are huge and visible to the eye. He took advantage of these when possible (as he did on his own property), using the drains as a correct way for water to exit the site. When this was not possible, he emphasized the great loss of wealth it could bring to the occupants—in some cases, total devastation. "You're already dead!" he'd say.

It is important to note that I am speaking of open and exposed drains, not those underground and invisible to the eye. To determine whether a site's drains will harm the occupants or business owners, we analyze two different and important considerations: location and direction. The safest course, however, is to avoid a home or a business near a storm drain, especially if you can see the drain from the front door.

Clients of mine in the Phoenix area experienced a classic example of what can happen when water leaves a site incorrectly. The problem began with a storm drain that sat in direct view of their front door, only about twenty feet away. Water flowed into a second drain and then the final water exit on the right side of the house. When I explained that these channels indicated poor money luck, they quickly confessed their experience. Within three years of living there, they had encountered problems in their relationship and with money. How can a simple drain indicate bad luck? As one client said, "Most people won't connect the dots." In other words, most people won't associate bad luck with land features (man-made or natural) or poorly planned living spaces.

These are just a few of the many secrets of harmonious environments and living the Chinese discovered. And it is hard to believe they are so accurate. This couple experienced almost three years of misery, primarily with money, which could have been spared. Had I come to do my assessment of this property two years before, the wife told me she would not have believed me. You need only to look at the history of a home to know these things are not only possible but true. The placement of water and its egress must be appropriate for your property. Needless to say, my clients moved to a better property.

MASTER'S TIP

If your home or business is near a huge drain, block it from view. If you have lost a great deal of money from such a site, relocate as soon as possible.

Homes Too Close to a Highway

In Feng Shui, roads and highways are considered virtual rivers. Imagine your home right on the banks of the Hudson, the mighty Mississippi, the great Thames, the Danube, or the Seine: these huge rivers are powerhouses of energy! Modern-day highways are equally powerful, if not more so. Cars are moving at fifty to eighty miles per hour, day after day, month after month, year after year. The longer a highway or road has existed, the more defined and established the energy.

When homes are too close to a highway, money will be lost because energy cannot be retained at your site. It's moving too fast, and the energy is too overwhelming, so the opposite effect comes into play. Single residences, even mansions, can't withstand this level of intensity. High-rises and other large structures, however, can. The placement of tall structures near real water or major highways works extremely well. It's a striking and awesome sight to see beautiful skyscrapers next to a large body of water—just think of Chicago, New York, San Francisco, Paris, Hong Kong, and Sydney. Now consider the great highways that define these cities: Lake Shore Drive, FDR Drive, Highway 101, Boulevard Périphérique, Connaught Road, and Cahill Expressway.

Highway energy is so powerful it can cause people to behave badly. Violent crimes often take place near major highways, a phenomenon that has been well documented in the media. In 2000, A & E's popular television series *American Justice* chronicled the murders of twenty-seven women over the span of thirty years along Interstate 45 between Galveston and Houston, Texas. Then there's Highway 16—the notorious Highway of Tears—that winds through central British Columbia. According to a 2006 PBS *Frontline* documentary, dozens of women, beginning in 1969, have gone missing, some of who were found murdered, along this 425-mile stretch of road. Police believe the victims are connected to one serial killer.

In addition to money loss, homes near a highway are vulnerable to all sorts of crimes and discord, including domestic disturbances and alcohol abuse (McDowell 1992). A quiet, sweet little neighborhood can change with the installation of a freeway near it, or even worse, over it. The energy may take twenty years or more to settle down again. People who live in a residence that backs up to a highway may experience the worst luck of all. In addition to a great loss of wealth, it also indicates the demise of a partner.

MASTER'S TIP

Create a sound wall, plant large trees, or add a water feature if possible, just make sure it is properly placed. Water will muffle the sound of the freeway and help hold the energy of a site. If you have experienced bad luck, consider relocating to a better property. Many realtors are aware that such sites have a lower resale value and will try to steer their clients away from such sites.

Robbery Mountain Sha

This negative formation, also known as Chor San Kibb Sart, will rob vital energy from a house, though money loss is merely one aspect of the trouble you might encounter. The Robbery Mountain Sha technique does not use the door direction or the facing of your home. Rather, it is based on the back of the property, which is referred to as the sitting direction.

For example, if your home sits in the east, and you have a negative feature located in the southwest, you could have the Robbery Mountain Sha formation. Negative features, such as high-tension electrical towers, a broken mountain (one that has been excavated, scarred, or marred), a quarry, a jagged cliff, lampposts, or a huge dead tree will activate the Robbery Mountain position. A jagged or broken mountain, however, is the most detrimental to the occupants. These attributes emit noxious and poisonous energies. If you have this unfortunate formation, your family could contract a strange disease, get hurt by knives, encounter all sorts of disasters, or even lose wealth.

MASTER'S TIP

To remedy this formation, a Feng Shui Master or practitioner will either block off the view of the negative feature (if possible), remove the dead tree, or suggest you relocate if you have experienced extremely bad luck. After all, mountains and electrical towers cannot be moved.

Homes and Businesses Near Water Towers, Electrical Towers, and Cemeteries

Wealth cannot grow if you live next to a cemetery because it is filled with dead energy. On the contrary, assets require vibrant, life-giving energy to thrive. There is an exception, however. A busy, dynamic road can counteract the dead energy of a graveyard. Even so, I wouldn't want my home or business next to one. I consulted with a developer who is building a major shopping center facing a bustling, six-lane road. He said a future tenant—the owner of a Chinese restaurant—told him the cemetery across the street was unlucky. Normally I would agree, but a dynamic, six-lane road stood between his property and the graveyard. This wide river of fast-moving energy totally negated the dead energy of the memorial park.

A high-tension electrical tower will also wreak havoc on a home or business. Depending on its proximity to your site, bad results can happen rather quickly. A cluster of high-tension towers and transformers is extremely intense and emits negative energy. I have seen one exception to this rule—a Shell station on a busy road in Scottsdale, Arizona, directly across from an electrical tower station. The tower location in relation to the gas station actually activates a great deal of energy for this business. A water tower, often the water supply for a community,

is also quite negative when situated too close to a house. Being located right under it is even worse. Water towers can be overpowering to a residence, causing money loss and sickness.

MASTER'S TIP

Large, tall trees can absorb a great deal of electromagnetic energy from electrical towers, as can water towers but to a lesser degree. There is no countermeasure for a private residence located next to a graveyard. If you find yourself suffering from depression after years of living next to a cemetery, it is likely to continue or get worse. Consider moving. If there is a busy road between your business and a cemetery, it is not likely the dead energy will affect you.

Death and Empty Lines or Void Lines

The Chinese identified specific door degrees that can bring disaster to a home or a business. The door degree means the exact compass direction that it faces. They call these disaster degrees Kong Wang or Kun Mang: Death and Empty Lines (DEL) or Void Lines. The most serious DELs fall on the exact cardinal points—90 degrees (east), 180 degrees (south), 270 degrees (west), and 360/0 degrees (north). Three levels of void lines actually exist. Secondary DELs, occur at the exact point when, for example, west changes to northwest (315) or south ends and southwest begins (225)[7]. *Any* level of the void line degrees will cause issues in the lives of the occupants

---

7. DELs have three levels. Major (level 1): These DELs comprise the exact cardinal points, such as 180 degrees, 90 degrees, and so on. Secondary (level 2): These DELs occur between Guas or the eight directions. Lesser (level 3): These DELs fall among the twenty-four divisions or mountains of the Luo Pan. Any level is harmful to occupants or business owners and can cause issues with money, health, and relationships. You will need a precise Luo Pan to determine whether your door has any of the DEL levels. Most Feng Shui Masters and practitioners consider even one or two degrees left or right of a DEL harmful. These degrees can be dangerous to yang dwellings—homes and businesses.

of a structure. I've seen more than sixty sites throughout the states languish from DEL-related energy. DELs are serious bad luck and will deplete your wealth.

These degrees, especially the major ones, are reserved for holy places and houses of worship. Many religions use these hallowed bearings as part of what is known as *sacred geometry*, which allows benevolent spirits (angels or ghosts) to enter during reverence, meditation, and prayer. Since DELs open a "window" in which energy, ghosts, or spirits can enter, they are best reserved for scared spaces, otherwise evil spirits or discarnate energy could enter, via these specific degrees, into your building.

Even if a ghosts or spirits do not enter, when these degrees appear in homes, disaster ensues, as the energy is extreme yin (dead chi). I have witnessed everything from divorce to bankruptcy, job loss, illness, and spiritual maladies in residences and business plagued by DELs. This is also why some properties don't sell. Classical Feng Shui provides techniques to change the door degree, but an entire foundation on a DEL is impossible to resolve. It is rare, but not unheard of. In my many years of consulting, I've only experienced two homes where the entire foundation was on a DEL. By the way, young children are very sensitive to the presence of spirits or ghosts in the house. Pay attention if they tell you "someone" came to visit them in their room.

MASTER'S TIP

Take a DEL-oriented door off of its hinges for about an hour and then re-hang it. I have had great success using this trick before resorting to tilting a door, which can be an involved and costly modification. Homes will settle over time and ease into these unlucky degrees if you are surrounded by a yin environment. Doors will go into a DEL if a structure has been closed up or empty for a while.

Homes Surrounded by Too Many Roads

When too many roads (four being the worst) surround a house, the property ostensibly becomes a floating island. Remember, roads are like swift rivers of energy. I have a client whose home was completely surrounded by virtual and real water, roads on two sides and two huge washes on the other sides. This home was a disaster the entire time that they owned it—money loss, multiple affairs, and eventually bankruptcy.

Though I've only encountered one house with four roads, I've seen many with three. This configuration will most definitely cause money loss, bankruptcy, illness, and misfortune for the occupants. From a practical standpoint, it is generally unsafe as well. Wayward vehicles collide with homes and businesses all the time. You can't accumulate wealth when your space is always in jeopardy of being impacted. A home or business on a collision course, energetically speaking, is no way to live and thrive. To build wealth, you must secure your site from unstable forces, such as roads and water—real or virtual. That's why it is important that your main door face a road to receive energy, as long as it's not too close and certainly not vulnerable to accidents.

MASTER'S TIP

Create a strong backing at the rear of the property. Also, insulate the site on the left- and right-hand sides from the roads.

Eight Roads of Destruction or Yellow Springs (Pa Loo Hwang Chuen)

It has many names—Eight Roads of Destruction, Eight Roads to Hell, Eight Roads to Disaster and Misfortune, Yellow Springs—but whatever you choose to call it, the consequences are the same: bad. The Chinese refer to the waters of the underworld, or hell, as *Yellow Springs*.

This situation applies to how water—real or virtual—comes to and exits the site, which, as with any form of energy, will affect your wealth.

Roads are the most common conduits of energy to a home or business. Real water is another way energy is dynamically brought to a site. Driveways and sidewalks also serve as channels of energy because cars and humans activate them with their chi; however, they do not have the same importance as roads and real water. The energy from a road or real water is a larger and more intense purveyor of energy. Roads can either determine the severity of problems or the level of fortune the occupants of a property will experience. A bad road or a poorly located main door can make or break a site. In the case of Eight Roads formations, people can encounter death, bankruptcy, divorce, affairs, and other hellish experiences.

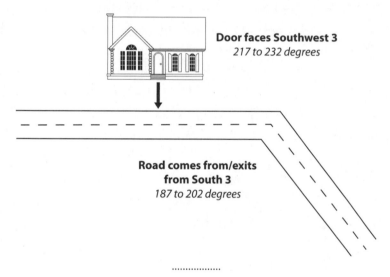

Fugure 16: Eight Roads of Destruction–
Can cause bankruptcy.

For example, if your home faces southwest, and a road, drain, stream, river, or driveway comes from the south, exits from the south, or both, you may have an Eight Roads of Destruction formation. These formations are specific to fifteen-degree increments. For instance, it won't apply to *all* homes that face southwest; they must face between 217.6 and 232.5 degrees. The road doesn't include the entire forty-five degrees of south either; it too only involves fifteen-degree increments.

MASTER'S TIP

Eight Roads of Destruction formations are serious and can harm the occupants. You can remedy the situation by changing the door or the road, but you will need the assistance of a Feng Shui Master or practitioner.

Four

·····················

Increasing Wealth Luck with Eight Mansions

·····················

*I hear and I forget. I see and I
remember. I do and I understand.*

Confucius

Ultimately, the true goal of Feng Shui is to improve every aspect of life, specifically to thrive. This is accomplished by analyzing the natural and man-made environment that is immediately in your sphere. Inside the home, important and key rooms, such as bedrooms, bathrooms, kitchens, and home offices, are also assessed as these will affect your efforts at building and securing wealth and prosperity.

Here's the shocking truth: In classical, traditional Feng Shui there is no such thing as the "wealth corner," "marriage corner," or "fame sector." The Eight Life Aspirations are not part of Classical Feng Shui nor is it part of the Eight Mansions system. This may be shocking to those who have read many books and perused numerous websites declaring this information as fact. When Grand Master Yap Cheng Hai was asked about this popular style of Feng Shui in his classes, he would passionately say "Don't ask me about this nonsense—this is NOT Feng Shui!"

In order to determine whether the energy is supportive or destructive, detailed information about the site and structure must be gathered. Without exception these will involve the facing direction, magnetic energy, water location, mountains in or around the site, and cycles of time. Positive energy will bring opportunities for business, romance, health, promotion, lucrative investments, and wealth luck. Negative energy can manifest in disease, poor health, divorce, bad relationships, poverty, and bankruptcy.

We can't talk about how to build wealth using Feng Shui without discussing the two most popular systems—Eight Mansions and Flying Stars (discussed in chapter 5). Both of these Feng Shui systems can yield fantastic results on their own, but together they can really deliver the goods. In this chapter we will discuss in detail how to use this excellent system.

You will be amazed at how a few simple changes can alter your life for the better. There are actually eight different styles of Eight Mansions. However, do not confuse Eight Mansions with the Eight Life Aspirations or Eight Life Stations of the Black Hat Sect or other Western styles of Feng Shui. They are neither in the same class of practice, nor are they derived from Eight Mansions. The Eight Life Aspirations/ Stations (faux Feng Shui) cannot be combined with Eight Mansions, Flying Stars or any other system of Classical Feng Shui.

Perhaps the most widely recognized style of Eight Mansions in the world, and certainly in Asia, is the Eight House Bright Mirror (Pa Chai Ming Jing). This style is described in the best-selling book *The Complete Idiot's Guide to Feng Shui*. The technique used in *this* book is from the Golden Star Classic or the Big Dipper Casting Golden Light (Kam Kwong Dou Lam King, also spelled Jin-Guang Dou Lin Jing) and is used a little differently.[8] I learned this style and its applications directly from Grand Master Yap Cheng Hai. Throughout his fifty years of practice, he has seen this method dramatically improve the lives of his clients. I too have seen incredible results with my clients, and in my public lectures I always include Eight Mansions as the jewel of my presentation. Eight Mansions—also known as Pa Chai or Ba Zhai—is a fairly simple and direct system of Feng Shui that dates back to the Tang Dynasty, beginning in the seventh century.

According to its premise, human life is influenced by the eight cardinal and intercardinal directions: four will support you and four won't. The auspicious directions address wealth and money luck, health, good relationships, and stability; the other four cover issues such as divorce, bankruptcy, betrayals, lawsuits, cancer, and so forth. Naturally, you will want to activate your positive directions and not use the negative ones.

No matter which Eight Mansions style is used, the formula to arrive at your personal Life Gua number is the same. The Life Gua (sometimes referred to as Ming Gua) is a number assigned to you based on your birthday and gender. Once you have this number, you know which four directions support you and the four that do not bring good luck. See, we're back to those all-important eight directions.

On the next page you'll find the actual formulas to determine your Life Gua number. Please note that in Classical Feng Shui, the Chinese solar calendar (Hsia) is used, which starts the new year on February 4. The Chinese use the lunar calendar for festivals and popular Chinese astrology systems, which is based on cycles of the moon. However, where timing is important, as in Feng Shui or agricultural purposes, the solar calendar is vastly more accurate. The lunar calendar may vary as much

---

8. Eight House Bright Mirror uses the sitting direction of the house, and the Golden Star Classic relies on the facing direction of the house; this is the main difference between these two styles. The sitting direction simply means the back of the house; for example, the house may face east but it sits in the west. Master Yap prefers the Golden Star Classic to all the other styles since it mixes well with Xuan Kong Fei Xing (Flying Stars).

as two weeks from the solar calendar. I've provided an Eight Mansions Reference Chart as a handy "cheat sheet" so you won't have to calculate, using the formula, a person's Life Gua. Nonetheless, the formula is also supplied below. The method to arrive at your Life Gua number is different for males and females.

Eight Mansions Formula for Males

Add the last two digits of your birth year until you reach a single digit. Subtract that number from 10. If you end up with 5, you will take the 2 Gua number. If you were born before February 4 in any given year, use the previous year.

Male example 1: Born January 29, 1945 will use the previous year, 1944. Add 4 + 4 = 8. Now subtract 10 - 8 = 2. This man is a 2 Gua.

Male example 2: Born June 21, 1964. Add 6 + 4 = 10, then 1 + 0 = 1. Now subtract 10 - 1 = 9. This man is a 9 Gua.

Males born in 2000 and after: Take the last two digits of your birth year and add them together until you reach a single digit. Subtract that number from 9. If you end up with 5, you will take the 2 Gua number. If you were born before February 4 in any given year, use the previous year.

Eight Mansions Formula for Females

Add the last two digits of your birth year until you reach a single digit. Add 5 to that number and add the last two digits again until you reach a single digit. If you end up with 5, you will take the 8 Gua number. If you were born before February 4 in any given year, use the previous year.

Female example 1: Born September 10, 1954. Add 5 + 4 = 9. Now add 9 + 5 = 14. Keep adding until you reach a single digit: 1 + 4 = 5. This woman is an 8 Gua.

Female example 2: Born March 15, 1962. Add 6 + 2 = 8. Now add 8 + 5 = 13. Keep adding until you reach a single digit: 1 + 3 = 4. This woman is a 4 Gua.

Females born in 2000 and after: add the last two digits of your birth year until you reach a single digit. Add 6 to that number. If you end up with 5, you will take the 8 Gua number. If you were born before February 4 in any given year, use the previous year.

The Eight Mansions chart has a male and female column, so be sure you are looking in the right one. The first Eight Mansion chart will help you find your Life Gua number based on your gender and birth date. **If you were born in any given year before February 4, use the previous year.** I've also indicated your birth year animal according to the Chinese zodiac—it is not part of Eight Mansions, just a point of interest. For example, a man born June 1, 1961 is a 3 Gua and was born in the Year of the Ox.

1933 to 1960				1961 to 1988				1989 to 2016			
Animal	Year	Male	Female	Animal	Year	Male	Female	Animal	Year	Male	Female
Rooster	1933	4	2	Ox	1961	3	3	Snake	1989	2	4
Dog	1934	3	3	Tiger	1962	2	4	Horse	1990	1	8
Pig	1935	2	4	Rabbit	1963	1	8	Goat	1991	9	6
Rat	1936	1	8	Dragon	1964	9	6	Monkey	1992	8	7
Ox	1937	9	6	Snake	1965	8	7	Rooster	1993	7	8
Tiger	1938	8	7	Horse	1966	7	8	Dog	1994	6	9
Rabbit	1939	7	8	Goat	1967	6	9	Pig	1995	2	1
Dragon	1940	6	9	Monkey	1968	2	1	Rat	1996	4	2
Snake	1941	2	1	Rooster	1969	4	2	Ox	1997	3	3
Horse	1942	4	2	Dog	1970	3	3	Tiger	1998	2	4
Goat	1943	3	3	Pig	1971	2	4	Rabbit	1999	1	8
Monkey	1944	2	4	Rat	1972	1	8	Dragon	2000	9	6
Rooster	1945	1	8	Ox	1973	9	6	Snake	2001	8	7
Dog	1946	9	6	Tiger	1974	8	7	Horse	2002	7	8
Pig	1947	8	7	Rabbit	1975	7	8	Goat	2003	6	9
Rat	1948	7	8	Dragon	1976	6	9	Monkey	2004	2	1
Ox	1949	6	9	Snake	1977	2	1	Rooster	2005	4	2
Tiger	1950	2	1	Horse	1978	4	2	Dog	2006	3	3
Rabbit	1951	4	2	Goat	1979	3	3	Pig	2007	2	4
Dragon	1952	3	3	Monkey	1980	2	4	Rat	2008	1	8
Snake	1953	2	4	Rooster	1981	1	8	Ox	2009	9	6
Horse	1954	1	8	Dog	1982	9	6	Tiger	2010	8	7
Goat	1955	9	6	Pig	1983	8	7	Rabbit	2011	7	8
Monkey	1956	8	7	Rat	1984	7	8	Dragon	2012	6	9
Rooster	1957	7	8	Ox	1985	6	9	Snake	2013	2	1
Dog	1958	6	9	Tiger	1986	2	1	Horse	2014	4	2
Pig	1959	2	1	Rabbit	1987	4	2	Goat	2015	3	3
Rat	1960	4	2	Dragon	1988	3	3	Monkey	2016	2	4

The next two charts of Eight Mansions is where—based on your Life Gua number—you will find your four good directions and four bad directions. You will be in either the East Life Group or the West Life Group. The "code" is explained a little later in this chapter.

Now that you have your Gua number, you will be able to see from this chart your four good directions and your four bad directions for those belonging to the **East Life** Group.

East Life Group Gua Numbers		1	3	4	9
	Gua Names	Kan	Chen	Xun	Li
Code:	Good Directions for:				
+90	Money and Wealth "Sheng Chi"	Southeast	South	North	East
+80	Health "Tien Yi" (Heavenly Doctor)	East	North	South	Southeast
+70	Relationships "Yen Nien"	South	Southeast	East	North
+60	Stability "Fu Wei"	North	East	Southeast	South
Code:	Bad Directions that will activate:				
-60	Nothing goes smooth "Wo Hai"	West	Southwest	Northwest	Northeast
-70	Lawsuits/ Bad Romance "Wu Gwei"	Northeast	Northwest	Southwest	West
-80	Bad Health and Betrayals "Liu Sha"	Northwest	Northeast	West	Southwest
-90	Divorce/Bankruptcy "Chueh Ming"	Southwest	West	Northeast	Northwest

Now that you have your Gua number, you will be able to see from this chart your four good directions and your four bad directions for those belonging to the **West Life** group.

West Life Group Gua Numbers		2	6	7	8
	Gua Names	Kun	Chien	Dui	Gen
Code:	Good Directions for:				
+90	Money and Wealth "Sheng Chi"	Northeast	West	Northwest	Southwest
+80	Health "Tien Yi" (Heavenly Doctor)	West	Northeast	Southwest	Northwest
+70	Relationships "Yen Nien"	Northwest	Southwest	Northeast	West
+60	Stability "Fu Wei"	Southwest	Northwest	West	Northeast
Code:	Bad Directions that will activate:				
-60	Nothing goes smooth "Wo Hai"	East	Southeast	North	South
-70	Lawsuits/ Bad Romance "Wu Gwei"	Southeast	East	South	North
-80	Bad Health and Betrayals "Liu Sha"	South	North	Southeast	East
-90	Divorce/ Bankruptcy "Chueh Ming"	North	South	East	Southeast

The Gua number is highly significant. From it, one can derive the directions that support you. Moreover, it is also indicative of several characteristics that can be used in important ways in Feng Shui—the compatibility of spouses, the relationship between parents and children, the dynamic between siblings, work mates, and business partners.

The Life Gua also gives clues to the emotional makeup and different personalities. Once you have located your best directions, you will be able to improve the Feng Shui of your home and business environments considerably, thereby maximizing the potential of the rooms in which you live and work.

East Life Group

If your Life Gua is 1, 3, 4, or 9, you belong to the East Life Group. Your four good directions are east, southeast, north, and south as indicated on the chart. Though everyone in this group shares the same good directions, the order of auspiciousness is different for each Life Gua. For example, east is the most favorable direction for a 9 Gua, while a 1 Gua should strive to activate the southeast. The other four directions are unfavorable to this life group. Refer to the Eight Mansions chart to see all eight directions and what they indicate.

West Life Group

If your Life Gua is 2, 6, 7, or 8, you belong to the West Life Group. Your four good directions are west, southwest, northwest, and northeast as indicated on the chart. Though everyone in this group shares the same good directions, the order of auspiciousness is different for each Life Gua. For instance, southwest is the most advantageous direction for an 8 Gua; northwest is best for a 7 Gua. The other four directions are inauspicious for this Life Group. Refer to the Eight Mansions chart to see all eight directions and what they indicate.

Whether you are male or female, the descriptions that begin on the next page apply to your Life Gua number. While there is much information about the good and bad directions for the Life Gua, there is virtually none regarding the inclinations and personalities. So, you'll be seeing this for the first time.

Just as in Western astrology, the eight different Life Guas have an element (water, wood, fire, earth, and metal) and ruling energy that will influence a person's behavior, habits, physical appearance, health issues, attraction to certain occupations, thinking process, and sexual desires. Western astrology would describe a Gemini as an air sign, for example. In the Eight Mansions system, we would say the 1 Gua is water, the 3 Gua is wood, the 9 Gua is fire, and so forth.

You will notice that there are positive and negative aspects—the yin and yang—as all humans exhibit both qualities at different times. Very evolved people will display the positive aspect most of the time. Those who have a lower energy will act out the negative aspects and I've included an infamous "criminal" for each Gua to demonstrate this. Famous movies stars, millionaires, and other celebrated people who share the same Life Gua number as you, are listed as well.

I'm the originator of the Life Gua Personalities™, which is a detailed description of each Life Gua. I created this expanded understanding based on a brief description given to me by Grand Master Yap Cheng Hai, the extensive information on the Guas themselves, the five elements theory, and my own decades of consulting with thousands of people.

The following descriptions are general and certainly do not tell the *whole* story of you, but I find them to be very accurate.

The 1 Life Gua

Trigram/Gua Name: Kan
Ruling Element or Sign: Water
Life Group: East
Best Personality Trait: Intellectual
Worst Personality Trait: Moody
Key Words: Sensuous, Moody, Intellectual

Famous 1 Gua: Brad Pitt, Dennis Quaid, Ang Lee, Chris Noth, Denzel Washington, Morgan Fairchild, Patti Austin, Cybil Shepherd, Elizabeth Taylor, Jackie Chan, Lindsay Lohan, Jude Law, John Travolta, Naomi Watts, Lady Gaga, and **criminal** Scott Peterson.

Personality: A 1 Gua has a cool exterior and appears to be together to the outside world. On the inside, however, they can have a deep and rich emotional landscape, at times moody, anxious, and high strung. Full of excellent ideas and concepts, 1 Gua people are highly intelligent, scholarly, and studious. Intuitive and able to size people up quickly, they are usually good at making money. Since their element is water, they can be hard to pin down and love their freedom. They are sensual and can be highly sexual. Tending to keep secrets below the surface, 1 Gua people are known to lead arcane lives.

The 2 Life Gua

Trigram/Gua Name: Kun
Ruling Element or Sign: Earth
Life Group: West
Best Personality Trait: Intuitive
Worst Personality Trait: Reclusive
Key Words: Intuitive, Reclusive, Nurturing

Famous 2 Gua: Luciano Pavarotti, Ashley Judd, Bill Murray, Billy Ocean, Dr. Phil McGraw, Jennifer Aniston, Ed Harris, Catherine Zeta-Jones, Rod Stewart, Pierce Brosnan, Michael Douglas, Jennifer Lopez, Will Smith, Tom Cruise, Daniel Radcliff, Rob Pattinson, Daniel Craig, and **criminal** Erik Menendez.

Personality: With their calm, relaxed demeanors, 2 Gua folks are dependable and tend to exhibit uncanny psychic abilities. Because of their nurturing qualities, they make great healers or doctors, plus they are family-oriented and maintain old-fashioned values. 2 Gua people are the most yin of all the Guas and they tend to enjoy and feel comfortable in dark spaces. A 2 Gua may fight depression, dark moods, and laziness. These grounded people relish activities that focus on the earth—gardening, farming, construction, and agriculture.

The 3 Life Gua

Trigram/Gua Name: Chen
Ruling Element or Sign: Big Wood
Life Group: East
Best Personality Trait: Progressive
Worst Personality Trait: Impatience
Key Words: Progressive, Outspoken, Organized

Famous 3 Gua: Kate Hudson, Naomi Campbell, Queen Latifah, Robin Williams, George Clooney, Sophia Loren, President Obama, Annette O'Toole, Christopher Reeve, Dan Aykroyd, Giada De Laurentiis, Petra Němcová, George Strait, and **criminal** Charles Manson.

Personality: Three Guas are highly organized, outspoken, and impatient. They tend to have a nervous nature punctuated by lots of energy and steam. They are always beginning, inventing, or crafting a new thing or venture and often attain a level of fame in their lives. 3 Gua individuals tend to self-punish, spread their energy too thin leading to collapse, and can be loud and brash. However, they are full of surprises, 3 Gua personalities have a sense of vitality and vigor that can overwhelm people.

The 4 Life Gua

Trigram/Gua Name: Xun
Ruling Element or Sign: Small Wood
Life Group: East
Best Personality Trait: Flexibility
Worst Personality Trait: Indecision
Key Words: Flexible, Indecisive, Gentle

Famous 4 Gua: Oprah Winfrey, Steve Wynn, Marlon Brando, Marilyn Monroe, Demi Moore, Michael Bloomberg, Hugh Grant, Tony Robbins, Antonio Banderas, Dina Lohan, Colin Firth, Jodie Foster, Jean-Claude Van Damme, Kelly Preston, Louise Hay, Alicia Keys, Kim Kardashian, Edward Norton, Zac Efron, Kenneth Branagh, Paul McCartney, Prince Andrew, and **criminal** Jeffery Dahmer.

Personality: Malleable, flexible, indecisive, and progressive, the 4 Gua is usually attractive with movie-star qualities. 4 Gua people can be controlled by sex through their partners or lovers more than other Life Guas. 4 Gua individuals often resist advice, can be extravagant, talk "big," self-destruct, and lean toward exaggeration. Their personalities are generally remote and distant, but they are gentle.

The 6 Life Gua

Trigram/Gua Name: Chien
Ruling Element or Sign: Big Metal
Life Group: West
Best Personality Trait: Authoritative
Worst Personality Trait: Over-thinking
Key Words: Authoritative, Over-thinkers, Protective

Famous 6 Gua: Bruce Lee, Teri Hatcher, Orlando Bloom, Andrea Bocelli, Warren Buffett, Richard Nixon, Wayne Dyer, Mother Teresa, Alec Baldwin, Bernie Mac, Chris Columbus, Connie Sellecca, Gary Oldman, Debra Winger, Ice-T, Jeff Foxworthy, Billy Joel, Devon Aoki, Sandra Bullock, Maria Shriver, and **criminal** John Gotti.

Personality: Though 6 Gua people tend to be noble, lofty, and in positions of authority, they are protective and want to take care of everyone. Because they can be self-absorbed and think too much, individuals with this Life Gua are often sleep-deprived and crave time alone. They are natural leaders and teachers, and have almost "heavenly" protection and blessings. They make excellent lawyers, judges, and CEOs, as their energy commands respect. 6 Gua types have a regal air that is naturally unpretentious.

The 7 Life Gua

Trigram/Gua Name: Dui
Ruling Element or Sign: Small Metal
Life Group: West
Best Personality Trait: Charisma
Worst Personality Trait: Excess
Key Words: Charismatic, Excessive, Lively

Famous 7 Gua: Rita Wilson, Daniel Day-Lewis, Mukesh Ambani, Clint Eastwood, Alice Cooper, Anderson Cooper, Bo Derek, Carrie Fisher, Dorothy Hamill, Spike Lee, Geena Davis, Harry Connick Jr., Ray Romano, Najee, Cameron Crowe, David Beckham, Penelope Cruz, Sarah Jessica Parker, and **criminal** Amy Fisher.

Personality: 7 Gua people tend to be youthful in appearance and demeanor. Attracted to metaphysical studies and arts, they can be talkative, lively, and nervous. 7s are usually very attractive, especially females. They often become movies stars or celebrated people—but they must avoid overindulging in the pleasures of life, such as food, drink, money, and sex. 7 Gua individuals are usually charming and engaging in stimulating conversation but can be fast- or smooth-talkers.

The 8 Life Gua

Trigram/Gua Name: GEN
Ruling Element or Sign: Mountain Earth
Life Group: West
Best Personality Trait: Nobility
Worst Personality Trait: Stubbornness
Key Words: Noble, Stubborn, Steadfast

Famous 8 Gua: Kate Winslet, Angelina Jolie, Angela Bassett, Bette Midler, Condoleezza Rice, Christie Brinkley, Princess Caroline, Beyoncé Knowles, Leonardo DiCaprio, Jessica Alba, Natalie Portman, Charlize Theron, Tom Hanks, Jennifer Hudson, Kristen Stewart, Andy Garcia, David E. Kelley, and **criminal** O. J. Simpson.

Personality: 8 Gua people have noble personalities coupled with stubbornness, dependability, and steadfastness. They are attracted to all things spiritual and can become monks or nuns. These earthy people are usually talented in matters of real estate, landscaping, or construction. An 8 Gua tends to resist change, but can handle trouble and pressure without falling apart. Unevolved 8s can hoard, be short-tempered, and self-righteous. The 8 Gua can attain riches, success, and fame.

The 9 Life Gua

Trigram/Gua Name: Li
Ruling Element or Sign: Fire
Life Group: East
Best Personality Trait: Brilliance
Worst Personality Trait: Radical
Key Words: Brilliant, Radical, Loyal

Famous 9 Gua: Russell Crowe, Jack Nicholson, Madhuri Dixit, Walt Disney, Sylvester Stallone, Julia Roberts, Steven Spielberg, Lilliane Bettencourt, Li Ka-shing, Bill Gates, Anna Nicole Smith, Faith Hill, Clive Owen, Keanu Reeves, Nicole Kidman, Michelle Pfeiffer, Linus Roache, and **criminal** Ted Bundy.

Personality: 9 Gua people generally have a fiery and highly developed intellect: they can also be wise, loyal, and sentimental. Women are usually beautiful like a diva or goddess but can be argumentative, aggressive, and rash. Blessed with an adventurous streak, a 9 Gua may possess an evolved consciousness. With focus and effort, a 9 Gua can attain great achievements, promotion, and status. Unevolved 9s will tend toward being radical, paranoid, and psychotic.

The eight Guas can be placed in four main categories based on their ruling elemental energy and what motivates them in general. Again, it is not the definitive, but gives you a little insight into your personality, your partner, children, parents, friends, boss, and coworkers.

The Four Categories of the Eight Life Guas

The Intellectuals	The Modernists	The Rebels	The Dependables
1 and 9 Guas *Water and Fire energy*	3 and 4 Guas *Wood energy*	6 and 7 Guas *Metal energy*	2 and 8 Guas *Earth energy*
These Guas tend to have a highly developed and sharp intellect; they can be scholarly, full of creative ideas, may be bright visionaries, and are constantly developing the mind. Very attracted to communications. Secondary key words are "I feel."	These Guas are modern and very progressive thinkers. These personalities tend to be highly organized, a bit outspoken and be full of surprises. They love to initiate start-up projects and thrive on growth or growing things. They are attracted to politics, acting, and writing. Secondary key words are "I analyze."	As natural leaders, these Guas tend to be rebels against authority. They have a talent for writing sharp papers or speaking out and can rally a group with their charm; they are often CEOs of firms. Attracted to metaphysics, corporate, and military power. Secondary key words are "I desire."	The earthy energy of these Guas marks them as steadfast, dependable, noble, and stubborn. They tend to gather wealth, are attracted to construction, healing arts, and metaphysics. Secondary key words are "I know."

Eight Mansions Descriptions

The detailed descriptions for the Eight Mansions system and what your good and bad directions could indicate are discussed below. Each of your auspicious directions will attract a slightly different kind of good luck to you. When you activate a direction, you're actually facing that direction, whether you're at your desk, sitting in a chair, or walking through a certain door on a regular basis. Doors are important in Feng Shui, and naturally you'll want your front door facing one of your four good directions, if at all possible.

In the following charts and descrptions, +90, +80, -80, -90, and so on is a numerical schematic code devised by my teacher, Grand Master Yap Cheng Hai as an easy way to remember the values of the corresponding Chinese terms, such as Sheng Chi, your best direction, and Chueh Ming, your least favorable direction. Throughout the rest of this book I will refer to these directions as +90, -80, +70, -60, and so forth. The one word or two that correlates to the numbers are highlighted in bold, and are the main indication or result for using that direction.

Your Four Best Directions

Wealth +90 *(Sheng Chi)*: Sheng Chi means "generating breath" or "life-giving energy." It is the best direction to activate wealth luck. Also known as millionaire chi, this direction is great for timing, opportunities, promotions, health, children, and money. Your Sheng Chi direction will help establish you in a position of authority or power.

Health +80 *(Tien Yi)*: Tien Yi means the "heavenly doctor," or "doctor form heaven." This is the best direction to improve or secure health. This direction brings unexpected wealth from the heavens, long life, good friends, social standing, and the power of speech. You will also garner government and VIP support.

Relationships +70 *(Yen Nien)*: This direction will bring great relationships, good health, and longevity. It is the best direction to activate for family love, romantic love, networking, and overall family harmony. You may have wealthy descendants or children who become specialized, rich, or famous. Activate this direction if you want to conceive quickly or encourage cooperative, obedient children.

Stability +60 *(Fu Wei)*: This direction will attract stability, moderate happiness, and wealth; it is a good alternative if your best directions aren't usable. Fu Wei indicates a middle-class family life, overall harmony, and peace. This energy will help grown children move on and out of the house.

Your Four Worst Directions

Total Disaster -90 *(Chueh Ming)*: This energy attracts the worst of
everything, including bankruptcy, bad health, fatalities, a death in
the family, divorce, business failures, loss of wealth, disharmony,
family breakups, accidents, and childlessness.

Backstabbing and Affairs -80 *(Liu Sha)*: Liu Sha is called the Six Killings direction and will attract backstabbing, thievery, injury, loss
of wealth, bad health, terrible money luck, grievous harm to you
and your family, business betrayals, accidents, love and relationship problems, and grave illness. If you use this direction, you may
become *unrecognized* in the world. That being said, this is a great
location for a toilet.

Lawsuits and Bad Romance -70 *(Wu Gwei)*: Wu Gwei is known as the
Five Ghosts direction, and its main indication if used is litigation.
Activating this direction can also bring trouble, disobedient and
rebellious children, romance issues, difficulty conceiving, gambling,
drug use, petty people, robberies, hot tempers, annoyances, betrayals, quarrels, disharmony, arguments, lack of employee support,
undermining, and gossip.

Nothing Goes Smoothly -60 *(Wo Hai)*: Activating this direction
will attract obstructions, persistent and irritating setbacks, and
loss of investments. It can bring disaster but not cataclysmic
tragedy. For instance, you may win a court case but lose the
monetary settlement.

Putting Your Life Gua into Action

Now that you know your Gua number, there are some significant ways
to use direction and location to get results. First, you will need a compass to take some directional readings of your home. Always start with
the house facing. Stand in front of your residence and find out what

direction it is facing. In most homes, the main door faces the road—if this is the case, stand near the front door and see what degree it is. If your front door does not face the road, take the compass reading from the center of your front yard or garden.

When you use and activate your good directions, it is said you "sail with the wind" rather than against it. Your bad directions will cause you to struggle in life; activate your good directions and life will propel you forward. The following suggestions will help you extract the most benefit from this system and the best results for building wealth using the +90, -90, and +70 directions. Pay close attention to specific features, such as doors, toilets, stoves, stove knobs, bedroom locations, and bed directions. The knobs of your stove are known as the fire mouth, or mouth of the fire. The direction it faces is extremely important in Classical Feng Shui because fire, just like water, is a powerful activator of energy. The suggestions below offer important, wealth-enhancing ideas to incorporate the Eight Mansions into your living space.

Doors

You must have a good door that brings you wealth luck. If you have a door facing one of your four good directions, use it. If you are currently using/activating a bad direction, frequent another door. Be sure to take a compass direction of the interior garage door if this is the door you primarily use.

Your house and front door should ideally face and receive energy from your +90. Your bedroom door should be one of your good directions, ideally your +90. If you have an attached garage, the door to enter the house should be a good direction, especially your +90. If the front of your house and the main front door face your -70, you may experience career failure, backstabbing, petty people, gossip, disloyalty, bickering, and lawsuits. High-traffic doors that face your -90 direction will hurt your money luck. The door you enter 100 percent of the time must face one of your four good directions. If not, use another door. For example, if your front door is excellent but your interior garage door is not, mix it up. Use your garage door only 20 percent of the time and your front door 80 percent of the time. This will immediately change your luck. If you have a door that faces your +90 wealth direction, use it.

Bedroom Locations and Bed Directions

In Classical Feng Shui, the master bedroom is one of the most important rooms in the house, normally occupied by the father and mother. A well-placed bed can affect the finances and harmony of the entire family. Since direction is more powerful than location, make sure your bed is angled toward a good direction. Sleeping to your +90 will attract opportunities, good career growth, and wealth. To capture the correct bed alignment, adjust your headboard toward that direction—the top of your head receives the energy while you are sleeping. Situate your bed toward your Sheng Chi, even if it means angling it.

Your bedroom should ideally be located in the +90 sector. The bed direction and headboard should face your +90 direction. If your bed direction is on your -70, you may experience lawsuits and betrayals. Your master bedroom door should be one of your four good directions. Whether you're married or single, make sure you have a headboard. A solid one is best because it offers support, protection, and stability.

Toilet Placement

Accruing money will be difficult if the toilet is located in your +90. Many people have the mistaken idea that the toilet will flush away something—money, relationships, and so on. This is not accurate. Toilets should not be located in your good sectors because of the *nature* and the *use* of the toilet. If you have a toilet in your -90, money luck will be good. A toilet located in your -70 is excellent for business and warding off betrayals and lawsuits.

The Stove

Finding a good location for the stove is one of the most powerful ways to use the Eight Mansions system. After all, fire can burn up a bad luck sector. The stove should be placed in any of your negative areas, especially on your -90 if you want to increase wealth. This is also known as burning up or depleting your bad luck.

If you have a stove in your -90, money luck will be excellent. It is best not to place a stove in your +90. Wealth luck will burn, and business deals will sour. If your stove is in your -70, you will not have betrayals or lawsuits. The knobs of the stove, or the fire mouth, should face one of your good directions, particularly your +90. Knobs are typically on the right-hand side or the front of the appliance.

Office and Desk

The location of a home office becomes important if you have a home-based business or you spend a great deal of time there. You will, at a minimum, need to face a good direction while sitting at your desk. To increase money luck, face your +90 direction; to improve relationships with clients, face your +70 direction. Using either of these directions will help with money, sales, and employee and client relationships. If you sit facing your -70, client relationships will be bad and family disputes will be common; you may also activate lawsuits and betrayals.

Getting Effective Results

To experience results with your money luck, you must implement change in at least three areas of your home. For example, use a door that faces your +90, position your bed toward your +90, and install the stove in your -90.

Advanced Eight Mansions
Used for People of Opposite Groups

The Eight Mansions system is flexible and powerful, offering many levels and techniques. The basic Eight Mansions help you arrive at your Life Gua to determine your good and bad directions. But the Advanced Eight Mansions (AEM) method takes it further by dividing the forty-five degrees of all the eight directions into fifteen-degree increments—giving you a total of twenty-four.

The benefit of this technique allows you to utilize certain increments of your bad directions. For instance, east is an inauspicious direction for members of the West Life Group (2, 6, 7, and 8). But according to AEM, the West Life Group can use the first and third fifteen degree of east, which means the bed direction, the fire mouth, or the desk can be aligned accordingly. If you are in the East Life Group (1, 3, 4, and 9), northwest is one of your unlucky directions. In AEM, however, the first and third fifteen-degree increments are available.

However this is not the case with the north direction and the West Life Group (2, 6, 7 and 8); the entire forty-five degrees is negative and cannot be used. Therefore, if you're in this group, you should avoid anything—including homes, doors, or beds—that faces this direction. It brings very inauspicious luck concerning money, relationships, and health.

When a couple belongs to different life groups, it can get tricky, and you may need a skilled Feng Shui Master to help you to adjust your home so both people are supported. However, if you follow the recommendations in chapters 6 and 7 where I've combined the Eight Mansions and Flying Star system, the Advanced Eight Mansions technique has already been factored—even if you and your partner are in different groups. So if you notice me suggesting a seemingly bad direction for you, remember that it is based on an auspicious fifteen-decree increment of Advanced

Eight Mansions. When following the suggestions in either chapter 6 or 7 for your home, if you and your partner are different Life Groups, you will need to use the recommendations where it indicates that the direction is good for all Guas. Choosing a great bed direction for mixed couples is really important, as this is the shared space.

Five

Flying Stars: The Power of Time Dimension

Ambition has one heel nailed in well, though she stretches her fingers to touch the heavens.
Lao Tzu

With more than 8,550,000 websites featuring the Flying Stars (*Xuan Kong Fei Xing*) system, it's likely the most recognized Classical Feng Shui system in the world. Most people who practice Feng Shui cannot imagine looking at a building without it, because it is so vital in determining a space's energy. While Eight Mansions may be the most recognized system in Southeast Asia, Flying Stars is the most *practiced* in the world. For most people embarking on the study of Classical Feng Shui, Flying Stars is usually where they start: it is well advertised, popular, and a bit of a brain-teaser. The Hong Kong masters are largely responsible for the worldwide proliferation of Flying Stars, and this system has enjoyed a major resurgence as a result of their work. Many who practice Western styles of Feng Shui often incorporate this particular system as part of their services, advertising that they offer Western and "Compass School" Feng Shui, not realizing it is only one system in the vast world of Classical Feng Shui.

Xuan Kong Fei Xing (pronounced "shoon kong fay sing") is the full name for this system. *Xuan kong* means "the subtle mysteries of time and space" or "the mysterious void," while *fei xing* translates to "Flying Stars." Flying Stars was designed to address the issue of time. During the development of this system, the great Feng Shui Masters pondered what would happen to a space or a structure as it moved through time. More importantly, they wanted to know how time would ultimately affect the building's occupants. Energy is in a constant state of change, and time never stands still. Whatever amount of fortune or adversity you're experiencing now won't apply in sixteen years, or even in two years, for that matter. That explains why no structure will forever enjoy good or bad Feng Shui as it cycles through time.

As with any Feng Shui system, specific changes made to the environment can alter your relationship to the world. Good Feng Shui can ward off times of bad luck and enhance opportunities for relationships, wealth, and health. Flying Stars removes the mystery of the seemingly random distribution of good and bad luck, enabling us to isolate variations in fortune. Feng Shui involves regular checkups and the periodic monitoring of the earth's subtle forces. Therefore, the time dimension of Feng Shui gives us the chance to deal with inauspicious forces and improve benevolent energy when the timing is advantageous. As superb as this system is, it should not be used in isolation or to the exclusion of other Feng Shui systems. That is why in chapters 6 and 7, Eight Mansions, Flying Stars, and other systems are all merged together for a comprehensive Feng Shui analysis.

The "stars" are simply the numbers 1 through 9, and a Flying Star chart is a box of nine squares containing three numbers in each square (see figure 17). The nine-square grid or box represents the eight directions plus the center square.

The purpose of a Flying Star chart is to overlay these important numbers onto your floor plan and examine the energy. In this system, every building has a natal Flying Star chart, which is the energy potential or energy map of a given space. Yes, a natal chart, just like the term used in astrology. Your home has a birthday—its chart, much like an astrological reading based on your birthday, holds energy in a way that influences you. A Flying Star chart has also been likened to the "numerology" of a building. Please keep in mind that you need not completely understand Flying Stars for it to work for you; with that being said, you may enjoy some behind-the-scenes information on this intriguing system that I've included in this chapter.

Because Flying Stars is an advanced system and there is quite a learning curve, I will not be teaching you how to *fly* the stars.[9] Plus, there is no need—I have provided the charts for you.

After all, acquiring a natal chart of a building is the sole purpose of flying the stars. Therefore, I will eliminate this aspect so that you may, without learning to fly the stars, improve your Feng Shui immediately. The Flying Star charts featured in this book are turned to the facing direction to easily transfer the information over your floor plan; they will look a little differently when "flown."

The primary and key aspects of Flying Stars are composed of spatial design, direction, time, and environmental forms; capturing the visible and unseen influences affecting the living environment. Flying Stars was developed during the Ming and Ching dynasties, beginning in the fourteenth century AD. Though there are six big schools of the Flying

---

9. The stars (the numbers one through nine) are "flown" by rearranging or moving them around on the nine-square grid of the Luo Shu (the magic square of fifteen). A specific path to this movement is prescribed, and if the computation of the stars is flown incorrectly, an inaccurate energy picture of the building results. It is much like having the wrong date and time of birth in an astrological chart. A star chart has a total of twenty-seven numbers or stars. The Flying Star charts for all twenty-four possible facing, are provided in chapters 6 and 7.

Star system, each method is similar in its approach to and interpretation of the classic texts.[10] The pedagogies of the Flying Stars, however, share one goal: to analyze the energy of a building or a home and adjust the energy to support its occupants.

Many famous masters contributed to the development of this system, which has always contained an air of mystery. The stars have a celestial correlation to the seven stars of the Big Dipper—also known as the Northern Ladle—and two imaginary ones for a total of nine.[11] Each star possesses a unique quality and energy that can influence behavior and events. For example, some stars indicate wealth, sickness, romance, scholarly pursuits, writing, fame, divorce, and so forth. It is obvious that some stars are auspicious and others are negative.

The Flying Star system is based on large-scale time cycles and planetary alignments. The Chinese have the longest recorded history of observing the movement of the planets, more than any other ancient culture. According to ancient Chinese scholars, the planets of the solar system align every 179 to 180 years. In Feng Shui, it is called a megacycle of time. Many historical sources believe that the first observation of this phenomenon occurred around 2500 BC. The Chinese then divided these 180-year cycles into three sixty-year cycles called upper, middle, and lower.

These sixty-year cycles were further grouped into twenty-year increments known as periods or ages. Each period is assigned a number—one through nine—and a Trigram (except Period 5, which has no Trigram) that exhibits a unique energy, and in turn, influences the world. Scholars

---

10. The six big schools of Flying Stars are Wu Chang Pai, Chen Nan Pai, Su Chou Pai, Shang Yu Pai, Siang Chuo Pai, and Kuang Tong Pai.

11. Ssu Ma Chien (145–87 BC), the great Chinese historian, described the Northern Ladle as "the chariot of the Emperor and effectuates his control over the four cardinal points by revolving around the center; it separates the yin and yang and regulates the four seasons; it maintains balance between the five elements; it regulates the moving of the celestial objects; it determines the timing and periods of the calendar."

also noted that the Milky Way shifts every twenty years, thus affecting the luck of a building and its occupants. See the chart below for an example of the nine twenty-year periods that constitute the 180-year mega-cycle of time that covers the years between 1864 and 2044.

The Current 180-Year Mega Cycle Used to Measure Time in the Flying Star System:

Cycle	Period	20-year Time Increment	Trigram/Gua of the Ruling Energy
Upper	1	1864 to 1884	Kan
	2	1884 to 1904	Kun
	3	1904 to 1924	Chen
Middle	4	1924 to 1944	Xun/Sun
	5	1944 to 1964	No Trigram
	6	1964 to 1984	Chien/Qian
Lower	7	1984 to 2004	Dui/Tui
	8*	2004 to 2024	Gen/Ken
	9	2024 to 2044	Li

The Eight Trigrams listed in both charts show the alternate spelling; we are currently in Period 8, which will end on February 3, 2024. The Chinese New Year—using the solar calendar—is February 4 in any given year, thus marking a new year or new period. Period 9 will start February 4, 2024. The ruling energy or influence is always the number and Trigram of the period. For example, the 8 Star reigns supreme in Period 8. Then again, eight is a lucky number in general regardless of the period. The Chinese believe it emits noble energy and represents wealth and prosperity.

The Next 180-Year Mega-Cycle Used to Measure Time in the Flying Star System:

Cycle	Period	20-year Time Increment	Trigram/Gua of the Ruling Energy
Upper	1	2044 to 2064	Kan
	2	2064 to 2084	Kun
	3	2084 to 2104	Chen
Middle	4	2104 to 2124	Xun/Sun
	5	2124 to 2144	No Trigram
	6	2144 to 2164	Chien/Qian
Lower	7	2164 to 2184	Dui/Tui
	8	2184 to 2204	Gen/Ken
	9	2204 to 2224	Li

Period 8 (Years 1824–1844, 2004–2024, 2184–2204)

The current Period 8 is ruled by the Gen Trigram. It represents a time of restitution, karmic laws, and limits. It also denotes the birth of a religious leader, wealth, young people meeting with success, uncovering the truth, and the strengthening of family values. With the collapse of the housing market and major financial institutions such as mortgage companies, the auto industry, and Wall Street, America (and the world) has had to revisit its values concerning money and debt.

As the global financial markets recover from the economic crisis of the late 2000s, humankind can look forward to an almost sixty-year span of great wisdom during Period 8, Period 9, and Period 1. These good Periods will usher in paradigm-changing benevolent energy. Oftentimes, a depression is needed to bring about equilibrium so that nature can achieve perspective and balance. When something is so polarized one way, energy will bring it into balance. Period 8 in particular uncovers falsehoods and foundations built on untruths (e.g., the mortgage industry and Enron scandal). It ultimately brings great wealth, a resolution to past mistakes and karma, and a rectification of excesses. The focus of this period is also on earth and land, including housing, real estate, large- and small-scale construction, mining, and conglomerates. Green living, conscious consumerism, Feng Shui, and preserving our planet are more popular than ever.

Components of a Flying Star Chart

As I stated earlier, the Flying Star Chart of a property is like an energy map or an astrological chart for a building. Flying Star experts, just from the analysis of the stars, can use this chart to make accurate predictions on relationships, wealth, and health—almost any matter that concerns humans. A Flying Star Chart is made up of three numbers in a nine-square grid. Throughout the book, I'll refer to the mountain and facing stars, as they are the most important aspect of a chart, even though there are actually three stars in each of the nine sectors. The third star—the time star—merely indicates the chart's time period. Although Feng Shui Masters will consider all three numbers, this type of analysis is beyond the scope of this book.

I have provided all of the Flying Star charts from 1984 to 2024. This covers two twenty-year periods—Period 8 and Period 7—since most homes fall into these two time periods.

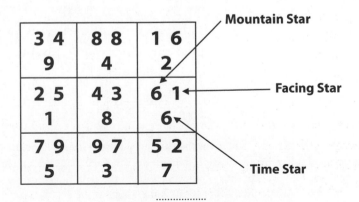

Figure 17: The Components of a Flying Star Chart.

Facing Star. Also known as water stars, these numbers are located in the upper right-hand corner in all nine palaces of the chart. These stars affect money, finance, and career. Good stars indicate wealth luck, while bad stars denote money loss.

Mountain Star. Also known as sitting stars, these numbers are located in the upper left-hand corner in all nine palaces of the chart. Mountain stars influence luck where people, health, career, fertility, and employees are concerned.

Time Star. Also known as the base star, this number indicates the period to which the chart belongs. It is the single star below the facing and mountain stars.

Throughout the book, I will use the terms "facing star" and "mountain star" for consistency. Meanwhile, to grasp fully the essence of the Flying Stars, you must understand the nature or meaning of each star. In this system, the good stars—which are also wealth stars—are 1, 6, 8, and 9, whether they are in the facing or mountain star position. The 4 Star is good for romance and writing. Watch out for 2, 3, 5, and 7—these bad stars indicate sickness, lawsuits, bankruptcy, and burglary, respectively. The 5 Star is the worst, followed by the 2.

The 5 Star is considered evil because it has no direction, thus making it dangerous and unpredictable.[12] It does, however, possess immense power. Bad stars are only good in their period; otherwise, they are considered inauspicious. In other words, the 5 Star is only advantageous in Period 5. The same goes for the 2, 3, and 7 stars.

---

12. Refer to the Luo Shu (also known as the Magic Square of Fifteen) located in chapter 2 and you will notice that the 5 Star resides in the middle. Because it has no direction—all of the other numbers represent the eight directions—it is dangerous. Specifically, this star is called the 5 Yellow. The Luo Shu is the foundation or the "Bible" of the Flying Star system.

When a Flying Star chart is analyzed, two important factors come into play: the nature of the star (good or bad) and the landforms in your immediate environmental landscape. If the external formations support the chart's energy, you will get a positive result. An auspicious formation can bring good fortune, while landforms that do not support the chart can attract misfortune. The chart can only come alive and bestow benevolent energy when the environment and landforms support it. The next most important level is the design layout and the internal distribution of chi.

The Nature of the Nine Stars and Their Effect on Behavior

Stars exert great influence—good and bad—on human behavior. Each of the nine stars of the Flying Star system has a positive and a negative aspect, which basically hinges on timing and how they are used (we call it being "activated") in your home. Stars will also combine with other stars to generate combined energy. Depending on the nearby landforms, the good or bad aspect of the stars will be exhibited. Bad land formations—such as sharp mountains, stagnant water, graveyards, T-junctions, heavily trafficked roads or highways, and negative-chi-attracting landmarks—activate the detrimental qualities of a star's energy. The stars will have the same attributes whether they are in the mountain or water position, as described below:

1 Star

Elemental Energy: Water
Color: White
Key Words: A good star that indicates knowledge, money, and sex

Positive aspects when timing and land formations are good: The basic nature of the 1 Star indicates research, thinking, knowledge, philosophy, intelligence, successful examinations, scholarship, promotions, studies, distinction, abundance, respect, flirtation, literature and writing, the chance for a new start, new romance, and the successful outcome of secret activities.

Negative effects when timing and land formations are bad: The nega-tive aspect of the 1 Star indicates wandering, divorce, detachment, robbery, sexual dysfunction, smuggling, conspiracy, imprisonment, robbery, illicit activities, and deception by friends and lovers. Love- and sex-related problems are also influenced by jealousy, isolation, poverty, or misery.

2 Star
Elemental Energy: Mother Earth
Color: Black
Key Words: A bad star indicating sickness, infertility, and widows

Positive aspects when timing and land formations are good: The 2 Star represents land, real estate; it possesses the energy of a doctor or a healer. Success at work, money, wealth, affluence, lots of children, military officers, women in authority, vibrant health. This star is only auspicious in Period 2 (begins 2064).

Negative effects when timing and land formations are bad: The nega-tive aspects and basic nature of the 2 Star are illness, miscarriages, disease, car accidents, laziness, unemployment, trouble in real estate dealings, misfortune in the family, the loss of the wife, greedy and petty women, low character, black magic, and gossip.

3 Star
Elemental Energy: Big Wood
Color: Jade
Key Words: A bad star indicating lawsuits, fighting, and gossip

Positive aspects when timing and land formations are good: The 3 Star influences the power of speech, linguistics, a good reputation, scholarship, a bright future, great success for the eldest son, and athletic achievement. This energy is also beneficial for industry, factories, and building a business from the ground up.

Negative effects when timing and land formations are bad: The negative nature of the 3 Star ignites arguments, litigation, gossip, quick tempers, slander, prosecution, lawsuits by the government, ruthlessness, conflict, the disclosure of secrets concerning money and taxes, self-punishment, persecution, and troubles with the opposite sex. A new enterprise is doomed to fail under the influence of this star.

4 Star
Elemental Energy: Small Wood
Color: Green
Key Words: A good star indicating romance, sex, and writing

Positive aspects when timing and land formations are good: The 4 Star primarily represents knowledge, passion, romance, wisdom, high officials, great wealth, bags of money, prosperity, land, officers, good workers, business that is three times as lucky, good success in government examinations, honor, and beautiful ladies in the house.

Negative effects when timing and land formations are bad: Suicide by hanging, scandals, extramarital affairs, adultery, broken families, a child who does drugs and gambles, the inability to accept advice, high expenses, demotion, rumors, fraud, problems revolving around the eldest daughter, divorce, exaggeration, damage by storm or hurricane, and self-destructiveness are the negative influences of the 4 Star.

5 Star
Elemental Energy: Universal Earth
Color: Yellow
Key Words: A bad star indicating bankruptcy, cancer, and disasters
This star is only good in Period 5; otherwise, it is considered the most devastating star of all, and if used continuously, it can lead to bankruptcy, cancer, serious illness, incurable tumors, and birth defects. The 5 Star also indicates the deterioration of physical and mental health, social and family

affairs, and financial circumstances. If and when it combines with the 2 Star, total loss is possible. When the 5 Star is in its element—Period 5— it is known to possess powerful kingmaker energy. The last Period 5 was between 1944 and 1964; the next one will not be for another 100 years.

Positive aspects when timing and land formations are good: The 5 Star represents power, authority, honesty, sincerity, accomplishments, prosperity, nobility, success, great wealth, and mysterious men who can run a country. Women in the family are highly respected, special, extraordinary, superhuman, mysterious, virtuous, and hold lots of power. The 5 Star is superb in its period and can be as powerful as a king.

Negative effects when timing and land formations are bad: Lawsuits, cancer, bankruptcy, boys who are always in legal trouble, cocky people, extremism, disasters, calamity, misfortune, accidents, avalanches, floods, the lonely star, the spinster, the widow, setbacks, and government lawsuits are the negative aspects of the 5 Star.

6 Star

Elemental Energy: Big Metal
Color: White
Key Words: A good star indicating power, leadership, government, authority

Positive aspects when timing and land formations are good: The 6 Star indicates power, authority, the government, nobility, leadership, good money decisions, a natural dealmaker, a diplomat, a good politician, the chief, world fame, riches, new enterprises, cooperation by the banks, a good senior officer construction activity, victory in a power struggle, respect, and honor.

Negative effects when timing and land formations are bad: The father hurting the wife and children; loneliness; poverty; the bachelor; accidents; the thief; capital, or permission from authorities; lack of support by banks or respect for the family; excessive desire to rule;

loss of land or real estate; gambling; trouble with the father; the victim of phony religion; rebelliousness; crime; and self-centeredness are the negative outcomes of the 6 Star.

7 Star

Elemental Energy: Small Metal
Color: Red
Key Words: A bad star indicating robbery, government lawsuits, and revolutions

Positive aspects when timing and land formations are good: The 7 Star represents spirituality; metaphysics; good authority and control; lots of money; military officers; wealth; mysticism; productivity; excellence in martial arts; socialism; revolutionism; a famous actor, author, artist, painter, or judge; and the pursuit of happiness.

Negative effects when timing and land formations are bad: The negative aspects and basic nature of the 7 Star represent robbery, government lawsuits, incarceration, fires, a deadly sweet-talker, psychosis, prostitution, brown-nosing and kissing up to the boss, the magician, voodoo, spiritual arts, fortune-telling, numerology, the mystic, metaphysical arts, failure in business, gambling debts, excessive drinking and eating, adultery, and bandits.

8 Star

Elemental Energy: Mountain Earth
Color: White
Key Words: An exceedingly good star indicating wealth, nobility, and real estate
Note: We are now in Period 8 (2004–2024), and this star is king!

Positive aspects when timing and land formations are good: The 8 Star represents riches, wealth, finance, good reserves, investments, loyalty, honor, cultivation, real estate and land, the gentleman, honor, success of the youngest son, a steady person, patriotism, honesty, firmness, thrift, good lawyers, stocks, high morals and virtue, change of lifestyle from bad to good, the end of misery and the beginning of a new life, healing from a troubled life, favorable address and job changes, graduation, marriage, inheritance, the restoration of business, the receipt of insurance money, earning money honestly, the ability to handle trouble and withstand pressure, and a solid countenance.

Negative effects when timing and land formations are bad: The youngest son dying at early age, short tempers, impulsiveness, stubbornness, self-centeredness, the hunchback, a limp, cancer, black magic, loss of money and property, stinginess, the failure to expand a business, bad checks, the bankruptcy of customers, the emergence of a powerful competitor, financial problems, falling from high places, forced address change, conflict among kin over an inheritance, reservation, and self-righteousness are the negative aspects and influences of the 8 Star.

9 Star

Elemental Energy: Fire
Color: Purple
Key Words: A good star indicating celebrations, promotions, and reputation

Positive aspects when timing and land formations are good: Advancement, graduation, reputation, emotion, intelligence, great achievements, promotions, accomplishments, status, litheness, high standards, honesty, nobility, prosperity, the sun, lucidity, tolerance, good luck, respect, prizes, honors, bonuses based on past efforts, the chance to become famous, a quick and favorable change of job, and fame through mass media are the results of an auspicious 9 Star.

Negative effects when timing and land formations are bad: When the 9 Star exhibits its negative side, there are problems with the government, fires, litigation, paranoia, psychosis, violence, fighting, physical disability, hypocrisy, public disgrace, an inability to rest quietly, exaggerated impatience, being the target of slander and suspicion, quarrelling, conflicts, the discovery of past illegal activities, losing face, loss of confidence or position, and deception by the opposite sex.

Flying Stars Feng Shui makes an essential connection between the orientation of a building, the move-in date, the present time, and the luck of the occupants. At the heart of analyzing a Flying Star chart properly is being able to extract and activate good stars and star combinations in important rooms, such as bedrooms, kitchens, home offices, and dining rooms. Another important facet of assessing a chart is gauging the entry points or doors and making sure these portals activate wealth stars.

Determining the Facing

You will need a fairly accurate compass to establish the correct degree of your home's facing. Buy one that has a square edge (protractor compass)—this will allow you to place it directly on your door. If you have a metal door, step away from the door at least six feet to get an accurate bearing. Take your compass measurement or degree from the front door if it faces the road. This design is prevalent in more than 80 percent of the circumstances, so your compass direction will be pretty straightforward. If not, the general rule to follow is to decide where the most vibrant (yang) energy is coming from—the road, ocean, lake, or park. For example, if an apartment building is facing a road, use the main entrance of the building as the facing direction. However, if one side of the building is near the ocean (extremely yang energy), use that direction as the facing. If your apartment building is overwhelmingly complex, just use the door direction of your suite as the facing direction.

If the front door of your home does not face the road, take the reading from the center of your front garden. This is the home's *facing direction*, even if the door does not face the road. Front doors located on the side of the house or an angled front door—even if it seems to face the road—cannot be used in this system to determine the facing of the building. Once you have that degree, check the Flying Star charts for your home in the next two chapters.

Figure 18: Determine the Facing.

According to Flying Stars, only twenty-four house-facing directions are possible. Each of the eight directions is subdivided into three sectors (8 x 3 = 24) and comprises a total of forty-five degrees. Each subsector is just fifteen degrees of that direction. As a result, you will have what is known in Feng Shui techno-talk as South 1, South 2, and South 3, for example. On the Luo Pan, this is known as the 24 mountain ring. Once a compass direction is taken of your home, it will fall into one of these twenty-four facings.

Even though there are twenty-four facings, only sixteen Flying Star charts for each period are available, since the last two subdivided sectors share the same natal chart. In other words, South 2 and South 3 will have the same chart in any given period. Once you know the facing degree, locating your chart is simple. All the charts are clearly indicated by degrees and will tell you which one is South 1, East 2, Southwest 1, and so forth. Make sure you have taken an accurate compass direction of your house so that you have the correct Flying Star chart.

Once you take your compass direction, look at the chart on the following page to see which facing direction it is; for example, 168 degrees means your house faces South 1 (S1 for short). If your house is Period 8, S1, go right to the chart that applies to your home and see the comprehensive recommendations.

The 24 Possible Facing
Directions for Homes or Buildings

Compass Reading at the Door or Facing	General Direction	Exact Direction in Feng Shui	Chinese Name for This Direction	Animal & Energy for This Direction
157.6–172.5	South	S1	Bing	Yang Fire
172.6–187.5		S2	Wu	HORSE
187.6–202.5		S3	Ting/Ding	Yin Fire
202.6–217.5	Southwest	SW1	Wei	GOAT
217.6–232.5		SW2	Kun	Earth
232.6–247.5		SW3	Shen	MONKEY
247.6–262.5	West	W1	Geng	Yang Metal
262.6–277.5		W2	You	ROOSTER
277.6–292.5		W3	Xin	Yin Metal
292.6–307.5	Northwest	NW1	Xu	DOG
307.6–322.5		NW2	Chien/Qian	Metal
322.6–337.5		NW3	Hai	PIG
337.6–352.5	North	N1	Ren	Yang Water
352.6–7.5		N2	Tzi/Zi	RAT
7.6–22.5		N3	Kwei/Gui	Yin Water
22.6–37.5	Northeast	NE1	Chou	OX
37.6–52.5		NE2	Gen/Ken	Earth
52.6–67.5		NE3	Yin	TIGER
67.6–82.5	East	E1	Jia	Yang Wood
82.6–97.5		E2	Mao	RABBIT
97.6–112.5		E3	Yi	Yin Wood
112.6–127.5	Southeast	SE1	Chen	DRAGON
127.6–142.5		SE2	Xun/Sun	Wood
142.6–157.5		SE3	Su/Si	SNAKE

Move-in Date

To this day, controversy abounds over whether to use the construction date (when the structure was built) or the move-in date (when the occupants moved into the home) in determining the period of a building. Feng Shui masters in Hong Kong and other areas of the world debate this notion, and according to Grand Master Yap, the conversations can get pretty heated. For the most part, masters in Hong Kong prefer the construction date, while those in Malaysia, Singapore, and Taiwan employ the move-in date (my personal camp and lineage.)

In my experience, the move-in date offers a more accurate assessment of the building's energy and the people who occupy it. To me this is quite logical. Human beings bring their powerful energy to a building; otherwise it's just an empty structure. Rare exceptions to this rule do crop up, but I've only seen one in my many years of consulting. In some instances, landforms are immutable and override the energy of the occupants. Dwellings constructed near vortices or where lei lines intersect, for instance, will bring bad luck no matter who lives there. In such homes, I use the construction date because these energies overpower the chi of the occupants, and this is extremely rare—it is prudent to always use the move-in date. The following guidelines will help you determine to which period your home belongs:

1. Your home is a **Period 7** if you moved in between February 4, 1984, and February 3, 2004.

2. Your home is a **Period 8** if you moved in between February 4, 2004, and February 3, 2024.

*Exceptions for Period 7 homes are if major renovations took place **after** February 4, 2004.* A major renovation includes removing the entire roof (a small percentage must be exposed to the open sky for at least a few hours); major remodeling of the interior; overhauling the front entrance and door; painting the entire inside and outside simultaneously; remodeling the kitchen or bathrooms; installing a skylight; changing all the floors at the same time; or adding an attached garage or room. These alterations will cause a major shift in energy, and therefore your Flying Star chart will change. Major remodeling will change the period of the house or building. So if you did any of these things or a combination thereof after February 4, 2004, and you moved in Period 7, your home now enjoys a Period 8 chart. If you moved into your house after 2004, and have done or are currently doing some renovations, your home is still a Period 8.

If you moved in between 1964 and 1984 and have made no renovations, then the home is a Period 6. The house is past good luck by two periods. Consider bringing the house current by using some of the above-mentioned methods such as remodeling, removing the roof, and so forth. The same applies to Period 7 homes; consider bringing them current as they are past good luck. In order to get the best wealth luck, your home should always be in the current period.

I have made recommendations and comments on all sixteen charts for Period 7 and Period 8. The suggestions will tell you how to activate the exterior and interior of your home, thus extracting the best wealth luck possible. So relax. Again, you need not completely understand the systems used for it to work for you. Correctly activating the exterior environment is one of the most important things you can do in Feng Shui.

You can have a perfectly wonderful, wealth-potential chart, but if you're dealing with bad landforms—such as those discussed in chapter 3—your great stars will be null and void. My recommendations also include water placement to activate the wealth stars (8, 1, and 9, respectively) in both periods, and I have not used the theory of Direct and

Indirect Spirit to do so.[13] Master Yap believes this aspect of the Direct and Indirect Spirit in old Xuan Kong texts could have been misinterpreted or is not entirely reliable, so I place water on the good, wealth stars regardless of their location.

All sixteen Flying Star charts in any given period will fall under four fundamental energy structures, which are explained and identified in the next section.

1. Double Stars Meet at Facing (Shuang Xing Dao Xiang)

2. Double Stars Meet at Sitting (Shuang Xing Dao Zuo)

3. Prosperous Sitting and Facing (Wang Shan Wang Shui)

4. Up the Mountain, Down the River (Shang Shan Xia Shui)

To extract the best energy from a chart, activation must be done correctly. I've identified how to activate all charts advantageously in Period 8 and Period 7 no matter which energy category your residence falls under. If the chart is exceptional for wealth luck, I've distinguished it with a star (*). Also note that in my following recommendations it may look as if I am suggesting a bad direction for your bed, desk, door, and so on. Remember, I am using Advanced Eight Mansions—some fifteen-degree increments actually support you.

Though I've given alternate water locations for some charts in the next chapters, keep in mind that these are not necessarily the best placements for water, or that you should add more water. In charts where no alternate water location is offered, the chart can only be properly activated as recommended. Otherwise, you will lose the potential wealth the chart may deliver.

---

13. The theory of Direct and Indirect Spirit restricts the use of water placement in some directions in certain periods. Some masters call this theory the Holy 1 and Holy 0. See the Glossary of Terms for more details.

Annual Visiting Stars

In addition to the permanent natal chart of a residence, visiting stars drop in or "fly" in for a finite amount of time, usually a month or a year. Daily and hourly stars are also part of the system, but this can get a bit fanatical and I have not included them in the book, as they have such a miniscule relevance. It is important to note that yearly and monthly stars will often trigger certain stars or combination of stars to release energy.

See the following chart for the annual visiting stars for the next four years and what they can indicate. When an annual star visits and combines with the facing stars in important areas, additional money luck can occur. No need to examine all eight sectors, just significant areas such as your main door, bed direction, or home office. When a 5 or 2 visits an important door, weaken the energy by placing metal there, such as a wind chime. No need to enhance the wealth stars (1, 6, 8, or 9)—just enjoy and reap the rewards of their visit.

Annual Visiting Stars and Indications				
Sectors or Directions	2012 Year of the Dragon	2013 Year of the Snake	2014 Year of the Horse	2015 Year of the Goat
Center Annual Star	6	5	4	3
Northwest	7 Rivals at work and thievery	6 Travel, good reputation, authority	5 Losing wealth and powerful positions	4 Romance, success in educational ideas and traveling
West	8 Wealth, marital bliss and romance	7 Injuries or robbery caused by small metal	6 Challenging authority and rebellious behavior	5 Friction that causes losing wealth, disasters, disease
Northeast	9 Money, festivities and achievements	8 Great wealth and lots of opportunities	7 Romance, good networking, and theft	6 Success in the political arena, power and authority
South	1 Being recognized at work and harmony	9 Promotions at work, fiery arguments	8 Achievements, wealth and weddings	7 Heated arguments and thievery
North	2 Sickness and worries	1 Good careers, wisdom, money	9 Harmony, good career-luck and money	8 Great wealth and success
Southwest	3 Gossip, lawsuits, theft and disharmony	2 Lots of sickness, especially in the stomach or reproductive organs	1 Divorce, dominating women, and some money luck	9 Heart and high blood pressure issues, achievements in real estate
East	4 Conflict in relationships and romance	3 Very aggressive male behavior, lawsuits and rebelliousness	2 Legal problems, sickness and bickering	1 Innovative changes, money luck, wisdom, career and start-up businesses
Southeast	5 Money loss, break-ups, disasters, and swelling	4 Romance, beauty, jet-set traveling and elegance	3 Quarrels, lawsuits and some travel	2 Sickness, especially in the stomach or reproductive organs

The Four Negative Annual Visiting Energies

Feng Shui is all about enhancing your luck and opportunities, so timing is an important factor to ensure continued harmony and prosperity. Every year brings with it certain taboos when it comes to renovations and major construction in and around your home. Four different yet inauspicious energies—the Grand Duke Jupiter (Tai Sui), the Three Killings (Sam Sart or San Sha), the annual 5 Yellow star, and the Year Breaker (Sui Po)—will visit your home and change locations every year. The Feng Shui New Year, February 4, marks the occasion. The phenomenon is similar to astrology when certain alignments can be malefic. Like many techniques and formulas, the theories of the Three Killings, the Grand Duke Jupiter, and the Year Breaker were adopted from the San He School and became part of the San Yuan system around the Ming Dynasty.

Not all Feng Shui Masters completely accept the validity of the negative energy theory. As for myself, I don't generally focus on the negative aspects of these sha energies, but I do exercise caution to not disturb them, or I implement countermeasures when the general Feng Shui of a home is not good. See the next chart, which gives you the sectors/directions that these four negative energies visit for the next few years. Awakening these energies can bring undesirable outcomes; negative effects will not occur without cause. To avoid this kind of activity, you must refrain from disturbing specific areas of your property. Unearthing certain areas in your garden/yard, or construction such as a room addition, during specific years will see the sha energy released. Pay close attention to earth-moving activities; if you are considering an outdoor water feature, such as a pool, pond, or waterfall per our recommendations or any other major digging or landscaping, consult a Feng Shui Master first. Simple gardening, however, is harmless.

The Three Killings

If the name sounds truly awful, it's for a reason. The Three Killings can be the most serious of the four negative energies. In 2012 it visits the entire south sector of your property. Disturbing the Three Killings has various levels of consequences. Some people have reported illnesses, accidents, marital problems, and money loss. Extreme bad luck is rare, but if unfavorable landforms are also present, it is possible. Place metal on well-used doors that face the Three Killings direction. Do not renovate, landscape, hang new doors, cut big trees from the roots, or install a pool or pond in this direction or location if you can avoid it. If this is not a frequented part of your home or yard, there is no need to implement a cure or countermeasure. Basic gardening will have no bearing on the Three Killings area of your yard because it does not displace enough dirt. If you must do repairs to the house or have planned a much-needed addition, consult a Feng Shui expert to select an auspicious date to begin construction, to protect you from any negative results.

It is common for Chinese people to place three bronze Chi Lin dragons, a turtle, or a laughing buddha in the affected area. I personally do not recommend that my clients place these countermeasures—simply avoiding major digging or construction is the best cure.

The 5 Yellow Star

The 5 star in the Flying Star system is the worst possible energy—but rest assured, the 5 annual star will visit one direction or sector of your house a year. If it takes up residence in the front of your home, you may experience difficulties with money, health, or relationships. By placing metal in this location, it can be countered or completely averted. In 2006, the 5 Yellow visited the front of my house (west). I placed wind chimes on the gate handle of my front entry, and I had a fantastic year. The 5 Yellow, however, can cause aggravations, so place metal there as a precaution for the year.

It is not advised to do major construction in the area the 5 visits; if you must, seek the advice of a Feng Shui Master or practitioner, who will give you good dates to begin construction. Replacing or tilting a main/front door is considered to be a major activity to engage in where the 5 is visiting and should also be avoided.

The Grand Duke and the Year Breaker

The Grand Duke and the Year Breaker are intangible stars, and are a more esoteric or spiritual aspect of Feng Shui. However, they are widely respected by the Chinese, and some attention is devoted to these visiting energies. The Grand Duke always corresponds to the ruling animal year; for example, 2012 is the year of the Dragon (location is Southeast 1). The Year Breaker is the exact opposite location, Northwest 1. As these energies are not as serious as the 5 Yellow and the Three Killings, you will just want to avoid facing these directions if possible.

If the earth is disturbed where the Grand Duke and Year Breaker are visiting, loss of money is possible. Before construction or repair projects are under way in these locations, refer to the Tong Shu, the Chinese almanac, for auspicious start dates to ensure good luck. Feng Shui practitioners can select a date using the Great Sun Formula to protect you from negative effects.[14] The Chinese have been known to place a metal Guan Di (the Chinese god of war) statue to protect them at these locations, especially if they plan to break the ground. In this case, they will bury the metal statue in the afflicted area, especially the Three Killings. The countermeasure or cure is really the metal, not the statue. Any metal (copper, brass, bronze, stainless steel, or pewter) can be used. If you are planning to install a pool or have major renovations in one or more of the afflicted area, you may

---

14. The Tong Shu (Chinese almanac) has been of great importance to the people of Asia since ancient times. It serves as a useful guide to everyday life, dispensing advice on auspicious days for burials, weddings, and business transactions. Even in modern times, millions consult the Chinese almanac daily.

want to consult professional to assist you. Please note that the Three Killings encompasses 75 degrees. It covers 45 degrees of the main direction (for example, all 45 degrees of South) plus two fifteen-degree increments left and right of it.

The Four Negative Energies
aka the Four Shas for the Next Seven Years

The Year	Grand Duke "Tai Sui"	The Year Breaker "Sui Po"	Three Killings "Sam Sart"	5 Yellow
2012 Dragon	Southeast 1	Northwest 1	South Plus SE3 & SW1	Southeast
2013 Snake	Southeast 3	Northwest 3	East Plus NE3 & SE1	Center
2014 Horse	South 2	North 1	North Plus NE1 & NW3	Northwest
2015 Goat	Southwest 1	North 1	West Plus NW1 & SW3	West
2016 Monkey	Southwest 3	Northeast 3	South Plus SE3 & SW1	Northeast
2017 Rooster	West 2	East 2	East Plus NE3 & SE 1	South
2018 Dog	Northwest 1	Southeast 1	North Plus NE1 & NW3	North

In order to proceed in properly activating the Feng Shui for your home, you will need to have an accurate compass direction and the right period using the date you moved in. All natal Flying Star charts for Period 8 and Period 7 are in the next two chapters.

Six

The Get-Rich Keys for Period 8 Buildings

There are many paths to the top of the mountain, but the view is always the same.

Chinese Proverb

The following data will help you best extract the wealth energy of Period 8 homes and buildings. Your house is a Period 8 if you moved in between February 4, 2004, and February 3, 2023. These suggestions are based on the Eight Mansions system, individual mountain and facing stars, Flying Star combinations, Advanced Eight Mansions (using specific fifteen-degree increments), the five elements, Later Heaven Ba Gua, San He formulas, San Yuan techniques, the nature of the stars, the timelessness of the stars, and location and direction—all of which focus on wealth. Because these recommendations are specific to the charts, they cannot be mixed and matched.

The recommendations I've outlined in this section take advantage of good locations *and* good directions. If you are unable to choose the auspicious location I've suggested (e.g., your office in the northwest area of the house), use the recommended **direction** instead. Remember, every single room in your house contains all eight directions, and directional energy will support you more powerfully than a particular room location. But, if you are able to do both, you will get a faster result. In Feng Shui we have a saying: "Direction rules!" You may notice that some of your good directions are not being used in the recommendations; this is because the Flying Stars in those directions are not good and using them could bring a negative outcome. For couples who are opposite Life Groups, pay special attention to the directions that work for all Guas. This is particularly important for the bed direction, as you are both sharing this space.

We are currently in the auspicious Period 8. Your Flying Star chart, however, must be properly set in motion to receive the benefit. The following information will help you activate the exterior and interior to accomplish that goal. It is important to remedy any bad formations discussed in chapter 3; otherwise, your great chart and its energy cannot be realized. When reviewing the recommendations, have your floor plan ready by doing the following:

1. Take a compass direction and determine the facing direction.

2. Divide your floor plan, with a yellow highlighter, into nine sectors. Place all eight directions—south, west, north, and so forth around your floor plan. The directions are identified in the black area of the star charts.

3. Place your +90, -80, +70, and so forth next to the palaces according to your Gua. Use the Eight Mansions chart in chapter 4 to find your +90, +80, -60, -90, and so forth.

4. Transpose the numbers of the correct natal Flying Star chart next to the eight directions.

5. See Figure 19, which demonstrates how to do this correctly.

While reading the suggestions for your home facing, have your completed floor plan in front of you to make notes. For example, place the bed here, install water there, create a mountain here, move the desk to face this direction, and so on. If you live in an apartment, high-rise, townhome, condo, or rented space and are unable to have an outdoor water feature, place one inside the recommended area. This will activate the wealth star and bring you good money luck. Wall and floor fountains are hugely popular and available everywhere. Water features should never be placed in the master bedroom.

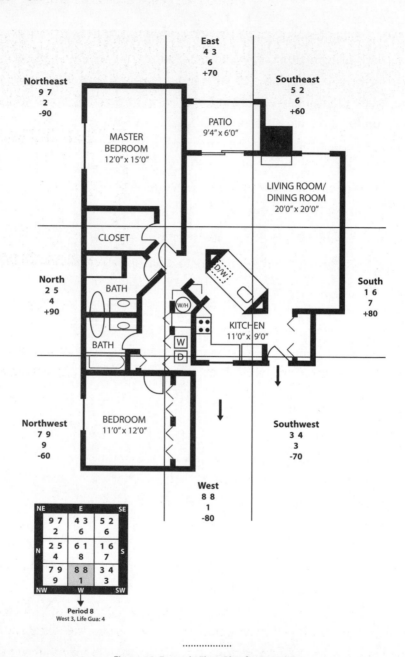

Figure 19: Example Floor Plan for Period 8–
Divide your floor plan into nine palaces or sectors.
Transfer the correct Natal Chart as indicated.

PERIOD 8
South 1
Li Trigram   Element: FIRE

South 1 (157.6° to 172.5°)
  Facing name: Bing

Chart: Double Stars Meet at Back
  (Shuang Xing Dao Zuo)

Warning: Possible Eight Roads Destruction
  and Robbery Mountain Sha

Level Two DEL: 157.5°

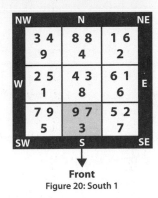

NW	N	NE
3 4 **9**	8 8 **4**	1 6 **2**
2 5 **1**	4 3 **8**	6 1 **6**
7 9 **5**	9 7 **3**	5 2 **7**
SW	S	SE

↓
Front
Figure 20: South 1

Figure 20 is the natal chart is for a south-facing property, between 157.6 and 172.5 degrees. Known as South 1, this is the first fifteen degrees of south. Note: The following recommendations are specific to this chart.

Activating the
Exterior Environment
Requires Water and Mountain in the North
Alternate Water Locations: East and Southwest
Bankruptcy Indicated: Water in the West
This house has the two prominent 8 stars in the back of the property known as Double Stars Meet at Sitting (Shuang Xing Dao Zuo). You need two important features to capture the energy properly—solid backing and big water. The water could be a pool, pond, waterfall, huge fountain, or lake. If you have a pool with a waterfall, the water should flow from the north. If your waterfall flows from the west or a water feature is located in the west, you could activate bankruptcy energy.

This chart must have solid backing, such as a fence (stone, brick, stucco, or a combination of wood and brick is best); high ground; landscape mounds; boulders (no sharp or jagged edges); a dense row of tall, stately trees; or any combination of these. If a natural mountain, high ground, or a hill is already at the back of your property, the layout is already quite auspicious.

A South 1 facing works great for the East Life Group (1, 3, 4, or 9 Guas) and the West Life Group (2, 6, 7, or 8 Guas). 6 and 7 Guas, however, may not thrive as well. Overall, if the energies are tapped correctly and the space is void of bad landforms, the house indicates good money luck, success in writing, and scholarly pursuits. South-facing properties can produce people in authority and charismatic, intelligent, and skilled entrepreneurs. Remedy any bad landforms discussed in chapter 3 such as T-junctures, sloping land, drains, and so forth using the Master's Tips as guidelines.

This house also has a potential Eight Roads of Destruction formation if your driveway or a nearby road approaches or exits from the southeast. Meanwhile, a jagged cliff, electrical tower, huge dead tree, lamppost, or a broken mountain in the southwest could produce a Robbery Mountain Sha formation.

Activating the Internal Environment
Master Bedroom

To enhance wealth luck, locate your bedroom in the south (second floor), north, northeast, or east. These sectors have good mountain stars with wealth energy. For additional money luck, place your headboard or bed toward the north (1, 3, 4, or 9 Guas only), northeast (2, 6, 7, or 8 Guas only), or east (all Guas); these directions have good mountain and facing star combinations.

Home Office

Establish your home office in the south (second floor), north, north-east, or east. These sectors/rooms have good mountain stars with wealth energy. While sitting at your desk, face toward the north (1, 3, 4, or 9 Guas only), northeast (2, 6, 7, or 8 Guas only), or east or southwest (all Guas), this will bring additional money luck.

Kitchen, Stove, Fire Mouth, and Toilets

North, east, and southwest are the best directions for the fire mouth; west is the worst and should be avoided to deter bankruptcy. If your kitchen is in the west or southeast sector, money loss is likely. A stove in the west of the kitchen is even more serious.

Review the Eight Mansions chart in chapter 4 to find your wealth/ power direction and location. Money struggles are likely if a stove or a toilet is located in your +90 sector. You can relocate a stove, but you must use another toilet if this is the case, so select a toilet in one of your negative sectors (-90, -80, -70, or -60). Also, if a toilet is in the area of your 8 facing star, wealth luck is diminished a great deal.

The Best Doors in the House (Interior and Exterior)

The best doors in the house to use are those that face north (1, 3, 4, or 9 Guas only), northeast (2, 6, 7, or 8 Guas only), or east and southwest (all Guas). Using these doors will activate wealth. Select one of the four doors based on your Life Gua. If one of these directions is also your +90, you will be lucky with money! Avoid using a door that faces the west; it will activate bankruptcy.

PERIOD 8
South 2 and South 3
Li Trigram   Element: FIRE

South 2 (172.6° to 187.5°)
Facing name: Wu and the Horse

South 3 (187.6° to 202.5°)
Facing name: Ting

Chart: Double Stars Meet at Front
(Shuang Xing Dao Xiang)

Warning: Possible Eight Roads of
Destruction, Eight Killing Forces
and Robbery Mountain Sha

Major DEL at 180°!

NW	N	NE
5 2 **9**	9 7 **4**	7 9 **2**
6 1 **1**	4 3 **8**	2 5 **6**
1 6 **5**	8 8 **3**	3 4 **7**

W (left) · E (right) · SW · S · SE

↓
Front
Figure 21: South 2 & 3

Figure 21 is the natal chart is for a house that is south-facing, between 172.6 and 202.5 degrees. Known as South 2 and South 3, these are the second and third fifteen degrees of south. Note: The following recommendations are specific to this chart.

Activating the External Environment
Requires Mountain and Water in the Front
Alternate Water Locations: West and Northeast
Bankruptcy Indicated: Water in the East
These south-facing homes feature the two prominent 8 stars in front known as **Double Stars Meet at Facing** (Shuang Xing Dao Xiang). You must activate this energy with two important features, a mountain and water. You can simulate a mountain (three feet or taller) with higher ground, landscape mounds, boulders (no sharp or jagged edges), or any combination thereof. Do not place boulders in direct alignment with the front door. Install a koi pond, a waterfall, a pond with a waterfall,

or a water fountain to activate the water element of this configuration. Some masters do not recommend water in the south; however, to fully capture the energy of the 8 facing star, water is a must. I've witnessed incredible results by activating the 8 facing star, regardless of its location.

Clients have reported money gains, business opportunities, financial windfalls, and unexpected inheritances. South-facing properties can produce people in authority and charismatic, intelligent, and skilled entrepreneurs. South 2 facings support the East Life Group (1, 3, 4, or 9 Guas) best. Homes that face South 3 work for both groups; 6 and 7 Guas, however, may not thrive as well. Overall, if the energies are tapped correctly and the space is void of bad landforms, this south-facing residence indicates good money luck, success in writing, and scholarly pursuits. Remedy any bad landforms discussed in chapter 3—such as T-junctures, sloping land, drains, and so forth—using the Master's Tips as guidelines.

South 2: A possible Eight Killings formation may occur if mountain energy comes from the northwest direction.

South 3: An Eight Roads of Destruction formation is likely if your driveway or a nearby road approaches or exits from the southwest.

Both facings (S2 and S3) may experience a Robbery Mountain Sha formation if a jagged cliff, electrical tower, huge dead tree, lamppost, or broken mountain is located in the southeast.

Activating the Internal Environment
Master Bedroom

To enhance wealth luck, choose a bedroom located in the south (second floor), north, west, or southwest. These sectors have good mountain stars with wealth energy. For additional money luck and if the home faces South 2, place your headboard or bed toward the south (1, 3, 4, or 9 Guas only), or west or southwest (2, 6, 7, or 8 Guas only). If the home faces South 3, position your headboard or bed toward the west, south, or southwest (all Guas); these directions have good mountain and facing star combinations.

Home Office

To enhance wealth luck, locate your office in the south (second floor), north, west, or southwest. These sectors have good mountain stars with wealth energy. For additional money luck and if the home faces South 2, the best directions to face while sitting at your desk are the south (1, 3, 4, or 9 Guas only), or west, northeast, or southwest (2, 6, 7, or 8 Guas only). In a South 3 home, orient your desk or face toward the northeast, west, south, or southwest (all Guas).

Kitchen, Stove, Fire Mouth, and Toilets

South, west, and northeast are the best directions for the fire mouth; east is the worst and should be avoided to deter bankruptcy. If your kitchen is in the northwestern or eastern sector, money loss is likely. A stove in the northwestern area of the kitchen is even more serious. Review the Eight Mansions chart to find your wealth/power direction and location. Money struggles are likely if a stove or a toilet is located in your +90 sector. You can relocate a stove, but you must use another toilet if this is the case, so select a toilet in one of your negative sectors (-90, -80, -70, or -60). Also, if a toilet is in the area of your 8 facing star, wealth luck is diminished a great deal.

The Best Doors in the House (Interior and Exterior)

In South 2 homes, use doors that face south (1, 3, 4, or 9 Guas only), or west, northeast, and southwest (2, 6, 7, or 8 Guas only). In a South 3 home, enter and exit doors that face northeast, west, south, and southwest (all Guas). Select one of these doors based on your Life Gua. If one of these directions is also your +90, you will be lucky with money. Avoid using doors that face the east direction; they will activate bankruptcy.

PERIOD 8
Southwest 1
Kun Trigram   Element: Mother EARTH

Southwest 1 (202.6° to 217.5°)

   Facing name: Wei and the Goat

*Very Special Chart: Combination
of Ten (He Shih Chu) and Prosperous
Sitting and Facing (Wang Shan Wang
Shui)

Warning: Possible Robbery Mountain Sha

Level Two DEL: 202.5°

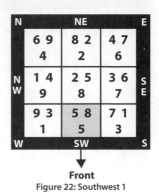

Front

Figure 22: Southwest 1

Figure 22 is the natal chart for southwest-facing properties, between 202.6 and 217.5 degrees. Known as Southwest 1, this is the first fifteen degrees of southwest. Note: The following recommendations are specific to this chart.

Activating the External Environment
Requires Mountain in Back, Water in Front

Alternate Water Location: North

This house has two special aspects for wealth luck—a Combination of Ten (He Shih Chu) and a Prosperous Sitting and Facing (Wang Shan Wang Shui). These features make this chart one of the luckiest in Period 8. It is extremely auspicious for employers, career climbers, entrepreneurs, sales, networking, joint-venture partnering, and Internet marketing. Southwest-facing properties are also known for turning bad fortunes into opportunities.

Combination of Ten charts are remarkably good for business relationships and partnering. To capture the luck your chart offers, an important and prominent backing to your property is paramount. If you are lucky enough to have a real mountain or hill in the back, you're ahead of the game. You can, however, simulate a mountain with a tall, solid fence; dense landscaping; high ground; and so forth. If you have water here, you will need to remove it if possible. Otherwise, serious illness in the house may occur, plus you could lose your opportunity to activate the wealth luck on your property correctly.

You will also need a beautiful water feature—such as a koi pond, waterfall, or fountain—in the front of the property. Center it as much as possible in the yard without being in direct alignment with or blocking the front door. If you already face a natural lake, pond, river, or the ocean, and you have a substantial backing, this chart is already fully activated and will bring great luck to you. This chart, however, is best served with more emphasis on the backing, so make it a priority and as substantial and solid as possible.

Overall, if the energies are tapped correctly and no adverse landforms are present, the house indicates great career luck, good networking, and strong partnerships in business. In the event of negative landforms, bad relationships—especially with business partners and employees—can ensue. Water in the back of the property can sour business deals. Review chapter 3 to make sure you are not experiencing any of the unfavorable formations mentioned there, especially sloping land in the back. The house may have a Robbery Mountain Sha formation if a jagged cliff, electrical tower, huge dead tree, lamppost, or broken mountain is in the southeast.

Activating the Internal Environment
Master Bedroom

To enhance wealth luck, locate your bedroom in the north, northwest, west, or northeast—these sectors have good mountain stars with wealth energy. For additional money luck, position your headboard or bed toward the north (1, 3, 4, or 9 Guas only) or northwest (all Guas); these directions have good mountain and facing star combinations.

Home Office

Establish your home office in the north, northwest, west, or northeast—these sectors have good mountain stars with wealth energy. For additional money luck, angle your desk, body, or both toward the north or southeast (1, 3, 4, and 9 Guas only), or south or southwest (all Guas).

Kitchen, Stove, Fire Mouth, and Toilets

Southwest and south are the best directions for the fire mouth, particularly the southwest for enhancing wealth. A kitchen in the north, or a kitchen or stove in the northwest with southeast-facing knobs, may hurt the father or man of the house. In both scenarios, he will feel exhausted and will work hard with little progress.

Review the chart to find your wealth/power direction and location. Money struggles are likely if a stove or a toilet is located in your +90 sector. You can relocate a stove, but you must use another toilet if this is the case, so select a toilet in one of your negative sectors (-90, -80, -70, or -60). Also, if a toilet is in the area of your 8 facing star, wealth luck is diminished a great deal.

The Best Doors in the House (Interior and Exterior)

The best doors in the house face north and southeast (1, 3, 4, or 9 Guas only), or south and southwest (all Guas). Using a west door will bring clients to high-powered lawyers, especially if this chart is properly activated by good landforms. Select one of these doors based on your Life Gua. If one of these directions is also your +90, you will be lucky with money.

PERIOD 8
Southwest 2 and Southwest 3
Kun Trigram   Element: Mother EARTH

Southwest 2 (217.6° to 232.5°)
  Facing name: Kun

Southwest 3 (232.6° to 247.5°)
  Facing name: Shen and the Monkey

*Special Chart: Parent String Formation
  (Fu Mo San Poon Gua)

Warning: Possible Eight Roads of
  Destruction, Eight Killing Forces
  and Robbery Mountain Sha

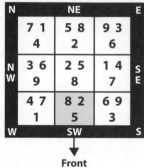

Front
Figure 23: Southwest 2 & 3

Figure 23 is the natal chart for southwest-facing properties facing between 217.6 and 247.5 degrees. Known as Southwest 2 and Southwest 3, these are the second and third fifteen degrees of southwest. Note: The following recommendations are specific to this chart.

Activating the External Environment
Requires Mountain in Front, Water in Back
These southwest-facing homes have a special chart known as a Parent String (Fu Mo San Poon Gua) formation. It is correctly activated by a mountain in the front and water in the back. It is said that the chi goes up the mountain, down the river. This simply means that the prominent mountain star (8) is in the front of the property, while the prominent facing star (8) is in back. To capture fully the special energy of this chart, the mountain star must be activated by a real or simulated mountain.

The mountain can be high ground, landscape mounds, massive boulders (no jagged or pointed edges), or any combination of these. Water in the back of the residence—a swimming pool, a spa, a waterfall, a large fountain, a lake, a pond, or the ocean—must also be present to tap into the area's natural good fortune. It is important that this house not have water in front. If it does, turn it off, or else it can bring a great deal of illness. Besides, you'll lose the chance to activate this chart correctly, which benefits businesses and entrepreneurs. Occupants are known to make vast fortunes with this type of chart, because the Parent String/Pearl String Formations are famous for turning bad luck into opportunities.

Southwest 2: Southwest 2 brings the best wealth luck to the West Life Group (2, 6, 7, or 8). Those living in Southwest 2 facing properties can become wealthy in a short period of time. An Eight Roads of Destruction is possible if your driveway or a nearby road approaches or exits from the west or south.

Southwest 3: These properties can be filled with abundance, erudition, and powerful families and so this is a good wealth-direction for all Life Guas. An Eight Killing formation may occur if a mountain comes from the east. A Robbery Mountain Sha formation is probable if a jagged cliff, an electrical tower, a huge dead tree, a lamppost, or a broken mountain is in the southwest.

Activating the Internal Environment
Master Bedroom

To enhance wealth luck, locate your bedroom in the south, southeast, southwest, or east—these areas have good mountain stars with wealth energy. For additional money luck and homes that face Southwest 2, position your headboard or bed toward the southeast or south (1, 3, 4, or 9 Guas only). In homes that face Southwest 3, orient the headboard or bed toward the southeast or south (all Guas); these directions have good mountain and facing star combinations.

Home Office

Establish your home office in the south, southeast, southwest, or east—these areas have good mountain stars with wealth energy. For additional money luck and homes that face Southwest 2, position your desk and body to face toward the northeast or northwest (2, 6, 7, or 8 Guas only), or north or south (1, 3, 4, or 9 Guas only). For Southwest 3 homes, angle your desk and body toward the northeast, northwest, or south (all Guas), or north (1, 3, 4, or 9 Guas only)—these directions have good facing stars with wealth energy.

Kitchen, Stove, Fire Mouth, and Toilets

Northeast, south, and north are the best directions for the fire mouth—these sectors have beneficial facing stars for wealth. The south is the worst location for the kitchen; it indicates problems for the breadwinner or the man of the house.

Review the Eight Mansions chart to find your wealth/power direction and location. Money struggles are likely if a stove or a toilet is located in your +90 sector. You can relocate a stove, but you must use another toilet if this is the case, so select a toilet in one of your negative sectors (-90, -80, -70, or -60). Also, if a toilet is in the area of your 8 facing star, wealth luck is diminished a great deal.

The Best Doors in the House (Interior and Exterior)

In Southwest 2 homes, the best doors in the house face northeast and northwest (2, 6, 7, or 8 Guas only), or north and south (1, 3, 4, or 9 Guas only). The occupants of Southwest 3 homes should use doors that face northeast, northwest, and south (all Guas), or north (1, 3, 4, or 9 Guas only)—these directions have good facing stars with wealth energy. Select one of these doors based on your Life Gua. If one of these directions is also your +90, you will be lucky with money. Note: Place metal at the front door and rarely use it; illness is indicated with everyday use or in the presence of real water.

PERIOD 8
West 1
Dui Trigram   Element: Small METAL

West 1 (247.6° to 262.5°)

   Facing name: Geng

Chart: Double Stars Meet at Sitting/Back
(Shuang Xing Dao Zuo)

Warning: Possible Eight Roads of
Destruction, Eight Killing Forces
and Robbery Mountain Sha

Level Two DEL: 247.5°

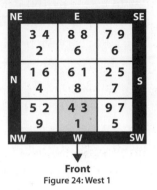

Front

Figure 24: West 1

Figure 24 is the natal chart for a west-facing property, between 247.6
and 262.5 degrees. Known as West 1, this is the first fifteen degrees of
west. Note: The following recommendations are specific to this chart.

Activating the External Environment
Requires Mountain and Water in Back
Bankruptcy Indicated: Water in the South

The prominent 8 stars meet at the back of this property (east). This chart
is called Double Stars Meet at Sitting (Shuang Xing Dao Zuo) and it
requires the following two features in back: an important, substantial
backing and a water feature. The backing could be a high, solid fence or
wall; dense landscaping against the wall; high ground (higher than the
front); or a natural mountain. As for the water element, a fountain, a pool,
a spa, a lake, or a pond will suffice. The 8 facing star, called the Water
Dragon, requires water to activate its potential fully. If this home has
water in the south, bankruptcy is likely.

Overall, if the energies are tapped correctly and no adverse landforms are present, the house indicates good wealth luck. This house has a possible Eight Roads of Destruction if your driveway or a nearby road approaches or exits from the southwest. This formation is serious and must be countered by a Feng Shui Master or practitioner. It can destroy good business relationships, devastate lives, and kill wealth luck. This house may also have a Robbery Mountain Sha formation if a jagged cliff, electrical tower, huge dead tree, lamppost, or broken mountain is in the south.

Activating the Internal Environment
Master Bedroom

To enhance wealth luck, locate your bedroom in the north, east, or southwest—these sectors have good mountain stars with wealth energy. If you want additional money luck, position your headboard or bed toward the north (1, 3, 4, or 9 Guas only), or east (all Guas); these directions have good mountain and facing star combinations.

Home Office

Establish your home office in the north, east, or southwest—these sectors have good mountain stars with wealth energy. If you want additional money luck, position your desk and body facing toward the north or southeast (1, 3, 4, or 9 Guas only), or east (all Guas); these directions have good facing stars with wealth energy.

Kitchen, Stove, Fire Mouth, and Toilets

East and southeast are the best directions for the fire mouth—these sectors have good facing stars for wealth. South indicates bankruptcy, making it the worst location for the kitchen, stove, and fire mouth.

Review the chart to find your wealth/power direction and location. Money struggles are likely if a stove or a toilet is located in your +90 sector. You can relocate a stove, but you must use another toilet if this is the case, so select a toilet in one of your negative sectors (-90, -80, -70, or -60). Also, if a toilet is in the area of your 8 facing star, wealth luck is diminished a great deal.

The Best Doors in the House (Interior and Exterior)

The best doors in the house face east (all Guas), or north and southeast (1, 3, 4, or 9 Guas only)—these directions will activate wealth when they are used. Select one of these doors based on your Life Gua. If one of these directions is also your +90, you will be lucky with money! Avoid south-facing doors; they will activate bankruptcy energy.

PERIOD 8

West 2 and West 3

Dui Trigram   Element: Small METAL

West 2 (262.6° to 277.5°)

   Facing name: You and the Rooster

West 3 (277.6° to 292.5°) Facing name: Xin

Chart: Double Stars Meet at Facing
   (Shuang Xing Dao Xiang)

Warning: Possible Eight Roads of
   Destruction, Eight Killing Forces
   and Robbery Mountain Sha

Major DEL at 270°!

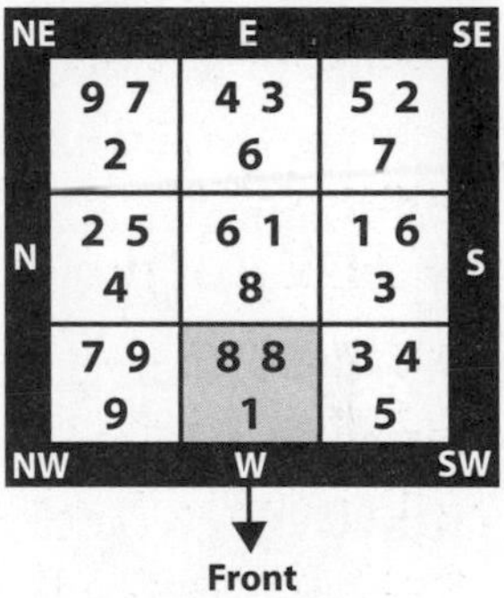

NE	E		SE
9 7	4 3	5 2	
2	6	7	
2 5	6 1	1 6	
4	8	3	
7 9	8 8	3 4	
9	1	5	
NW	W		SW

Front

Figure 25: West 2 & 3

Figure 25 is the natal chart for a west-facing property facing between 262.6 and 292.5 degrees. Known as West 2 and West 3, these are the second and third fifteen degrees of west Note: The following recommendations are specific to this chart.

Activating the External Environment
Requires Mountain and Water in Front

Bankruptcy Indicated: Water in the North

These West-facing properties feature a pair of 8 stars in the front of the property known as the **Double Stars Meet at Facing** (Shuang Xing Dao Xiang). For maximum results, place a mountain and a water feature in the front. A mountain could be higher ground than the back, landscaping mounds, or huge boulders (no sharp or jagged edges). You can install a fountain, koi pond, or waterfall near the front door. In general, many masters are opposed to placing water in the west, but I have had incredible results by activating the 8 stars, regardless of the location.

A large body of water—natural or man-made—in the north will activate huge money loss, bankruptcy, a dishonest business partner, or business scandals made public. It is important in this residence (West 2 and West 3) that the center, or the heart of the house, remain free of a staircase, fire (stove or fireplace), and water (toilet, laundry room, or fountain). The energy here is quite excellent (1, 6, 8 stars).

If you live in an apartment, high-rise, townhome, condo, or rented space and are not able to place an outdoor water feature, install one inside the recommended area. This will activate the wealth star and bring you good money luck. Wall and floor fountains are hugely popular and available everywhere. Water features do not belong in the bedroom.

West 2: With the correct external landforms, these properties can produce dynamic individuals who will be successful and able to amass great wealth in a short period time. West 2 homes also have a possible Eight Killing Forces if mountain chi comes from the southeast or a Robbery Mountain Sha formation if a jagged cliff, electrical tower, huge dead tree, lamppost, or broken mountain is in the south.

West 3: With the proper landforms, West 3 properties can produce outstanding academic achievements, exceptional athletes, and power in the political arena. An Eight Roads of Destruction formation is possible if your driveway or a nearby road approaches or exits from the northwest. These residences may also experience a Robbery Mountain Sha formation if a jagged cliff, an electrical tower, a huge dead tree, a lamppost, or a broken mountain is in the southwest.

Overall, if the energies are tapped correctly and no adverse landforms are present, these houses indicate good money luck with the 8 facing star in front.

Activating the Internal Environment
Master Bedroom
To enhance wealth luck, locate your bedroom in the west (second floor), south, or northeast. For additional money luck and in homes that face West 2, position your headboard or bed toward the south (1, 3, 4, or 9 Guas only) or west (2, 6, 7, or 8 Guas only). In homes that face West 3, place your headboard or bed toward the south or west (all Guas); these directions have good mountain and facing star combinations.

Home Office
Establish your home office in the west (second floor), south, or northeast. For additional money luck and in homes that face West 2, angle your desk and body facing toward the west or northwest (2, 6, 7, or 8 Guas only), or south (1, 3, 4, or 9 Guas only). In homes that face West 3, position your desk and body facing toward the south, west, or northwest (all Guas)—these directions have good facing stars with wealth energy.

Kitchen, Stove, Fire Mouth, and Toilets

West and northwest are the best directions for the fire mouth; the north is the worst and should be avoided to deter bankruptcy. If the kitchen is in the north or southeast sector, money loss is likely. Stoves in the north or southeast areas of the kitchen are even more serious.

Review the Eight Mansions chart to find your wealth/power direction and location. You will struggle with money if a stove or a toilet is located in your +90 sector of the house. You can relocate a stove, but you must use another toilet if this is the case, so select a toilet in one of your negative sectors (-90, -80, -70, or -60). Also, if a toilet is in the area of your 8 facing star, wealth luck is diminished a great deal.

The Best Doors in the House (Interior and Exterior)

In West 2 homes, the best doors in the house face west and northwest (2, 6, 7, or 8 Guas only) or south (1, 3, 4, or 9 Guas only). Use doors that face south, west, and northwest (all Guas) in West 3 homes—these directions have good facing stars with wealth energy. Select one of these doors based on your Life Gua. If one of these directions is also your +90, you will be lucky with money. Avoid using doors that face the North direction; they will activate bankruptcy.

PERIOD 8
Northwest 1
Chien Trigram   Element: Big METAL

Northwest 1 (292.6° to 307.5°)
  Facing name: Xu and the Dog

*Special Chart: Pearl String
  (Lin Cu San Poon Gua)

Warning: Possible Robbery Mountain Sha

Level Two DEL: 292.5 degrees

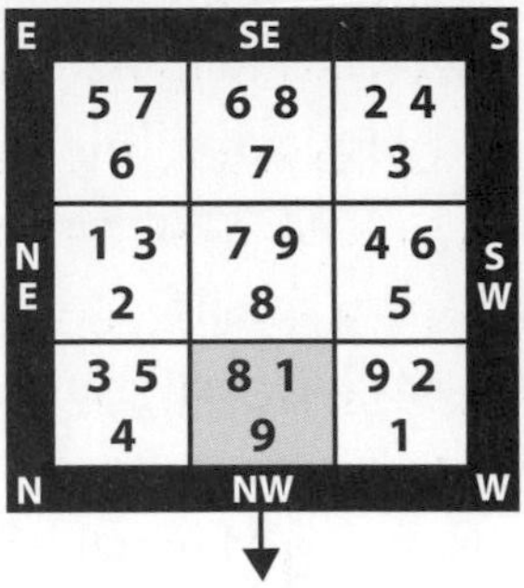

E	SE		S
5 7 **6**	**6 8** **7**	**2 4** **3**	
1 3 **2**	**7 9** **8**	**4 6** **5**	
3 5 **4**	**8 1** **9**	**9 2** **1**	
N	NW		W

Front

Figure 26: Northwest 1

Figure 26 is the natal chart for a northwest-facing property between 292.6 and 307.5 degrees. Known as Northwest 1, this is the first fifteen degrees of northwest. Note: The following recommendations are specific to this chart.

Activating the External Environment
Requires Mountain in Front, Water at the Back

This house has a special chart known as a **Pearl String** (Lin Cu San Poon Gua). A mountain in the front and water in the back will correctly activate this chart. According to lore, chi travels up the mountain, down the river. This simply means that the prominent mountain star (8) is in the front of the property while the prominent facing star (8) is in the back. So, to capture the special energy of this chart fully, the mountain star must be activated by a real or simulated mountain. The mountain can be high ground, landscape mounds, massive boulders (no jagged or pointed edges), or any combination of these; it should be as centered as possible without blocking the front door. Water in the back—proportional to the residence and centered in your backyard or garden—can include a swimming pool, a spa, a waterfall, a large fountain, a lake, a pond, or the ocean.

There are two different types of Pearl String Formations—one that enhances luck with people and relationships and one that brings wealth luck. This particular Pearl String Formation builds wealth. It must, however, be activated properly; otherwise, this formation is not considered auspicious. This chart is extremely lucky, because all the front stars (8, 1, 9) are wealth stars. Properly activated Pearl Strings in Period 8 have the potential to turn almost everything into an advantage. This is especially true if it involves business. In other periods, when the landforms are good, people can become rich indeed. The house may have a Robbery Mountain Sha formation if a jagged cliff, electrical tower, huge dead tree, lamppost, or broken mountain is in the southwest.

Activating the Internal Environment
Master Bedroom

To enhance wealth luck, locate your bedroom in the southeast, west, northeast, or northwest (second floor)—these rooms have good mountain stars with wealth energy. For additional money luck, position your headboard or bed toward the northwest or southwest (all Guas), or southeast (1, 3, 4, or 9 Guas only); these directions have good mountain and facing star combinations.

Home Office

Establish your home office in the southeast, west, northeast, or northwest (second floor)—these rooms have good mountain stars with wealth energy. For additional money luck, angle your desk and body facing toward the northwest or southwest (all Guas), or southeast (1, 3, 4, or 9 Guas only).

Kitchen, Stove, Fire Mouth, and Toilets

Northwest and southeast are the best directions for the fire mouth; north should be avoided to deter bankruptcy. The east sector is one of the worst locations for a kitchen in this house, and an east-facing fire mouth could rob you of business deals, promotions, and intellectual property.

Review the Eight Mansions chart to find your wealth/power direction and location. Money struggles are likely if a stove or a toilet is located in your +90 sector. You can relocate a stove, but you must use another toilet if this is the case, so select a toilet in one of your negative sectors (-90, -80, -70, or -60). Also, if a toilet is in the area of your 8 facing star, wealth luck is diminished a great deal.

The Best Doors in the House (Interior and Exterior)

The best doors in the house face northwest and southwest (good for all Guas), or southeast (1, 3, 4, or 9 Guas only). Select one of these three doors based on your Life Gua. If one of these directions is also your +90, you will be lucky with money! Avoid using an angled door that faces north; it will activate bankruptcy.

PERIOD 8
Northwest 2 and Northwest 3
Chien Trigram   Element: Big METAL

Northwest 2 (307.6° to 322.5°)
Facing name: Chien

Northwest 3 (322.6° to 337.5°)
Facing name: Hai and the Pig

*Special Chart: Prosperous Sitting and
Facing (Wang Shan Wang Shui)

Warning: Possible Eight Roads of
Destruction, Eight Killings and
Robbery Mountain Sha

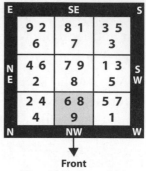

Front
Figure 27: Northwest 2 & 3

Figure 27 is the natal chart for northwest-facing properties facing between 307.6 and 337.5 degrees. Known as Northwest 2 and Northwest 3, these are the second and third fifteen degrees of northwest. Note: The following recommendations are specific to this chart.

Activating the External Environment
Requires Water in Front, Mountain in Back
Bankruptcy Indicated: Water in the South
These northwest-facing homes have a special chart known as a Prosperous Sitting and Facing (Wang Shan Wang Shui), which is good for money and people luck. This is considered the perfect placement for these stars. You will need a good backing to activate the 8 mountain star properly. A pool in the back is lucky for money, but you will get mixed results if you do not have an excellent backing or a significant mountain—even a simulated one. Water should be placed in the front of the house to activate the 8 facing star. Some masters do not recommend

water in the northwest, but to capture the energy of the 8 facing star (prominent wealth star and current water dragon) fully, water is a must. I've witnessed incredible results by activating the 8 facing star, regardless of its location. Clients have reported money gains, business opportunities, financial windfalls, and unexpected inheritances.

Northwest 2: Overall, if the energies are tapped correctly and no adverse landforms are present, the house indicates excellent money luck potential. An Eight Roads of Destruction formation (see chapter 3 for more details) is possible if a road approaches the house from the west or north. A Robbery Mountain Sha formation could also occur if a jagged cliff, an electrical tower, a huge dead tree, a lamppost, or a broken mountain is in the north.

Northwest 3: These homes may have an Eight Killing Forces formation if mountain energy/chi comes to the home from the south or a Robbery Mountain Sha formation if a jagged cliff, an electrical tower, huge dead tree, lamppost, or broken mountain is in the west.

Activating the Internal Environment
Master Bedroom

To enhance wealth luck, locate your bedroom in the east, southeast, southwest, or northwest (second floor)—these rooms have good mountain stars with wealth energy. For additional money luck and in homes that face Northwest 2, position your headboard or bed toward the northwest or northeast (2, 6, 7, or 8 Guas only), or southeast (1, 3, 4, or 9 Guas only). In homes that face Northwest 3, place your headboard or bed toward the northwest, southeast, or northeast (all Guas); these directions have good mountain and facing star combinations.

Home Office

Establish your home office in the east, southeast, southwest, or northwest (second floor)—these rooms have good mountain stars with wealth energy. For additional money luck and in homes that face Northwest 2, situate your desk and body facing toward the northwest or northeast (2, 6, 7, or 8 Guas only), or southeast (1, 3, 4, or 9 Guas only). In Northwest 3 homes, angle your desk and body facing toward the northwest, southeast, or northeast (all Guas)—these directions have good facing stars with wealth energy.

Kitchen, Stove, Fire Mouth, and Toilets

Northwest and southeast are the best directions for the fire mouth (stove knobs)—these are good facing stars and the fire will activate them perfectly. A south-facing fire mouth, however, could attract bankruptcy. If your kitchen is in the west of the house, money loss is likely. Stoves in the west of the kitchen are even more serious.

Review the Eight Mansions chart to find your wealth/power direction and location. Money struggles are likely if a stove or a toilet is located in your +90 sector. You can relocate a stove, but you must use another toilet if this is the case, so select a toilet in one of your negative sectors (-90, -80, -70, or -60). Also, if a toilet is in the area of your 8 facing star, wealth luck is diminished a great deal.

The Best Doors in the House (Interior and Exterior)

In Northwest 2 homes, the best doors face northwest and northeast (2, 6, 7, or 8 Guas only), or southeast (1, 3, 4, or 9 Guas only). If your residence faces Northwest 3, use northwest, northeast, and southeast (all Guas) doors. Using a southwest door will bring clients to high-powered lawyers, especially if this chart is properly activated by good landforms. If you are not a lawyer, do not use the southwest door or you may experience unfair lawsuits, conflicts, and issues with legal contracts. Select one of these three doors based on your Life Gua. If one of these directions is also your +90, you will be lucky with money.

PERIOD 8
North 1
Kan Trigram   Element: WATER

North 1 (337.6° to 352.5°)
    Facing name: Ren

Chart: Double Stars Meet at
    Facing (Shuang Xing Dao Xiang)

Warning: Possible Eight Roads of
    Destruction and Robbery Mountain Sha

Level Two DEL: 337.5°

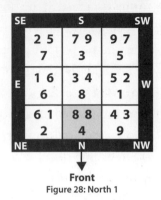

Front
Figure 28: North 1

SE	S	SW
2 5 7	7 9 3	9 7 5
1 6 6	3 4 8	5 2 1
6 1 2	8 8 4	4 3 9

(E on left, W on right; NE, N, NW across bottom)

Figure 28 is the natal chart of a north-facing properties facing between 337.6 and 352.5 degrees. Known as North 1, this is the first fifteen degrees of north. Note: The following recommendations are specific to this chart.

Activating the External Environment
Requires Water and Mountain in Front
Alternate Water Location: South
Bankruptcy Indicated: Water in the Southeast
This chart features the two prominent 8 stars in the front of the property known as Double Stars Meet at Facing (Shuang Xing Dao Xiang). Both of the 8 stars must be represented in the environment by a mountain and a water in front to capture the wealth potential of this chart fully. The mountain can be high ground, landscape mounds, massive boulders or moss rocks (no jagged or pointed edges), or any combination of these. Keep these simulated mountains as centered as possible, but do not align with the front door. The water element can include a

waterfall, a large fountain, a gorgeous slate or granite water wall near the main door, or a koi pond. Water in the southeast or water flowing from a southeastern direction indicates bankruptcy.

Overall, if the energies are tapped correctly and no adverse landforms are present, the house indicates excellent wealth luck. If activated properly, North 1 charts can bring success to businesses and indicate charismatic people, depending on your life group. This residence may be unlucky for those born in the years of the Tiger, the Horse, or the Dog. Not one single degree of luck is available for 2, 6, 7, or 8 Guas, so north should be avoided altogether. If you belong to the West Life Group and live in a north-facing house, avoid entering your home from north-facing doors. Use alternate doors as much as possible, at least 80 percent of the time. This change alone will bring you some luck.

North is one of the best facings for those in the East Life Group (1, 3, 4, or 9 Guas), and you will benefit greatly from living in one of these residences. If you have a natal Flying Star chart that profits from water in the front (such as this one), a north-facing house can attract lots of wealth luck.

An Eight Roads of Destruction formation is possible if your driveway or a nearby road approaches or exits from the northwest. The house may also have a Robbery Mountain Sha formation if a jagged cliff, electrical tower, huge dead tree, lamppost, or broken mountain is in the west.

Activating the Internal Environment
Master Bedroom

To enhance wealth luck, locate the master bedroom in the east, southwest, north (second floor), or northeast sector of the house—these areas have good mountain stars with wealth energy. For additional money luck, place your headboard or bed toward the north (1, 3, 4, or 9 Guas only), east (all Guas) or northeast (2, 6, 7, or 8 Guas only); these directions have good mountain and facing star combinations. Rooms located in the southeast and west are the worst for money luck. If your master bedroom is located in either of these areas, incorporate metal, such as a stunning metal bed. Do not use a fireplace or add too much red to this room. Make sure you position yourself in a good direction as mentioned previously.

Home Office
Establish your home office in the east, southwest, north (second floor), or northeast—these areas are good mountain stars with wealth energy. Angle your desk and body facing toward the north (1, 3, 4, or 9 Guas only), east (all Guas), northeast (2, 6, 7, or 8 Guas only), or south (all Guas except 6 and 7)—these directions have good facing stars for wealth.

Kitchen, Stove, Fire Mouth, and Toilets
North, northeast, and south are the best directions for the fire mouth because fire stimulates the wealth energy of these facing stars. A west- or southeast-facing fire mouth is problematic and must be corrected. If your kitchen is located in the west or southeast sector, money loss is likely. Stoves in the west area of the kitchen are even more serious. These scenarios indicate cancer, huge financial loss, bankruptcy, and business breakups.

Review the Eight Mansions chart to find your wealth/power direction and location. Money struggles are likely if a stove or a toilet is located in your +90 sector. You can relocate a stove, but you must use another toilet if this is the case. Select a toilet in one of your negative sectors (-90, -80, -70, or -60). Also, if a toilet is in the area of your 8 facing star, wealth luck is diminished a great deal.

The Best Doors in the House (Interior and Exterior)
The best doors in this house face north (1, 3, 4, or 9 Guas only), east (all Guas), northeast (2, 6, 7, or 8 Guas only), or south (all Guas except 6 and 7)—these will activate wealth when used. Select one of these four based on your Life Gua. If one of these directions is also your +90, you will be lucky with money! Avoid using an angled door that faces southeast; it will activate bankruptcy.

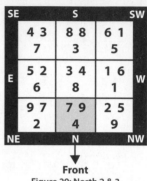

PERIOD 8
North 2 and North 3
Kan Trigram   Element: WATER

North 2 (352.6° to 7.5°)
   Facing name: Tzi and the Rat

North 3 (7.6° to 22.5) Facing name: Kwei

Chart: Double Stars Meet at Sitting
   (Shuang Xing Dao Zuo)

Warning: Possible Eight Roads of
   Destruction and Robbery Mountain Sha

Major DEL at 0/360°!

Front

Figure 29: North 2 & 3

Figure 29 is the natal chart for north-facing properties facing between 352.6 and 22.5 degrees. Known as North 2 and North 3, these are the second and third fifteen degrees of north. Note: The following recommendations are specific to this chart.

Activating the External Environment
Requires Mountain and Water in the Back
Alternate Water Locations: Southwest and North
Bankruptcy Indicated: Water in Northwest
These north-facing homes feature two 8 stars in the back of the property; this chart is known as Double Stars Meet at Sitting (Shuang Xing Dao Zuo). You will need two important features to capture the energy properly—a solid backing and big water. The water can be a pool, a pond, a waterfall, a huge fountain, or a lake. If you incorporate a waterfall, make sure it flows in a southern direction. The water feature should be in proportion to the size of the house. A solid backing—such as a solid fence, high ground, landscape mounds, boulders, a dense row of tall, stately trees,

or any combination thereof—is necessary. If a natural mountain or high ground is already part of the landscape, this is excellent. Some masters do not recommend water in the south, but to capture the energy of the 8 facing star (prominent star and current water dragon) fully, water is a must. I've seen incredible results by activating the 8 facing star, regardless of its location. Clients have reported money gains, business opportunities, financial windfalls, and unexpected inheritances.

North 2: Occupants of these homes can successfully run their own businesses and enjoy good fortune—their careers will take them all over the world. Bad landforms, however, can produce alcoholics and injurious gossip. North 2 residences may also have a Robbery Mountain Sha formation if a jagged cliff, electrical tower, huge dead tree, lamppost, or broken mountain is in the west.

North 3: When these properties have good landforms, long life and prosperity are indicated. Bad landforms, however, suggest loneliness and bankruptcy for the inhabitants of the residence. An Eight Roads of Destruction formation is possible if your driveway or a nearby road approaches or exits from the northeast. These residences may also experience a Robbery Mountain Sha formation if a jagged cliff, electrical tower, huge dead tree, lamppost, or broken mountain is in the northeast.

Activating the Internal Environment
Master Bedroom

To enhance wealth luck, locate your bedroom in the south, southwest, west, or northeast—these areas have good mountain stars with wealth energy. For additional money luck and in homes that face North 2, position your headboard or bed south (1, 3, 4, or 9 Guas only), or southwest or west (2, 6, 7, or 8 Guas only). In North 3 residences, position your headboard or bed toward the south, west, or southwest (all Guas); these directions have good mountain and facing star combinations. Rooms located in the northwest and east are the worst areas for money luck. If your master bedroom is located in either sector, incorporate metal, such as a stunning metal bed. Do not use a fireplace or add too much red to this room. Make sure you place yourself in a good direction as mentioned previously.

Home Office

Establish your home office in the south, southwest, west, or northeast—these areas have good mountain stars with wealth energy. For additional money luck and in homes that face North 2, angle your desk and body toward the south or north (1, 3, 4, or 9 Guas only), or southwest or west (2, 6, 7, or 8 Guas only). If your home faces North 3, orient your desk and body facing toward the south, west, or southwest (all Guas), or north (1, 3, 4, or 9 Guas only)—these directions have good facing stars with wealth energy.

Kitchen, Stove, Fire Mouth, and Toilets

South, north, and southwest are the best directions for the fire mouth (stove knobs), because fire stimulates the wealth energy of these good facing stars. An east- or northwest-facing fire mouth should be remedied; otherwise, huge financial devastation, cancer, or the breakdown of your business, especially where entrepreneurs are concerned, could occur. If your kitchen is in the east or northwest sector, money loss is likely. Stoves in the east or the northwest of the kitchen are even more serious. If this is the case, consider changing the stove location, the knobs, or both, depending on the severity of the placement.

Review the Eight Mansions chart to find your wealth/power direction and location. Money struggles are likely if a stove or a toilet is located in your +90 sector. You can relocate a stove, but you must use another toilet if this is the case, so select a toilet in one of your negative sectors (-90, -80, -70, or -60). Also, if a toilet is in the area of your 8 facing star, wealth luck is diminished a great deal.

The Best Doors in the House (Interior and Exterior)

South and north (1, 3, 4, or 9 Guas only), or southwest and west (2, 6, 7, or 8 Guas only) are the best doors in a North 2 residence. In North 3 homes, use doors that face south, west, and southwest (all Guas), or north (1, 3, 4, or 9 Guas only)—these directions have good facing stars with wealth energy. Select one of these doors based on your Life Gua. If one of these directions is also your +90, you will be lucky with money! Do not use an angled door that faces northwest; it will activate bankruptcy energy.

PERIOD 8
Northeast 1
Gen Trigram   Element: Mountain EARTH

Northeast 1 (22.6° to 37.5°)

   Facing name: Chou and the Ox

*Very Special Chart: Combination of Ten (He Shih Chu) and Prosperous Sitting and Facing (Wang Shan Wang Shui)

Warning: Possible Robbery Mountain Sha

Level Two DEL: 22.5°

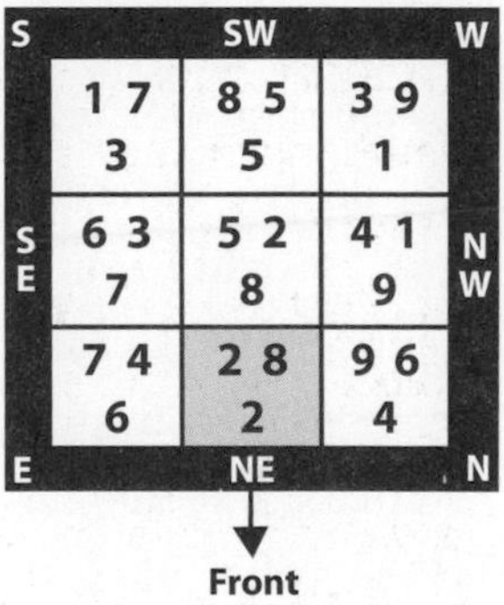

S	SW	W
1 7 3	**8 5** 5	**3 9** 1
6 3 7	**5 2** 8	**4 1** 9
7 4 6	**2 8** 2	**9 6** 4
E	NE	N

Front
Figure 30: Northeast 1

    Figure 30 is the natal chart for northeast-facing properties facing between 22.6 and 37.5 degrees. Known as Northeast 1, this is the first fifteen degrees of northeast. Note: The following recommendations are specific to this chart.

Activating the External Environment
Requires Water in Front, Mountain in Back

This house has two powerful opportunities for wealth indicated in the chart with the Combination of Ten (He Shih Chu) and the Prosperous Sitting and Facing (Wang Shan Wang Shui), making it one of the most auspicious charts in Period 8. Notice how the facing stars and the time stars add to ten in all nine palaces. They add to ten toward the facing stars, which indicate huge money luck. Another version of the Combination of Ten relates to people, relationship, and career luck. These add to ten toward the mountain star. Read chapter 8 to learn more about the two types of Combinations of Ten.

This chart requires great support in the back, such as a tall, solid fence, high ground (higher than the front), a mountain, dense landscaping, or any combination thereof. Water in front is one of the most important aspects of this special wealth-producing chart—a water fountain; a water wall constructed of slate, granite, or stone near the front door; a waterfall; or a koi pond is also a must. Though the water feature should be proportionate to the size of the home, it should possess the Wow! factor. Water does not belong in the back of the property: it could activate bankruptcy!

This site should have none of the bad landforms described in chapter 3. If so, you could lose the lucrative potential of this exceptional chart. Remedy any injurious landforms, such as T-junctures, sloping land, drains, and so forth, using the Master's Tips as guidelines. This house may also have a Robbery Mountain Sha formation if a jagged cliff, electrical tower, huge dead tree, lamppost, or broken mountain is in the north.

Activating the Internal Environment
Master Bedroom

To enhance wealth luck, locate your bedroom in the south, southwest, north, or southeast—these areas possess good mountain stars with wealth energy. For additional money luck, position your headboard or bed toward the northwest (all Guas) or north (1, 3, 4, or 9 Guas only); these directions have good mountain and facing star combinations.

Home Office
Establish your home office in the south, southwest, north, or southeast—these areas have good mountain stars with wealth energy. While sitting at your desk, face northeast (2, 6, 7, or 8 Guas only), northwest or west (all Guas), or north (1, 3, 4, or 9 Guas only). These directions have good facing stars for wealth luck.

Kitchen, Stove, Fire Mouth, and Toilets
Northeast, northwest, and west are the best directions for the fire mouth. Review the Eight Mansions chart to find your wealth/power direction and location. Money struggles are likely if a stove or a toilet is located in your +90 sector. You can relocate a stove, but you must use another toilet if this is the case, so select a toilet in one of your negative sectors (-90, -80, -70, or -60). Also, if a toilet is in the area of your 8 facing star, wealth luck is diminished a great deal.

The Best Doors in the House (Interior and Exterior)
The best doors in the house face northeast (2, 6, 7, or 8 Guas only), northwest and west (all Guas), or north (1, 3, 4, or 9 Guas only). These directions have good facing stars for wealth luck and will be activated when used. Select one of these doors based on your Life Gua. If one of these directions is also your +90, you will be lucky with money! Avoid as much as possible a back door facing southwest—it will activate bankruptcy energy with regular use.

PERIOD 8
Northeast 2 and Northeast 3
Gen Trigram   Element: Mountain EARTH

Northeast 2 (37.6° to 52.5°)
  Facing name: Gen

Northeast 3 (52.6° to 67.5°)
  Facing name: Yin and the Tiger

*Special Chart: Parent String
  (Fu Mu San Poon Gua)

Warning: Possible Eight Roads of
  Destruction, Eight Killing Forces,
  and Robbery Mountain Sha

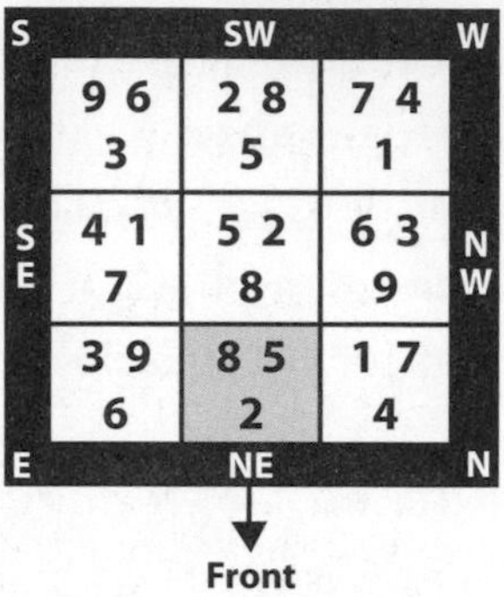

S	SW	W
9 6 3	2 8 5	7 4 1
4 1 7	5 2 8	6 3 9
3 9 6	8 5 2	1 7 4

(SE on left, NW on right; E bottom-left, NE bottom-center, N bottom-right)

↓
Front
Figure 31: Northeast 2 & 3

Figure 31 is the natal chart for northeast-facing properties facing between 37.6 and 67.5 degrees. Known as Northeast 2 and Northeast 3, these are the second and third fifteen degrees of northeast. Note: The following recommendations are specific to this chart.

Activating the External Environment
Requires Mountain in Front, Water in Back
This house has a special chart known as a Parent String (Fu Mu San Poon Gua), which is auspicious for wealth luck. It is an Up the Mountain, Down the River formation—which simply means that the prominent mountain star (8) is in the front of the property, while the prominent facing star (8) is in the back. In this case, the mountain gets activated first, and the water second. This is known as a reverse formation. The perfect placement is the prosperity facing star at the front/facing and the prosperity mountain star at the sitting or back.

Its shelf life, however, is only twenty years. To extract this chart's potential it must be activated properly because of the 5 facing star in front. To capture the special energy of this chart fully, the mountain star must be activated by a real or a simulated mountain; it should be as centered as possible without blocking the front door. High ground, landscape mounds, massive boulders (no jagged or pointed edges), or any combination of these will suffice. Water in the back—proportional to the residence and centered in your backyard or garden—can include a swimming pool, spa, waterfall, large fountain, lake, pond, or the ocean.

Northeast 2: With correct external formations, this type of property will produce smart and intelligent children and humble, open-minded, kindhearted, wealthy, and respected people. The occupants will use international businesses to accumulate assets. If, however, the landforms are bad, gambling and drinking, coupled with loneliness, may occur. Overall, if the energies are tapped properly and no adverse landforms are present, this house creates excellent potential for wealth luck. This chart, however, has a 5 facing star in the northeast and it needs to be cured with metal, such as wind chimes. An Eight Roads of Destruction formation is possible if your driveway or a nearby road approaches or exits from the north or east. These homes may also have a Robbery Mountain Sha formation if a jagged cliff, electrical tower, huge dead tree, lamppost, or broken mountain is in the east.

Northeast 3: These properties may experience a possible Eight Killing Forces if a mountain is in front, or a Robbery Mountain Sha formation if a jagged cliff, electrical tower, a huge dead tree, lamppost, or a broken mountain is in the north.

Activating the Internal Environment
Master Bedroom

To enhance wealth luck, locate your bedroom in the south, north, north-west, or northeast (second floor)—these areas have good mountain stars with wealth energy. For additional money luck and in homes that face Northeast 2, place your headboard or bed toward southeast or south (1, 3, 4, or 9 Guas only). In homes that face Northeast 3, position your head-board toward the southeast or south (all Guas); these directions have good mountain and facing star combinations.

Home Office

Establish your home office in the south, north, northwest, or northeast (second floor)—these areas have good mountain stars with wealth energy. In homes that face Northeast 2, angle your desk and body facing toward the southwest (2, 6, 7, or 8 Guas only), or southeast, south, or east (1, 3, 4, or 9 Guas only)—these directions have good facing stars with wealth energy. For Northeast 3 homes, orient your desk and body facing toward the southwest, southeast, south, or east—these support all Guas.

Kitchen, Stove, Fire Mouth, and Toilets

Southeast, southwest, and east are the best directions for the fire mouth. Review the chart to find your wealth/power direction and location. Money struggles are likely if a stove or toilet is located in your +90 sector. You can relocate a stove, but you must use another toilet if this is the case, so select a toilet in one of your negative sectors (-90, -80, -70, or -60). Also, if a toilet is in the area of your 8 facing star, wealth luck is diminished a great deal.

The Best Doors in the House (Interior and Exterior)

The best doors in a Northeast 2 home face southwest (2, 6, 7, or 8 Guas only), or southeast, south, and east (1, 3, 4, or 9 Guas only)—these directions have good facing stars with wealth energy. If you live in a Northeast 3 home, use southwest, southeast, south, and east doors—these support all

Guas. Frequenting a northwest-facing door will bring clients to high-powered lawyers, especially if this chart is properly activated by good landforms. Select one of these doors based on your Life Gua. If one of these directions is also your +90, you will be lucky with money! Avoid using a northeast-facing door on a regular basis; otherwise, it will activate bankruptcy energy. Place high-grade metal, such as bronze, brass, or copper, on or near the door, and use it less than 5 percent of the time.

PERIOD 8
East 1
Chen Trigram   Element: Big WOOD

East 1 (67.6° to 82.5°) Facing name: Jia

Chart: Double Stars Meet at Facing
   (Shuang Xing Dao Xiang)

Warning: Possible: Eight Roads of
   Destruction and Robbery
   Mountain Sha

Level Two DEL: 67.5°

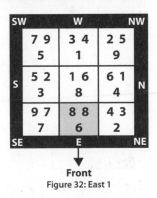

Front
Figure 32: East 1

Figure 32 is the natal chart is for east-facing properties facing between 67.6 to 82.5 degrees. Known as East 1, this is the first fifteen degrees of east. Note: The following recommendations are specific to this chart.

Activating the External Environment
Requires Water and Mountain in Front
Alternate Water Location: North

Bankruptcy Indicated: Water in the Northwest

This house features the prominent 8 stars—known as Double Stars Meet at Facing (Shuang Xing Dao Xiang)—in the front. To capture the full wealth potential of this chart, both of the 8 stars must be represented and activated in the environment by a mountain and a water in the front of the property. The mountain can be high ground, landscape mounds, massive boulders or moss rocks (no jagged or pointed edges), or any combination of these. Try to keep the simulated mountain as centered as possible without blocking the front door. The water can be a waterfall; a large fountain; a gorgeous slate, granite, or rock water wall near the main door; or a koi pond.

Overall, if the energies are tapped correctly and no adverse landforms are present, the house indicates good potential for money luck. An Eight Roads of Destruction formation is possible if your driveway or a nearby road approaches or exits from the northeast. The house may have a Robbery Mountain Sha formation if a jagged cliff, electrical tower, huge dead tree, lamppost, or broken mountain is in the south.

Activating the Internal Environment
Master Bedroom
To enhance wealth luck, locate your bedroom in the north, east, or southeast—these areas have good mountain stars with wealth energy. For the best money luck, position your headboard or bed toward the north (1, 3, 4, or 9 Guas only) or east (all Guas).

Home Office

Establish your home office in the north, east, or southeast—these areas have good mountain stars with wealth energy. While sitting at your desk, face north (1, 3, 4, or 9 Guas only), or east or southwest (all Guas)—these are good facing stars and will activate luck when used.

Kitchen, Stove, Fire Mouth, and Toilets

North, southwest, and east are the best directions for the fire mouth because fire stimulates the wealth energy of these good facing stars. To deter bankruptcy, avoid a northwest-facing fire mouth. If your kitchen is in the northwestern or southern sector, money loss is likely. Stoves in the southern part of the kitchen are even more serious.

Review the Eight Mansion chart to find your wealth/power direction and location. Money struggles are likely if a stove or a toilet is located in your +90 sector. You can relocate a stove, but you must use another toilet if this is the case, so select a toilet in one of your negative sectors (-90, -80, -70, or -60). Also, if a toilet is in the area of your 8 facing star, wealth luck is diminished a great deal.

The Best Doors in the House (Interior and Exterior)

The best doors in the house face north (1, 3, 4, or 9 Guas only), east and southwest (all Guas)—these directions have good facing stars and using them will activate wealth luck. Select one of these doors based on your Life Gua. If one of these directions is also your +90, you will be lucky with money! Avoid using an angled door that faces northwest—it will activate bankruptcy.

PERIOD 8
East 2 and East 3
Chen Trigram   Element: Big WOOD

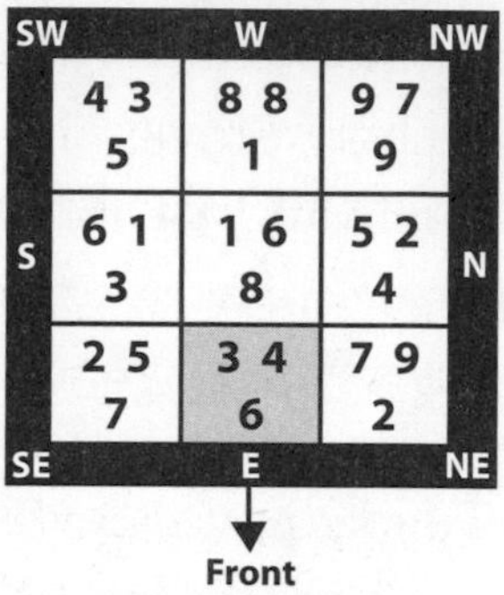

East 2 (82.6° to 97.5°)

    Facing name: Mao and the Rabbit

East 3 (97.6° to 112.5°) Facing name: Yi

Chart: Double Stars Meeting at the
    Sitting/Back (Shuang Xing Dao Zuo)

Warning: Possible Eight Roads of
    Destruction, Eight Killing Forces,
    and Robbery Mountain Sha

Major DEL at 90°!

SW	W	NW
4 3	8 8	9 7
5	1	9
6 1	1 6	5 2
3	8	4
2 5	3 4	7 9
7	6	2

S (left side), N (right side), SE (bottom left), E (bottom center), NE (bottom right)

↓
Front
Figure 33: East 2 & 3

Figure 33 is the natal chart for east-facing properties facing between 82.6 and 112.5 degrees. Known as East 2 and East 3, these are the second and third fifteen degrees of east. Note: The following recommendations are specific to this chart.

Activating the External Environment
Requires Mountain and Water in Back
Alternate Water Location: South
Bankruptcy Indicated: Water in the Southeast
These east-facing properties have a chart known as Double Stars Meet at Sitting (Shuang Xing Dao Zuo), this chart features a pair of prominent 8 stars in the back of the property. You will need two important features to capture the energy properly—solid backing and big water. The water in proportion to the residence could be a pool, pond, waterfall, huge fountain, or lake. If you incorporate a waterfall, the water should flow from a southern direction. Install a solid backing, such as a solid fence, high

ground, landscape mounds, boulders, a dense row of tall, stately trees, or any combination thereof. A natural mountain or high ground already on your property is excellent. Some masters do not recommend water in the west, but to capture fully the energy of the 8 facing star (prominent star and current water dragon), water is a must. I've witnessed incredible results by activating the 8 facing star, regardless of its location. Clients have reported money gains, business opportunities, financial windfalls, and unexpected inheritances.

East 2: These homes will produce wealthy, noble, righteous, charismatic, loyal, and faithful professionals, such as doctors, lawyers, and philosophers. If the landforms are bad, the opposite is true—the occupants will be involved in destructive behavior, such as gambling, taking unnecessary risk, and engaging in immoral activity. East 2 homes have a possible Eight Killings formation if mountain energy comes from the southwest or a Robbery Mountain Sha formation if a jagged cliff, electrical tower, huge dead tree, lamppost, or broken mountain is in the northeast.

East 3: With good landforms, these properties will bear kind-hearted, smart, and responsible children, who will become charming leaders. Money loss and legal problems, however, will arise in properties near bad land formations. An Eight Roads of Destruction is possible if your driveway or a nearby road approaches or exits from the southeast. These residences may also experience a Robbery Mountain Sha formation if a jagged cliff, electrical tower, huge dead tree, lamppost, or a broken mountain is in the northeast.

Activating the Internal Environment
Master Bedroom
To enhance wealth luck, locate your bedroom in the south, northwest, or west—these areas have good mountain stars with wealth energy. For the best money luck in homes that face East 2, place your headboard

or bed toward the west (2, 6, 7, and 8 Guas only) or south (1, 3, 4, or 9 Guas only). In homes that face East 3, position your headboard or bed toward the west or south (all Guas); these directions have good mountain and facing star combinations.

Home Office

The south, northwest, and west are great locations for your home office— these areas have good mountain stars with wealth energy. For the best money luck in homes that face East 2, angle your desk and body facing toward the west or northeast (2, 6, 7, or 8 Guas only), or south (1, 3, 4, or 9 Guas only). In homes that face East 3, position your desk and body facing toward the west, northeast, or south (all Guas). These directions have good facing stars that provide wealth energy.

Kitchen, Stove, Fire Mouth, and Toilets

West, south, and northeast are the best directions for the fire mouth, because fire stimulates the wealth energy of these good facing stars. To deter bankruptcy, avoid a southeast-facing fire mouth. If your kitchen is in the northern or southeastern sector, money loss is likely—stoves in the northern area of the kitchen are even more serious.

Review the Eight Mansions chart to find your wealth/power direction and location. Money struggles are likely if a stove or a toilet is located in your +90 sector. You can relocate a stove, but you must use another toilet if this is the case, so select a toilet in one of your negative sectors (-90, -80, -70, or -60). Also, if a toilet is in the area of your 8 facing star, wealth luck is diminished a great deal.

The Best Doors in the House (Interior and Exterior)

In East 2 homes, use doors that face west and northeast (2, 6, 7, or 8 Guas only), or south (1, 3, 4, or 9 Guas only) to activate money luck. If you live in an East 3 residence, west, northeast, and south (all Guas) doors are best. These directions have good facing stars with wealth energy. Select one of these doors based on your Life Gua. If one of these directions is also your +90, you will be lucky with money! Avoid using an angled door that faces the southeast direction; it will activate bankruptcy energy.

PERIOD 8
Southeast 1
Xun Trigram   Element: Small WOOD

Southeast 1 (112.6° to 127.5°)
   Facing name: Chen and the Dragon

*Special Chart: Pearl String
   (Lin Cu San Poon Gua)

Warning: Possible Eight Killing
   Forces and Robbery Mountain Sha

Level Two DEL: 112.5

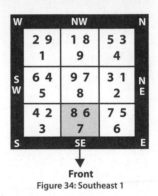

Front
Figure 34: Southeast 1

Figure 34 is the natal chart for southeast-facing properties facing between 112.6 and 127.5 degrees. Known as Southeast 1, this is the first fifteen degrees of southeast. Note: The following recommendations are specific to this chart.

Activating the External Environment
Requires Mountain in Front, Water in Back

This house has a special chart known as a Pearl String (Lin Cu San Poon Gua)—a mountain in front and water in back will correctly activate this chart. This formation is an Up the Mountain, Down the River (Shang Shan Hsia Shui). This simply means that the prominent mountain star (8) is in the front of the property and gets activated first, while the prominent facing star (8) is in the back and is activated second. Ideally, the placement of the stars should be reversed; however, these special charts offer a great deal of wealth luck. So, to capture fully the special energy of this chart, the mountain star must be activated by a real or simulated mountain. The mountain can be high ground, landscape mounds, massive boulders (no jagged or pointed edges), or any combination of these; it should be as centered as possible without blocking the front door. Water in the back—proportional to the residence and centered in your backyard or garden—can include a swimming pool, spa, waterfall, large fountain, lake, pond, or the ocean.

There are two different types of Pearl String Formations—one that enhances luck with people and relationships, and one that brings wealth luck. This one builds wealth through relationships, partnerships, and joint ventures. It must, however, be activated properly; otherwise, this chart will not attract fortune. Pearl Strings have a maximum shelf life of twenty years. If the right landforms are in place, the property can indicate great talent in sports and martial arts. The children who live in these residences excel in sciences, especially those requiring technical expertise.

An Eight Killings formation is possible if mountain energy comes to the house from the north. The house may also have a Robbery Mountain Sha formation if a jagged cliff, electrical tower, huge dead tree, lamppost, or broken mountain is in the northeast.

Activating the Internal Environment
Master Bedroom

To enhance wealth luck, locate your bedroom in the southwest, northwest, or southeast (second floor)—these areas have good mountain stars with wealth energy. For the best money luck, position your headboard or bed toward the southwest or northwest (all Guas) or to the southeast (1, 3, 4, or 9 Guas only); these directions have good mountain and facing star combinations.

Home Office

Establish your home office in the southwest, northwest, or southeast (second floor)—these areas have good mountain stars with wealth energy. While sitting at your desk, face northwest or west (all Guas), northeast (2, 6, 7, or 8 Guas only), or southeast (1, 3, 4, or 9 Guas only). These directions have good facing stars with wealth energy.

Kitchen, Stove, Fire Mouth, and Toilets

Northwest, northeast, and west are the best directions for the fire mouth, because fire stimulates the wealth energy of these good facing stars. A kitchen or stove in the northeast, however, may trigger lawsuits.

Review the Eight Mansions chart to find your wealth/power direction and location. Money struggles are likely if a stove or a toilet is located in your +90 sector. You can relocate a stove, but you must use another toilet if this is the case, so select a toilet in one of your negative sectors (-90, -80, -70, or -60). Also, if a toilet is in the area of your 8 facing star, wealth luck is diminished a great deal.

The Best Doors in the House (Interior and Exterior)

The best doors in the house face northwest and west (all Guas), northeast (2, 6, 7, or 8 Guas only), or southeast (1, 3, 4, or 9 Guas only). These directions have good facing stars that produce wealth energy. Select one of these doors based on your Life Gua. If one of these directions is also your +90, you will be lucky with money! Avoid using an angled door that faces the east direction; it will activate bankruptcy.

PERIOD 8
Southeast 2 and Southeast 3
Xun Trigram   Element: Small WOOD

Southeast 2 (127.6° to 142.5°)
  Facing name: Xun

Southeast 3 (142.6° to 157.5°)
  Facing name: Su and the Snake

Chart: Prosperous Sitting and
  Facing (Wang Shan Wang Shui)

Warning: Possible Eight Roads of
  Destruction, Eight Killing Forces,
  and Robbery Mountain Sha

Level Two DEL: 157.5°

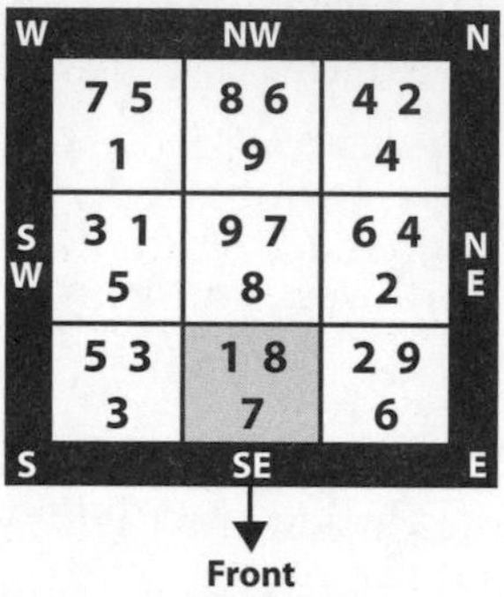

W		NW		N
7 5		8 6		4 2
1		9		4
SW 3 1		9 7		6 4 **NE**
5		8		2
5 3		1 8		2 9
3		7		6
S		SE		E

↓
Front
Figure 35: Southeast 2 & 3

Figure 35 is the natal chart for southeast-facing properties facing between 127.6 and 157.5 degrees. Known as Southeast 2 and Southeast 3, these are the second and third fifteen degrees of southeast. Note: The following recommendations are specific to this chart.

Activating the External Environment
Requires Water in Front, Mountain in Back
Alternate Water Location: Southwest
Bankruptcy Indicated: Water in the West
These southeast-facing homes have a special chart known as a Prosperous Sitting and Facing (Wang Shan Wang Shui), which is good for money, wealth, and people. This chart has the perfect placement for these stars—the 8 facing star in front and the 8 mountain in back. To activate this chart properly, you will need a beneficial backing to activate the 8 mountain star and water in front to activate the 8 facing star. Though a pool

in the back is potentially lucky for money, mixed results are possible too. For instance, the man of the house might not feel supported at work or at home. Though he could make money, he might have trouble hanging on to it, depending on the nearby landforms and other factors. If you already have small children and water in the back, do not install a water feature in the front. If you're lucky, your home faces the road and your main door activates the 8 facing star: use it as much as possible.

Southeast 2: With the right landforms, these properties will produce noble and trustworthy people. If bad landforms are present, families could break apart. An Eight Roads of Destruction is a possibility if your driveway or a nearby road approaches or exits from the south or east. These homes may also have a Robbery Mountain Sha formation if a jagged cliff, electrical tower, huge dead tree, lamppost, or broken mountain is in the east.

Southeast 3: Properties facing this direction produce people with high morals and values. These facings are best suited for philosophers, performers, singers, and artists. An Eight Killings formation is possible if mountain energy comes to the house from the west. These homes may also experience a Robbery Mountain Sha formation if a jagged cliff, electrical tower, huge dead tree, lamppost, or broken mountain is in the east.

Activating the Internal Environment
Master Bedroom

To enhance wealth luck, locate your bedroom in the northwest, northeast, or southeast (second floor)—these have good mountain stars with wealth energy. For the best money luck in homes that face Southeast 2, position your headboard or bed toward the southeast (1, 3, 4, or 9 Guas only), northeast or northwest (2, 6, 7, or 8 Guas only). In homes that face Southeast 3, position your headboard or bed toward the southeast, northwest, or northeast (all Guas); these directions have good mountain and facing star combinations.

Home Office

Establish your home office in the northwest, northeast, or southeast (second floor)—these have good mountain stars with wealth energy. For the best money luck in homes that face Southeast 2, angle your desk and/or body facing toward the southeast or east (1, 3, 4, or 9 Guas only), or northwest or southwest (2, 6, 7, or 8 Guas only). In Southeast 3 homes, orient your desk and body toward the southeast, northwest, southwest, or east (all Guas). These directions have good facing stars and bring wealth luck when used for desk directions.

Kitchen, Stove, Fire Mouth, and Toilets

Southeast, east, and southwest are the best directions for the fire mouth, because fire stimulates the wealth energy of these good facing stars. To deter bankruptcy, avoid a west-facing fire mouth. Kitchens and stoves in the southwest may attract lawsuits. Review the Eight Mansions chart to find your wealth/power direction and location. You will struggle with money if a stove or a toilet is located in your +90 sector of the house. You can relocate the stove, but must use another toilet if this is the case, so select a toilet in one of your negative sectors (-90, -80, -70, or -60).

The Best Doors in the House (Interior and Exterior)

The best doors in the house face southwest, southeast, east, and northwest (all Guas); these will activate wealth energy when used. Select one of these four based on your Life Gua. If one of these directions is also your +90, you will be lucky with money! Avoid using an angled door that faces west; it will activate bankruptcy.

Seven

....

The Get-Rich Keys for Period 7 Buildings

....

The wise adapt themselves to circumstances,
as water moulds itself to the pitcher.

Chinese Proverb

The following data will help you best extract the wealth energy of Period 7 homes. Your house is a Period 7 if you moved in between February 4, 1984, and February 3, 2004. These suggestions are based on the Eight Mansions system, individual mountain and facing stars, Flying Star combinations, Advanced Eight Mansions (with fifteen-degree increments), the five elements, Later Heaven Ba Gua, San He formulas, San Yuan techniques, the nature of the stars, the timelessness of the stars, and location and direction—all of which focus on wealth. Because these recommendations are specific to the charts, they cannot be mixed and matched.

The recommendations I've outlined in this section take advantage of good locations *and* good directions. If you are unable to choose the auspicious location I've suggested (e.g., locate your office in the northwest area of the house), use the recommended direction instead. Remember, every single room in your house contains all eight directions, and directional energy will support you more powerfully than a particular room location. But, if you are able to do both, you will get a faster result. In Feng Shui we have a saying: "Direction rules!" You may notice that some of your good directions are not being used in the recommendations; this is because the Flying Stars in those directions are not good and using them could bring a negative outcome. For couples who are opposite Life Groups, pay special attention to the directions that work for all Guas. This will ensure that both Life Guas get the benefits from the bed direction, doors, and so forth.

For the most part, Period 7 homes are now out of luck. Some fortune, however, can be extracted depending on the nearby landforms, the location of current prosperity (the 8 facing star and other wealth stars), and the effectiveness of the Eight Mansion for the occupants. Period 7 homes will negatively experience robbery energy and can attract lots of lawsuits, conflict, and a sense of hopelessness.

When reviewing the recommendations, have your floor plan ready by doing the following:

1. Take a compass direction and determine the facing direction.

2. Divide your floor plan, with a yellow highlighter, into nine sectors. Place all eight directions—south, west, north, and so forth around your floor plan. The directions are identified in the black area of the star charts.

3. Place your +90, -80, +70, and so forth next to the palaces according to your Gua. Use the Eight Mansions chart in chapter 4 to find your +90, +80, -60, -90, and so forth.

4. Transpose the numbers of the correct natal Flying Star chart next to the eight directions.

5. See the example on p. 180, which demonstrates how to do this correctly.

While reading the suggestions for your home facing, have your completed floor plan in front of you to make notes. For example, place the bed here, install water here, create a mountain here, move the desk to face this direction, and so on. You do not need a deep understanding of Eight Mansions and Flying Stars because the work has been done for you. Just follow the suggestions as described below. If you live in an apartment, high-rise, townhome, condo, or rented space and are not able to have an outdoor water feature, place one inside the recommended area. This will activate the wealth star and bring you good money luck. Wall and floor fountains are hugely popular and available everywhere. Water features should never be placed in the master bedroom.

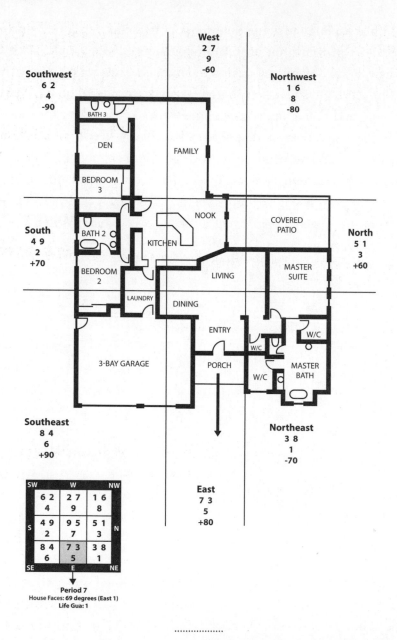

West
2 7
9
-60

Southwest
6 2
4
-90

Northwest
1 6
8
-80

BATH 3

DEN

FAMILY

BEDROOM
3

NOOK

COVERED
PATIO

South
4 9
2
+70

BATH 2

KITCHEN

North
5 1
3
+60

MASTER
SUITE

BEDROOM
2

LIVING

LAUNDRY

DINING

3-BAY GARAGE

ENTRY

W/C

W/C

MASTER
BATH

PORCH

W/C

Southeast
8 4
6
+90

Northeast
3 8
1
-70

East
7 3
5
+80

SW	W	NW
6 2 4	2 7 9	1 6 8
4 9 2	9 5 7	5 1 3
8 4 6	7 3 5	3 8 1
SE	E	NE

S · N

Period 7
House Faces: 69 degrees (East 1)
Life Gua: 1

....

Figure 36: Example Floor Plan for Period 7–
Divide your floor plan into nine palaces or sectors. Transfer the correct Natal Chart as indicated.
Refer to the Eight Mansions Chart for information on your Gua Number. The example is a 1 Gua.

PERIOD 7
South 1
Li Trigram   Element: FIRE

South 1 (157.6° to 172.5°)
Facing Name: Bing

Chart: Past Luck! Double Stars Meet at
Facing (Shuang Xing Dao Xiang)

Warning: Possible Eight Roads of
Destruction and Robbery Mountain Sha

Level Two DEL: 157.5°

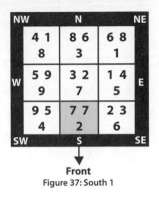

Front
Figure 37: South 1

Figure 37 natal chart is that of south-facing properties facing between 157.6 and 172.5 degrees. Known as South 1, this is the first fifteen degrees of south. Note: The following recommendations are specific to this chart and this facing direction.

Activating the External Environment
Requires Water in the Northeast, Mountain in the North
Alternate Water Locations: Northwest and West
Bankruptcy Indicated: Water in the Southwest
This facing is known as Double Stars Meet at Facing (Shuang Xing Dao Xiang) with a pair of 7 stars in the front. In Period 7, this was quite auspicious, but now it's considered unfavorable. However, the 7 stars are not strong in the south, and no cure or countermeasure is needed. To extract luck from this home, install a solid backing, such as a fence (stone, brick, stucco, or a combination of wood and brick are best); high ground, landscape mounds; boulders (no sharp or jagged edges), a dense row of tall,

stately trees; or any combination of these in the north. A natural mountain, high ground, or a hill in the back of your property is auspicious. Place water—a pool, pond, waterfall, huge fountain, or lake—in the northeastern area of the yard or garden. If water flows, it should meander from the northeast.

Water in the southwest can activate bankruptcy. If you live in an apartment, a condo, or a rented space and cannot install an outdoor water feature, place one inside in the angled in the northeast corner of the living room, dining room or home office. This will also activate a wealth star and bring you good money luck. Wall and floor fountains are hugely popular and available everywhere.

This home also has a potential Eight Roads of Destruction if your driveway or a nearby road approaches or exits from the southeast. This house may have a Robbery Mountain Sha formation if a jagged cliff, electrical tower, huge dead tree, lamppost, or broken mountain is in the southwest.

The South 1 facing works well for the East Life Group (1, 3, 4, or 9 Guas) and the West Life Group (2, 6, 7, or 8 Guas), though 6 and 7 Guas may not thrive as well. Overall, if the energies are tapped correctly and no adverse landforms are present, the house indicates good money luck and success in writing and scholarly pursuits. South-facing properties can produce people in authority, and charismatic, intelligent, and skillful entrepreneurs. Remedy any injurious landforms discussed in chapter 3—such as T-junctures, sloping land, drains, and so forth—using the Master's Tips as guidelines.

Consider updating the energy/chi of the house with extensive and major renovations. A major renovation includes removing the entire roof (a small percentage must be exposed to the open sky for at least a few hours); overhauling the front entrance and door; painting the entire inside and outside simultaneously; remodeling the kitchen or bathrooms; installing a skylight; changing all the floors at the same time; or adding an attached garage or room. These alterations will cause a major shift in energy, thereby transforming your Flying Star Chart into a South 1, Period 8 dwelling rather than a South 1, Period 7. Refer to those charts for more information.

Activating the Internal Environment
Master Bedroom
To enhance wealth luck, locate your bedroom in the north, northeast, east, or southwest—these areas have good mountain stars with wealth energy. For the best money luck, position your headboard or bed toward the north (1, 3, 4, or 9 Guas only), northeast (2, 6, 7, or 8 Guas only), or east or northwest (all Guas); these directions have good mountain and facing star combinations.

Home Office
Establish your home office in the north, northeast, east, or southwest— these areas have good mountain stars with wealth energy. For the best money luck, angle your desk and/or body facing toward the north (1, 3, 4, or 9 Guas only), northeast (2, 6, 7, or 8 Guas only), or west or northwest (all Guas). These directions have good facing stars with wealth energy.

Kitchen, Stove, Fire Mouth, and Toilets
Northeast, northwest, and west are the best directions for the fire mouth, because fire stimulates the wealth energy of these good facing stars. To deter bankruptcy, avoid a southwest-facing fire mouth.

Review the Eight Mansions reference chart in chapter 4 to find your wealth/power direction and location. Money struggles are likely if a stove or a toilet is located in your +90 sector. You can relocate a stove, but you must use another toilet if this is the case, so select a toilet in one of your negative sectors (-90, -80, -70, or -60). Also, if a toilet is in the area of your 8 facing star, wealth luck is diminished a great deal.

The Best Doors in the House (Interior and Exterior)

The best doors in the house face north (1, 3, 4, or 9 Guas only), north-east (2, 6, 7, or 8 Guas only), or west and northwest (all Guas). These doors have good facing stars that will activate wealth luck when used, so select one of them based on your Life Gua. If one of these directions is also your +90, you will be lucky with money. Avoid using doors that are angled to the southwest direction; it will activate bankruptcy.

PERIOD 7
South 2 and South 3
Li Trigram   Element: FIRE

South 2 (172.6° to 187.5°)
   Facing Name: Wu and the Horse

South 3 (187.6° to 202.5°)
   Facing Name: Ting

Special Chart: Past Luck! Combination of
   Ten and Double Stars Meeting at Back

Warning: Eight Roads of Destruction,
   Eight Killing Forces and Robbery
   Mountain Sha

Major DEL at 180°!

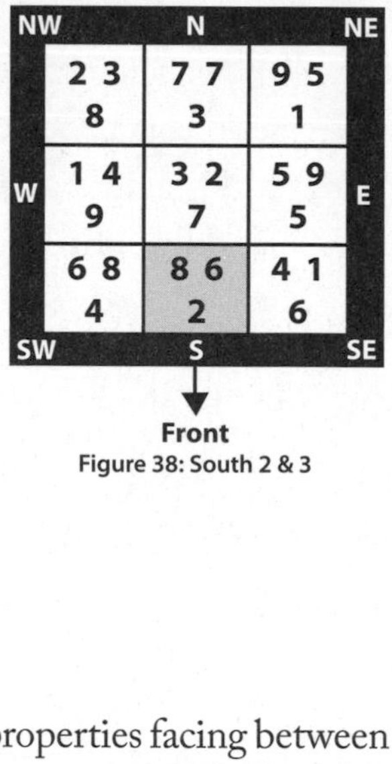

NW	N	NE
2 3 8	7 7 3	9 5 1
1 4 9	3 2 7	5 9 5
6 8 4	8 6 2	4 1 6

W (left side), E (right side), SW, S, SE (corners)

↓
Front
Figure 38: South 2 & 3

Figure 38 is the natal chart for south-facing properties facing between 172.6 and 202.5 degrees. Known as South 2 and South 3, these are the second and third fifteen degrees of south. Note: The following recommendations are specific to this chart and this facing direction.

Activating the External Environment
Requires Water in the Southwest, Mountain in the South
Alternate Water Locations: Southeast and East
Bankruptcy Indicated: Water in the Northeast
This house features a pair of 7 stars in the back, known as Double Stars Meet at Sitting, and a Combination of Ten formation. In its day, this was a remarkable auspicious chart with two wealth-producing aspects, though it is out of luck in the current Period 8. The 7 stars are ruinous stars, indicating robbery and thief energy, which can take things away from you. To improve your fortune, simulate a mountain in the front with high ground, landscape mounds, or boulders (no sharp or jagged edges) in the southern area of your front yard. Do not align the boulders with the front door. Encourage money and wealth by placing a water feature—such as a fountain, a small pond, or a waterfall—in the southwest. Water in the northeast could attract bankruptcy, bad land deals, or huge money loss. A pool is in the back (north) may weaken the 7 stars and attract robberies to the house—not only stealing in the literal sense, but the theft of promotions, ideas, intellectual property, and even your job.

Overall, if the energies are tapped and extracted correctly and no adverse landforms are present, the house indicates success in writing and scholarly pursuits, and good money luck. South-facing properties can produce people in authority, and charismatic, intelligent, and skilled entrepreneurs. If you were born in the year of the Snake, Rooster, or Ox, or are a 6 or 7 Life Guas (both are metal), a south-facing home can bring you harm.

In South 2 homes, an Eight Killing Force formation is possible if a mountain comes from the northwest. South 3 residences could experience an Eight Roads of Destruction if your driveway or a nearby road approaches or exits from the southwest. Both facings (S2 and S3) may have a Robbery Mountain Sha formation if a jagged cliff, electrical tower, huge dead tree, lamppost, or broken mountain is in the southeast.

Activating the Internal Environment
Master Bedroom

To enhance wealth luck, locate your bedroom in the west, northeast, south, or southwest—these sectors have good mountain stars with wealth energy. For the best money luck in homes that face South 2, place your headboard or bed toward the south or southeast (1, 3, 4, or 9 Guas only), or southwest or west (2, 6, 7, or 8 Guas only). In homes that face South 3, position your headboard or bed toward the south, southwest, west, or southeast (all Guas); these directions have good mountain and facing star combinations.

Home Office

Establish your home office in the west, northeast, south, or southwest—these sectors have good mountain stars with wealth energy. For the best money luck in homes that face South 2, angle your desk and/or body facing toward the south, east, or southeast (1, 3, 4, or 9 Guas only), or southwest (2, 6, 7, or 8 Guas only). In homes that face South 3, position your desk and/or body facing toward the south, southwest, east, or southeast (all Guas). These directions have good facing stars that will enhance wealth luck.

Kitchen, Stove, Fire Mouth, and Toilets

Southwest, southeast, and east are the best directions for the fire mouth; northeast is the worst and should be avoided to deter imminent financial ruin. A kitchen or stove in the east will bring money problems and possible bankruptcy.

Review the Eight Mansions chart to find your wealth/power direction and location. Money struggles are likely if a stove or a toilet is located in your +90 sector. You can relocate a stove, but you must use another toilet if this is the case, so select a toilet in one of your negative sectors (-90, -80, -70, or -60). Also, if a toilet is in the area of your 8 facing star, wealth luck is diminished a great deal.

The Best Doors in the House (Interior and Exterior)

The best doors in a South 2 home face south, east, and southeast (1, 3, 4, or 9 Guas only), or southwest (2, 6, 7, or 8 Guas only). If your residence is a South 3, doors that face south, southwest, east, and southeast (all Guas) offer the best results and will enhance wealth luck when used. Select one of these doors based on your Life Gua. If one of these directions is also your +90, you will be lucky with money! Avoid using east-facing doors; they will activate bankruptcy.

PERIOD 7
Southwest 1
Kun Trigram   Element: Mother EARTH

Southwest 1 (202.6° to 217.5°)

   Facing Name: Wei and the Goat

Chart: Past Luck! Double Stars Meet at
   Facing (Shuang Xing Dao Xiang)

Warning: Possible Robbery Mountain Sha

Level Two DEL: 202.5°

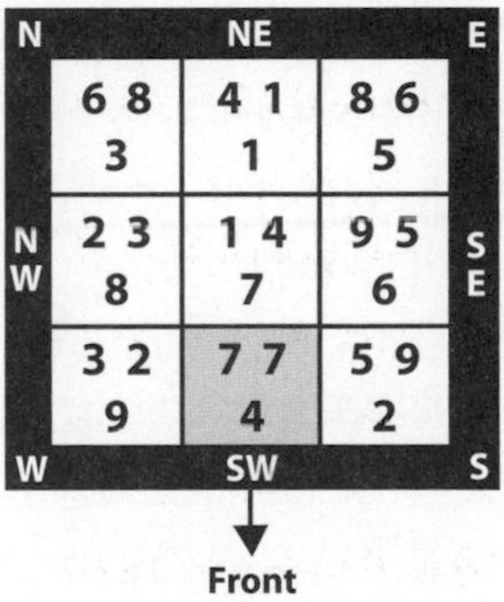

Figure 39: Southwest 1

   Figure 39 is the natal chart for southwest-facing properties facing between 202.6 and 217.5 degrees. Known as Southwest 1, this is the first fifteen degrees of southwest. Note: The following recommendations are specific to this chart.

Activating the External Environment
Requires Water in the North, Mountain in the East
Alternate Water Locations: Northeast and South
Bankruptcy Indicated: Water in the Southeast

This chart is known as Double Stars Meet at Facing (Shuang Xing Dao Xiang) because of the two 7 stars featured in the front of this property. Unfortunately, this chart is no longer auspicious. The 7 stars are quite strong in the southwest, but they can be weakened by placing small water near the front door (no larger than a desk fountain), or you can paint the front door blue or black. Metal doors will fortify these stars and make the situation worse, so it is best to switch to wooden ones.

You must create a strong backing: Higher ground in the east will activate the good mountain star there. Also, position a water feature, such as a small pond or water fountain, in the north. If you live in an apartment, high-rise, townhome, condo, or rented space and are not able to place an outdoor water feature, install one inside the recommended area. This will activate the wealth star and bring you good money luck. Wall and floor fountains are hugely popular and available everywhere. Water features do not belong in the bedroom.

The house may have a Robbery Mountain Sha formation if a jagged cliff, electrical tower, huge dead tree, lamppost, or broken mountain is in the southeast.

Activating the Internal Environment
Master Bedroom

To enhance wealth luck, locate your bedroom in the north, east, or southeast—these areas have good mountain stars with wealth energy. For the best money luck, angle your headboard or bed toward the north (1, 3, 4, or 9 Guas only), northeast (2, 6, 7, or 8 Guas only), or east (all Guas); these directions have good mountain and facing star combinations. Do not position your headboard or bed toward the southeast; it will activate money loss.

Home Office

Establish your home office in the north, east, or southeast—these areas have good mountain stars with wealth energy. For the best money luck, angle your desk and/or body facing north (1, 3, 4, or 9 Guas only), northeast (2, 6, 7, or 8 Guas only), or east or south (all Guas); these directions have good facing stars for wealth.

Kitchen, Stove, Fire Mouth, and Toilets

North, northeast, and south are the best directions for the fire mouth; southeast is the worst and should be avoided to deter bankruptcy. A kitchen or stove in the northwest or west, however, could trigger lawsuits and conflicts with and among business associates.

Review the Eight Mansions chart to find your wealth/power direction and location. Money struggles are likely if a stove or a toilet is located in your +90 sector. You can relocate a stove, but you must use another toilet if this is the case, so select a toilet in one of your negative sectors (-90, -80, -70, or -60). Also, if a toilet is in the area of your 8 facing star, wealth luck is diminished a great deal.

The Best Doors in the House (Interior and Exterior)

The best doors in the house face north (1, 3, 4, or 9 Guas only), northeast (2, 6, 7, or 8 Guas only), or east and south (all Guas); these directions have good facing, wealth stars. A northwest-facing door will bring clients to high-powered lawyers, especially if this chart is properly activated by good landforms. Select good doors to use based on your Life Gua. If one of these directions is also your +90, you will be lucky with money! Avoid using a southeast facing door; it will activate bankruptcy.

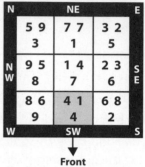

Figure 40: Southwest 2 & 3

Southwest 2 (217.6° to 232.5°)
Facing Name: Kun

Southwest 3 (232.6° to 247.5°)
Facing name: Shen and the Monkey

Chart: Past Luck! Double Stars Meet
at Sitting (Shuang Xing Dao Zuo)

Warning: Eight Roads of Destruction,
Eight Killing Forces and Robbery
Mountain Sha

Figure 40 is the natal chart for southwest-facing properties facing between 217.6 and 247.5 degrees. Known as Southwest 2 and Southwest 3, these are the second and third fifteen degrees of southwest. Note: The following recommendations are specific to this chart and this facing direction.

Activating the External Environment
Requires Water in the South, Mountain in the West
Alternate Water Locations: Southwest and North
Bankruptcy Indicated: Water in the Northwest
This chart features a pair of 7 stars, known as Double Stars Meet at Sitting (Shuang Xing Dao Zuo), in the rear of the property. In Period 7, this was an excellent chart, particularly if it had a mountain or strong support in the back. The 7 Star, however, is out of luck in the current Period 8. To increase your fortune by mitigating the energy of the 7 Star, install a

small water feature (the size of a desk fountain) near the back door or paint the back door a blue color.

Big water, such as a pool, should not be placed in the back of the property—bankruptcy, bad land deals, or huge money loss could result. Though a pool in the backyard (northeast) will weaken the 7 stars, it may attract robberies to your home or workplace. This could manifest in others stealing your promotions, ideas, intellectual property, or even your job.

To extract some luck from the current period, create high ground with landscape mounds and/or large boulders in the west. Also, place a water fountain in the south of your front yard to activate wealth. Some masters do not recommend water in the south, but to capture the energy of the 8 facing star (prominent wealth star) fully, it requires water. I've witnessed incredible results by activating the 8 facing star, regardless of its location. Clients have reported money gains, business opportunities, financial windfalls, and unexpected inheritances.

Southwest 2 homes may experience an Eight Roads of Destruction formation if your driveway or a nearby road approaches or exits from the south or west. Southwest 3 residences may also have an Eight Killings formation if a mountain comes from the east or a Robbery Mountain Sha formation if a jagged cliff, electrical tower, huge dead tree, lamppost, or broken mountain is in the southwest. Overall, if the energies are tapped correctly and no adverse landforms are present, Southwest 2 or Southwest 3 homes indicate good money luck. These types of dwellings can turn bad situations into opportunities.

Activating the Internal Environment
Master Bedroom

To enhance wealth luck, locate your bedroom in the northwest, south, or west—these sectors have good mountain stars with wealth energy. For the best money luck in homes that face Southwest 2, angle your headboard or bed toward the south (1, 3, 4, or 9 Guas only), southwest or west (2, 6, 7, or 8 Guas only). For the best money luck in homes that face

Southwest 3, position your headboard or bed toward the south, southwest, or west (all Guas); these directions have good mountain and facing star combinations.

Home Office

Establish your home office in the northwest, south, or west—these sectors have good mountain stars with wealth energy. For the best money luck in homes that face Southwest 2, position your desk and body toward the north or south (1, 3, 4, or 9 Guas only), or southwest or west (2, 6, 7, or 8 Guas only). For the best money luck in homes that face Southwest 3, angle your desk and body toward the north (1, 3, 4, or 9 Guas only), or south, southwest, or west (all Guas). These directions have good facing stars with wealth energy.

Kitchen, Stove, Fire Mouth, and Toilets

South, southwest, and north are the best directions for the fire mouth; northwest is the worst and should be avoided to deter bankruptcy. A kitchen in the north may trigger money loss, but stoves in the northern area of the kitchen are even more serious.

Review the chart to find your wealth/power direction and location. Money struggles are likely if a stove or a toilet is located in your +90 sector. You can relocate a stove, but you must use another toilet if this is the case, so select a toilet in one of your negative sectors (-90, -80, -70, or -60). Also, if a toilet is in the area of your 8 facing star, wealth luck is diminished a great deal.

The Best Doors in the House (Interior and Exterior)

In Southwest 2 homes, use doors that face north and south (1, 3, 4, or 9 Guas only), or southwest and west (2, 6, 7, or 8 Guas only). If your residence is a Southwest 3, the best doors face north (1, 3, 4, or 9 Guas only), or south, southwest, and west (all Guas). These doors have good facing stars with wealth energy, which are activated by continual use.

Select one of these doors based on your Life Gua. If one of these directions is also your +90, you will be lucky with money! Avoid using a door that faces northwest; it will activate bankruptcy.

PERIOD 7
West 1
Dui Trigram   Element: Small METAL

West 1 (247.6° to 262.5°)
   Facing Name: Geng

Chart: Past Luck! Up the Mountain,
   Down the River

Warning: Possible Eight Roads of
   Destruction, Eight Killing Forces
   and Robbery Mountain Sha

Level Two DEL: 247.5°

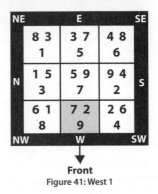

Figure 41: West 1

Figure 41 is the natal chart for west-facing properties facing between 247.6 and 262.5 degrees. Known as West 1, this is the first fifteen degrees of west. Note: The following recommendations are specific to this chart.

Activating the External Environment
Requires Water in the Southeast, Mountain in the Northeast
Alternate Water Location: Northwest
Bankruptcy Indicated: Water in the North
This house, though not a Pearl or Parent String, has an Up the Mountain, Down the River formation in Period 7, which simply meant that the prominent mountain star of the period (7) was in front, while the

prominent facing star of the period (7) was in back. This is known as a reverse formation. In its time of Period 7 (between February 4, 1984, and February 3, 2004), it needed a mountain in the front and water in the back, as all Pearl and Parent Strings require. In Period 8, however, the current prosperity must be activated to extract wealth energy. This house should have good support in the back in general with a high fence, dense landscaping, or higher ground than the front. You must simulate a mountain or high ground in the northeast of your backyard.

Install a water feature—such as a small pond, a waterfall, or a water fountain—in the southeast sector of your backyard, or the northwest area of your front yard, to activate wealth luck. The southeast offers the most powerful wealth luck or 8 facing star, but if you can't utilize this space, use the alternate water location.

To counteract the negative facing star for this residence, place metal near or on the front door.[15] If you had water near your front door in the past, or even now, extensive illness in the home is a possibility; building wealth will be difficult when you are constantly struggling with your health. Remove it and relocate the water feature elsewhere.

Overall, if the energies are tapped correctly and no adverse land-forms are present, the house indicates good money luck. The house does have a possible Eight Roads of Destruction formation if your driveway or a nearby road approaches or exits from the southwest. A Robbery Mountain Sha formation is possible if a jagged cliff, electrical tower, huge dead tree, lamppost, or broken mountain is in the south.

Activating the Internal Environment
Master Bedroom

To enhance wealth luck, locate your bedroom in the north, northeast, south, or northwest—these sectors have good mountain stars with wealth energy.

---

15. The energy of the 5 and 2 stars are reduced with a high quality metal, such as bronze, copper, or brass. The 5 facing star is the most dangerous, particularly if a door faces that direction. A 5 facing star cannot be completely cured with metal—only weakened. The use of the door will always activate this disaster star.

For the best money luck, angle your headboard or bed toward the northwest, south (all Guas), or southeast (1, 3, 4, or 9 Guas only); these directions have good mountain and facing star combinations.

Home Office

Establish your home office in the north, northeast, south, or northwest—these sectors have good mountain stars with wealth energy. For the best money luck, angle your desk and body toward the northwest or southwest (all Guas), or southeast (1, 3, 4, or 9 Guas only); these directions have good facing stars for wealth.

Kitchen, Stove, Fire Mouth, and Toilets

Southeast and northwest are the best directions for the fire mouth. A north-facing fire mouth could trigger bankruptcy; a west-facing fire mouth could activate health issues. When it comes to this chart, severe money and health problems stem from a kitchen or stove in the center of the house.

Review the chart to find your wealth/power direction and location. Money struggles are likely if a stove or a toilet is located in your +90 sector. You can relocate a stove, but you must use another toilet if this is the case, so select a toilet in one of your negative sectors (-90, -80, -70, or -60). Also, if a toilet is in the area of your 8 facing star, wealth luck is diminished a great deal.

The Best Doors in the House (Interior and Exterior)

The best doors in the house face northwest and southwest (all Guas), or southeast (1, 3, 4, or 9 Guas only); these directions have good facing stars and will activate wealth with continual use. Select one of these doors based on your Life Gua. If one of these directions is also your +90, you will be lucky with money! Avoid using a north-facing door; it will activate bankruptcy.

PERIOD 7
West 2 and West 3
Dui Trigram   Element: Small METAL

West 2 (262.6° to 277.5°)
Facing Name: You and the Rooster

West 3 (277.6° to 292.5°)
Facing Name: Xin

Chart: Past Luck! Prosperous Sitting
and Facing (Wang Shan Wang Shui)

Warning: Possible Eight Roads of
Destruction, Eight Killing Forces
and Robbery Mountain Sha

Major DEL at 270°!

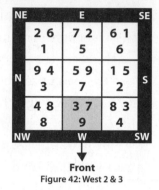

Front
Figure 42: West 2 & 3

Figure 42 is the natal chart for west-facing properties facing, between 262.6 and 292.5 degrees. Known as West 2 and West 3, these are the second and third fifteen degrees of west. Note: The following recommendations are specific to this chart and this facing direction.

Activating the External Environment
Requires Water in the Northwest, Mountain in the Southwest
Alternate Water Location: Southeast
Bankruptcy Indicated: Water in the South
This chart was lucky for money, wealth, and prosperity in Period 7 with its Prosperous Sitting and Facing (Wang Shan Wang Shui). The 7 stars, however, are no longer lucky in Period 8, when the 8s are king! To extract some luck from this house install a water feature, such as a small pond, a waterfall, or a fountain, in the northwestern section of your

front yard, and simulate a mountain or higher ground in the south-west region of your front yard. These two additions will activate wealth energy. Water directly centered at the back of the property will create serious illness, particularly if it is a large body of water, such as a swimming pool. With the 7 facing star in the front of the house, frequent robberies may be an issue. Activating the northwest with water and the southwest with high ground will counterbalance this negative energy.

Overall, if the energies are tapped correctly and no adverse land-forms are present, the house indicates good money luck. West 2 homes have a possible Eight Killing Forces if mountain chi comes from the southeast, or a Robbery Mountain Sha if a jagged cliff, an electrical tower, a huge dead tree, a lamppost, or a broken mountain is in the south. When it comes to West 3 residences, an Eight Roads of Destruction formation is possible if your driveway or a nearby road approaches or exits from the northwest. A Robbery Mountain Sha formation is also a threat if a jagged cliff, an electrical tower, a huge dead tree, a lamppost, or a broken mountain is in the southwest.

Activating the Internal Environment
Master Bedroom

To enhance wealth luck, locate your bedroom in the north, southwest, south, or southeast—these sectors have good mountain stars with wealth energy. For the best money luck in homes that face West 2, angle your headboard or bed toward the northwest (2, 6, 7, or 8 Guas only), southeast or north (1, 3, 4, or 9 Guas only). For the best money luck in West 3 residences, position your headboard or bed toward the north (1, 3, 4 or 9 Guas only), southeast or northwest (all Guas); these directions have good mountain and facing star combinations.

Home Office

Establish your home office in the north, southwest, south, or southeast—these sectors have good mountain stars with wealth energy. For the best money luck in homes that face West 2, angle your desk and body toward the northwest or northeast (2, 6, 7, or 8 Guas only), or southeast (1, 3, 4, or 9 Guas only). For the best money luck in West 3 residences, orient your desk and body toward the northwest, northeast, or southeast (all Guas); these directions have good facing stars with wealth energy.

Kitchen, Stove, Fire Mouth, and Toilets

Northwest and southeast are the best directions for the fire mouth; south is the worst and should be avoided to deter bankruptcy.

Review the Eight Mansions chart to find your wealth/power direction and location. Money struggles are likely if a stove or a toilet is located in your +90 sector. You can relocate a stove, but you must use another toilet if this is the case, so select a toilet in one of your negative sectors (-90, -80, -70, or -60). Also, if a toilet is in the area of your 8 facing star, wealth luck is diminished a great deal.

The Best Doors in the House (Interior and Exterior)

In West 2 homes, the best doors face northwest and northeast (2, 6, 7, or 8 Guas only), or southeast (1, 3, 4, or 9 Guas only). In a West 3 residence, northwest, northeast, and southeast (all Guas) doors are most auspicious; these directions have good facing stars with wealth energy. Select one of these door directions based on your Life Gua. If one of these directions is also your +90, you will be lucky with money! Avoid using doors that face south; they will activate bankruptcy.

PERIOD 7
Northwest 1
Chien Trigram   Element: Big METAL

Northwest 1 (292.6° to 307.5°)
  Facing Name: Xu and the Dog

Chart: Past Luck! Prosperous Sitting and
  Facing (Wang Shan Wang Shui)

Warning: Possible Robbery Mountain Sha

Level Two DEL: 292.5°

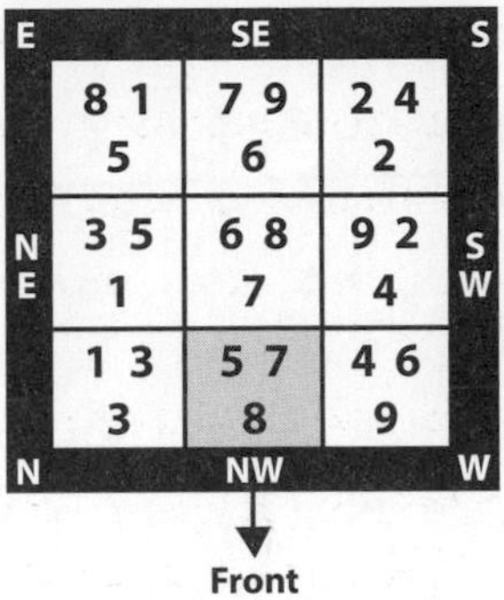

E		SE		S
	8 1	**7 9**	**2 4**	
	5	6	2	
NE	**3 5**	**6 8**	**9 2**	**SW**
	1	7	4	
	1 3	**5 7**	**4 6**	
	3	8	9	
N		NW		W

↓
Front
Figure 43: Northwest 1

Figure 43 is the natal chart for north-west-facing properties facing between 292.6 and 307.5 degrees. Known as Northwest 1, this is the first fifteen degrees of northwest. Note: The following recommendations are specific to this chart and this facing direction.

Activating the External Environment
Requires Water and Mountain in the East
Alternate Water Location: Southeast

With a Prosperous Sitting and Facing (Wang Shan Wang Shui), this chart was lucky for money, wealth, and prosperity in Period 7. The 7 stars, however, are no longer auspicious in Period 8, when the eights are king! Unfortunately, the 8 facing star is trapped in the middle of the house, where no water can be placed. Keep this area, such as a great room, as open as possible. If the center of your house has many small rooms or walls, money will be tight and restricted. To extract some luck from this house, install a water feature, such as a small pond, a waterfall, or a fountain, in the eastern region of your backyard. Since this area also requires a real or simulated mountain, consider erecting a natural rock or stone waterfall—five to six feet tall—that flows into a small pool from the east. If you opt for a fountain, make sure it has the same dimensions and flow direction as the waterfall, and is fashioned from natural stone, concrete or cement. These additions will activate wealth luck for the home.

Water in the rear of the property (southeast), such as a lake, a pond, a swimming pool, a meandering stream, a waterfall, or a koi pond, will also bring you wealth luck. If you already have a pool in the southeast, simulate a mountain in the eastern area of your backyard with landscape mounds or boulders (no sharp or pointed edges). With the 7 facing star in the front of the house, frequent robberies may be an issue. Activating the east, southeast, or both with water and a mountain will counterbalance this negative energy.

Overall, if the energies are tapped correctly and no adverse landforms are present, the house indicates good money luck. The house may have a Robbery Mountain Sha formation if a jagged cliff, an electrical tower, a huge dead tree, a lamppost, or a broken mountain is in the southwest. Remedy any bad landforms discussed in chapter 3—such as T-junctures, sloping land, drains, and so forth—using the Master's Tips as guidelines.

Activating the Internal Environment
Master Bedroom

To enhance wealth luck, locate your bedroom in the north, southwest, or east—these sectors have good mountain stars with wealth energy. For the best money luck, angle your headboard or bed toward the east or west (all Guas); these directions have good mountain and facing star combinations.

Home Office

Establish your home office in the north, southwest, or east—these sectors have good mountain stars with wealth energy. For the best money luck, angle your desk and body toward the east or west (all Guas), or southeast (1, 3, 4, or 9 Guas only); these directions have good facing stars with wealth energy.

Kitchen, Stove, Fire Mouth, and Toilets

East and southeast are the best directions for the fire mouth, because fire stimulates the wealth energy of these good facing stars. To deter bankruptcy, a northeast-facing fire mouth should be avoided. A kitchen or stove in the northeast may attract lawsuits, especially over land deals, home construction, or properties.

Review the Eight Mansions chart to find your wealth/power direction and location. Money struggles are likely if a stove or a toilet is located in your +90 sector of the house. You can relocate a stove, but you must use another toilet if this is the case, so select a toilet in one of your negative sectors (-90, -80, -70, or -60). Also, if a toilet is in the area of your 8 facing star, wealth luck is diminished a great deal.

The Best Doors in the House (Interior and Exterior)

The best doors in the house face east and west (all Guas), or southeast (1, 3, 4, or 9 Guas only); these directions have good facing stars with wealth energy. Continual use of an auspicious door will stimulate good fortune. Select one of these doors based on your Life Gua. If one of these directions is also your +90, you will be lucky with money! Avoid using doors that face northeast; they activate bankruptcy.

PERIOD 7
Northwest 2 and Northwest 3
Chien Trigram   Element: Big METAL

Northwest 2 (307.6° to 322.5°)
Facing Name: Chien

Northwest 3 (322.6° to 337.5°)
Facing Name: Hai and the Pig

Special Chart: Past Luck! Pearl String
Formation (Lin Cu San Poon Gua)

Warning: Possible Eight Roads of
Destruction, Eight Killings and
Robbery Mountain Sha

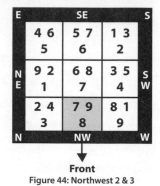

Front
Figure 44: Northwest 2 & 3

Figure 44 is the natal chart for northwest-facing properties facing between 307.6 and 337.5 degrees. Known as Northwest 2 and Northwest 3, these are the second and third fifteen degrees of northwest. Note: The following recommendations are specific to this chart and this facing direction.

Activating the External Environment
Requires Water in the Northwest, Mountain in the West
Alternate Water Location: West
This house has a special formation known as a Pearl String (Lin Cu San Poon Gua). The shelf life of a Pearl String, which is only auspicious in its periods, is no more than twenty years. In Period 7 it was extremely lucky for money if it had a mountain in front and water in back. Unfortunately, the 8 facing star is trapped in the middle of the house and water cannot be placed there to activate it. Keep the center open and free as possible. This is a perfect location for a great room for family and guests to gather.

Northwest Pearl Strings, however, have a good facing star (9) in the front of the property, and this brings some good luck, especially with money. A water fountain in the front yard (northwest), or near the front door will attract some wealth and business opportunities. High ground in the front should be lowered and landscape boulders removed. If you have water out back, this may stimulate robberies, bad business deals, and people stealing your ideas or getting your promotions. Simulate a mountain in the western area of your lawn or yard with high ground, landscape mounds, or boulders (no sharp or jagged edges)—this will activate wealth luck for your home. You should also consider installing water in the west with a combination feature, such as a tall waterfall made of natural stone. This will activate the good mountain and the facing stars here, thereby attracting money luck. Overall, if the energies are tapped correctly and no adverse landforms are present, the house indicates good money luck.

Northwest 2: These homes could experience an Eight Roads of Destruction formation if a nearby road approaches your residence from the west or the north. A Robbery Mountain Sha formation is possible if a jagged cliff, an electrical tower, a huge dead tree, a lamppost, or a broken mountain is in the north.

Northwest 3: An Eight Killing Forces formation is possible if mountain energy/chi comes from the south. This type of home could also experience a Robbery Mountain Sha formation if a jagged cliff, an electrical tower, a huge dead tree, a lamppost, or a broken mountain is in the west. Remedy any bad landforms discussed in chapter 3—such as T-junctures, sloping land, drains, and so forth—using the Master's Tips as guidelines.

Activating the Internal Environment
Master Bedroom

To enhance wealth luck, locate your bedroom in the south, west, or north-east—these sectors have good mountain stars with wealth energy. For the best money luck, and in homes that face Northwest 2, angle your head-board or bed toward the west (2, 6, 7, or 8 Guas only), or east (1, 3, 4, or 9 Guas only). In Northwest 3 homes, angle your headboard or bed toward the west or east (all Guas); these directions have good mountain and facing star combinations.

Home Office

Locate your home office in the in the south, west, or northeast as these sectors have good mountain stars with wealth energy. For the best money luck, and for homes that face Northwest 2, face your desk to the north-west or west (2, 6, 7, or 8 Guas only), or east (1, 3, 4, or 9 Guas only); these directions have good facing stars with wealth energy. For homes that face Northwest 3, face your desk to the northwest, west or east (all Guas).

Kitchen, Stove, Fire Mouth, and Toilets

West and northwest are the best directions for the fire mouth because fire stimulates the wealth energy of these good facing stars. To deter bankruptcy, avoid a southwest-facing fire mouth. Review the Eight Mansions chart to find your wealth/power direction and location. Money struggles are likely if a stove or a toilet is located in your +90 sector. You can relocate a stove, but you must use another toilet if this is the case, so select a toilet in one of your negative sectors (-90, -80, -70, or -60). Also, if a toilet is in the area of your 8 facing star, wealth luck is diminished a great deal.

The Best Doors in the House (Interior and Exterior)

For the best money luck in Northwest 2 homes, use doors that face northwest and west (2, 6, 7, or 8 Guas only), or east (1, 3, 4, or 9 Guas only); these directions have good facing stars with wealth energy. In Northwest 3 residences, use doors that face northwest, west, and east (all Guas). If one of these directions is also your +90, you will be lucky with money! Avoid using a door that faces southwest direction; it will activate bankruptcy.

PERIOD 7
North 1
Kan Trigram   Element: WATER

North 1 (337.6° to 352.5°)
  Facing Name: Ren

Chart: Past Luck! Double Stars Meet
  at Sitting (Shuang Xing Dao Zuo)

Warning: Possible Eight Roads of
  Destruction and Robbery Mountain Sha

Level Two DEL: 337.5°

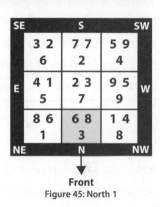

Front
Figure 45: North 1

Figure 45 is the natal chart for north-facing properties facing between 337.6 and 352.5 degrees. Known as North 1, this is the first fifteen degrees of north. Note: The following recommendations are specific to this chart.

Activating the External Environment

Requires Water in the North, Mountain in the Northeast
Alternate Water Locations: East and Southwest
Bankruptcy Indicated: Water in the West

In this chart, known as Double Stars Meet at Sitting (Shuang Xing Dao Zuo), two 7 stars are in the back of the property, and these are past any good luck. However, the 8 wealth star is at the facing, and it is the only Period 7 chart that has this lucky feature. You have a great opportunity to extract wealth luck from this Period 7 house because the north can handle lots of water when the facing stars are good. Activate this formation with a prominent and beautiful water feature, such as a small koi pond, a waterfall, or a fountain. Make sure it is in proportion to the size of the home. Create higher ground in the northeastern area of your front yard with landscape mounds or massive boulders (no sharp or jagged edges). If a pool is in the southeast, you will experience lots of fighting and bickering with your business associates or partners; water in the south can generate bad business deals.

Overall, if the energies are tapped correctly and no adverse landforms are present, the house indicates good wealth luck, even in Period 8. If activated properly, North 1 charts can bring success to business people and charismatic people. The house may be unlucky for those born in the years of the Tiger, the Horse, and the Dog. For 8 Life Guas, north-facing properties can bring incredibly bad personal and business relationship luck, such as divorces from hell, messy partnerships, and miscommunications. Not one single degree of luck is available for 2, 6, 7, or 8 Guas, so avoid north altogether. If you are a member of the West Life Group and live in a north-facing residence, do not enter your home from north-facing doors. Use alternate doors 80 percent of the time and northern doors 20 percent of the time. This alone will alter your luck for the better. North is one of the best facings for members of the East Life Group (1, 3, 4, or 9 Guas), and you will reap great rewards. If you have a natal Flying Star chart that benefits from water in the front, such as this one, a north-facing residence will bring you lots of luck.

An Eight Roads of Destruction is possible if your driveway or a nearby road approaches or exits from the northwest. The house may have a Robbery Mountain Sha formation if a jagged cliff, an electrical tower, a huge dead tree, a lamppost, or a broken mountain is in the west. Remedy any bad landforms discussed in chapter 3—such as T-junctures, sloping land, drains, and so forth—using the Master's Tips as guidelines.

Activating the Internal Environment
Master Bedroom
To enhance wealth luck, locate your bedroom in the west, northwest, north (second floor), or northeast—these sectors have good mountain stars with wealth energy. For the best money luck, angle your headboard or bed toward the northwest or east (all Guas), northeast (2, 6, 7, or 8 Guas only), or north (1, 3, 4, or 9 Guas only); these directions have good mountain and facing star combinations.

Home Office
Establish your home office in the west, northwest, north (second floor), or northeast—these sectors have good mountain stars with wealth energy. For the best money luck, angle your desk and body toward the southwest or east (all Guas), northeast (2, 6, 7, or 8 Guas only), or north (1, 3, 4, or 9 Guas only)—these directions have good facing stars with wealth energy.

Kitchen, Stove, Fire Mouth, and Toilets
North, east, or southwest are the best directions for the fire mouth; west is the worst and should be avoided to deter bankruptcy. A stove in the southwest area of a kitchen indicates loss of wealth.

Review the Eight Mansions chart to find your wealth/power direction and location. Money struggles are likely if a stove or a toilet is located in your +90 sector. You can relocate a stove, but you must use another toilet if this is the case, so select a toilet in one of your negative sectors (-90, -80, -70, or -60). Also, if a toilet is in the area of your 8 facing star, wealth luck is diminished a great deal.

The Best Doors in the House (Interior and Exterior)

The best doors in the house face southwest and east (all Guas), north-east (2, 6, 7, or 8 Guas only), or north (1, 3, 4, or 9 Guas only)—these directions have good facing stars with wealth energy. Select one of these doors based on your Life Gua. If one of these directions is also your +90, you will be lucky with money! Avoid using doors that face west on a daily basis; they will activate bankruptcy.

PERIOD 7

North 2 and North 3

Kan Trigram   Element: WATER

North 2 (352.6° to 7.5°)

Facing name: Tzi and the Rat

North 3 (7.6° to 22.5°) Facing name: Kwei

Chart: Past Luck! Combination of Ten

Warning: Possible Eight Roads of
Destruction and Robbery Mountain Sha

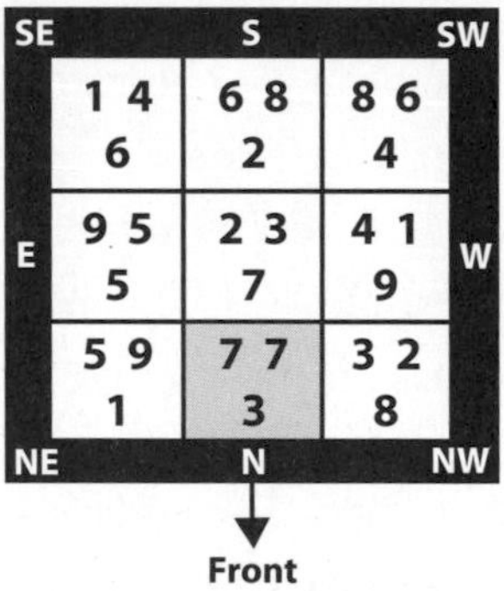

Figure 46: North 2 & 3

Figure 46 is the natal chart for north-facing properties facing between 352.6 and 22.5 degrees. Known as North 2 and North 3, these are the second and third fifteen degrees of north. Note: The following recommendations are specific to this chart.

Activating the External Environment

Requires Water in the South, Mountain in the Southwest

Alternate Water Locations: West and Northeast

Bankruptcy Indicated: Water in the East

In Period 7, this house had the auspicious chart Combination of Ten (He Shih Chu). It is, however, past its prime now and should not be activated by water, low ground, or vast, open space in the front. To extract the good luck this home offers now, place a large water feature—such as a pool, waterfall, fountain, pond, or lake—in the south. You can also create higher ground in the southwest sector of your backyard with mounds or boulders (no sharp or jagged edges).

Overall, if the energies are tapped correctly and no adverse landforms are present, the house indicates good money luck and scholarly pursuits. This residence supports professors, writers, teachers, or those in communications. North-facing properties are not good for members of the West Life Group (2, 6, 7, or 8 Guas), particularly the breadwinner. The house may also be unlucky for those born in the years of the Tiger, Horse, and Dog (fire trine). For 8 Life Guas, however, north-facing properties can bring incredibly bad personal or business relationships.

North 2: People who live in North 2 properties often run successful businesses, enjoy good fortunes, and pursue careers that take them all over the world. If the landforms are unfavorable, alcoholics and injurious gossip ensue. These residences may have a Robbery Mountain Sha formation if a jagged cliff, an electrical tower, a huge dead tree, a lamppost, or a broken mountain is in the west.

North 3: When these homes are coupled with good landforms, expect long life and prosperity. Negative landforms, however, can produce loneliness and bankruptcy. An Eight Roads of Destruction is possible if your driveway or a nearby road approaches or exits from the northeast. The potential also exists for a Robbery Mountain Sha formation if a jagged cliff, an electrical tower, a huge dead tree, a lamppost, or a broken mountain is in the northeast.

Activating the Internal Environment
Master Bedroom

To enhance wealth luck, locate your bedroom in the east, southeast, south, or southwest—these sectors have mountain stars with wealth energy. For the best money luck in homes that face North 2, angle your headboard or bed toward the west or southwest (2, 6, 7, or 8 Guas only), south or southeast (1, 3, 4, or 9 Guas only). In North 3 residences, angle your headboard or bed toward the south, southeast, west, or southwest (all Guas); these directions have good mountain and facing star combinations.

Home Office

Establish your home office in the east, southeast, south, or southwest— these sectors have good mountain stars with wealth energy. For the best money luck in homes that face North 2, angle your desk and body toward the northeast, west, or southwest (2, 6, 7, or 8 Guas only), or south (1, 3, 4, or 9 Guas only). In North 3 residence, angle your desk and body toward the northeast, west, southwest, or south (all Guas); these directions have good facing stars with wealth energy.

Kitchen, Stove, Fire Mouth, and Toilets

South, west, and northeast are the best directions for the fire mouth, because fire stimulates the wealth energy of these good facing stars. To deter bankruptcy, avoid an east-facing fire mouth. If your kitchen is in the northeast sector of the house, money loss is likely.

Review the Eight Mansions chart to find your wealth/power direction and location. Money struggles are likely if a stove or toilet is located in your +90 sector. You can relocate a stove, but you must use another toilet if this is the case, so select a toilet in one of your negative sectors (-90, -80, -70, or -60). Also, if a toilet is in the area of your 8 facing star, wealth luck is diminished a great deal.

The Best Doors in the House (Interior and Exterior)

In North 2 homes, the best doors face northeast, west, and southwest (2, 6, 7, or 8 Guas only), or south (1, 3, 4, or 9 Guas only). In North 3 residences, northeast, west, southwest, and south (all Guas) doors activate money fortune; continual use stimulates the wealth energy of these good facing stars. The worst door in this chart faces east and will activate bankruptcy energy. If one of these directions is also your +90, you will be lucky with money! Avoid using doors that face east; they will activate bankruptcy.

PERIOD 7
Northeast 1
Gen Trigram   Element: Mountain EARTH

Northeast 1 (22.6° to 37.5°)

　Facing name: Chou

Chart: Past Luck! Double Stars Meet
　at Sitting (Shuang Xing Dao Zuo)

Warning: Possible Robbery Mountain Sha

Level Two DEL: 22.5°

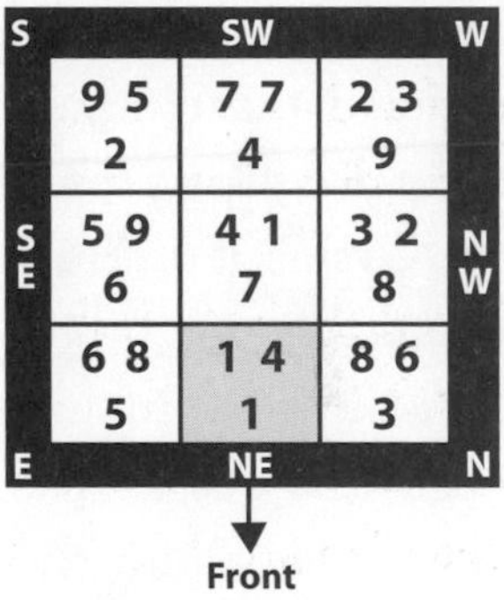

S	SW		W
9 5 2	7 7 4	2 3 9	
5 9 6	4 1 7	3 2 8	N W (SE)
6 8 5	1 4 1	8 6 3	
E	NE		N

Front

Figure 47: Northeast 1

　Figure 47 is the natal chart for northeast-facing properties facing between 22.6 and 37.5 degrees. Known as Northeast 1, this is the first fifteen degrees of northeast. Note: The following recommendations are specific to this chart and this facing direction.

Activating the External Environment
Requires Water in the East, Mountains in the North
Alternate Water Location: Southeast

Bankruptcy Indicated: Water in the South

This house features a pair of 7 stars in the back of the property—that's why this chart is known as Double Stars Meet at Sitting (Shuang Xing Dao Zuo). Unfortunately, this chart and the 7 stars that define it are no longer lucky. Water anywhere in the back of this property will produce inauspicious events, such as money loss, lawsuits, fighting, and theft. So, if you have a large water feature in your backyard, you may want to consider changing and updating the star chart of this building. This is accomplished through a major remodel of the interior or exterior of the house. But if you can't afford an overhaul, focus your attention on the front of the house to extract wealth luck from this property. Install a small pond, a waterfall, or a fountain in the eastern sector of your front yard and create higher ground, no more than four feet tall, in the north region of the front yard. This can easily be done with landscape mounds or large boulders (no sharp or jagged edges).

Overall, if the energies are tapped correctly and no adverse landforms are present, the house indicates good money luck. This residence may have a Robbery Mountain Sha formation if a jagged cliff, electrical tower, huge dead tree, lamppost, or broken mountain is in the north. Remedy any bad landforms discussed in chapter 3—such as T-junctures, sloping land, drains, and so forth—using the Master's Tips as guidelines.

Activating the Internal Environment
Master Bedroom
To enhance wealth luck, locate your bedroom in the south, north, northeast, or east—these sectors have good mountain stars with wealth energy. For the best money luck, angle your headboard or bed toward the north or southeast (1, 3, 4, or 9 Guas only), or east (all Guas); these directions have good mountain and facing star combinations.

Home Office

Establish your home office in the south, north, northeast, or east—these sectors have good mountain stars with wealth energy. For the best money luck, angle your desk and body toward the north or southeast (1, 3, 4, or 9 Guas only), or east (all Guas); these directions have good facing stars with wealth energy.

Kitchen, Stove, Fire Mouth, and Toilets

East and southeast are the best directions for the fire mouth, because fire stimulates the wealth energy of these good facing stars. To deter bankruptcy, avoid a south-facing fire mouth. If your kitchen is in the southeast sector of the house, money loss is likely. A stove in the southeast area of the kitchen is even more serious.

Review the chart to find your wealth/power direction and location. Money struggles are likely if a stove or a toilet is located in your +90 sector. You can relocate a stove, but you must use another toilet if this is the case, so select a toilet in one of your negative sectors (-90, -80, -70, or -60). Also, if a toilet is in the area of your 8 facing star, wealth luck is diminished a great deal.

The Best Doors in the House (Interior and Exterior)

The best doors in the house face north and southeast (1, 3, 4, or 9 Guas only), or east (all Guas); these directions have good facing stars with wealth energy. Using auspicious doors on a continual basis will stimulate money luck. Select one of these doors based on your Life Gua. If one of these directions is also your +90, you will be lucky with money!

PERIOD 7
Northeast 2 and Northeast 3
Gen Trigram   Element: Mountain EARTH

Northeast 2 (37.6° to 52.5°)
　　Facing name: Gen

Northeast 3 (52.6° to 67.5°)
　　Facing name: Yin and the Tiger

Chart: Past Luck! Double Stars Meet
　　at Facing (Shuang Xing Dao Xiang)

Warning: Possible Eight Roads of
　　Destruction, Eight Killing Forces
　　and Robbery Mountain Sha

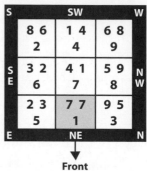

Front
Figure 48: Northeast 2 & 3

Figure 48 is the natal chart for northeast-facing properties facing between 37.6 and 67.5 degrees. Known as Northeast 2 and Northeast 3, these are the second and third fifteen degrees of northeast. Note: The following recommendations are specific to this chart.

Activating the External Environment
Requires Water in the West, Mountain in the South
Alternate Water Location: Northwest
Bankruptcy Indicated: Water in the North
This chart is known as Double Stars Meet at Facing (Shuang Xing Dao Xian) with two 7 stars at the front of the property. Though lucky in Period 7, this chart is now past its prime; therefore, its wealth energy must be extracted properly to promote good fortune. A water feature—such as a small koi pond, a waterfall, or a large fountain—is needed in the western sector of the backyard. Some masters do not recommend water in the west, but to capture the energy of the 8 facing star (prominent wealth

star) fuller, water is a must. I've witnessed incredible results by activating the 8 facing star, regardless of its location. Clients have reported money gains, business opportunities, financial windfalls, and unexpected inheritances. You must also simulate a mountain with high ground, landscape mounds, or boulders (no sharp or jagged edges) in the back southern area of the backyard.

This site should possess none of the bad landforms described in chapter 3. Don't hesitate to apply the solutions found in the Master's Tips to remedy unfavorable landforms, such as T-junctures, sloping land, drains, and so forth.

Northeast 2: An Eight Roads of Destruction formation is possible if your driveway or a nearby road approaches or exits from the north or east. You may also experience a Robbery Mountain Sha formation if a jagged cliff, electrical tower, huge dead tree, lamppost, or broken mountain is in the east.

Northeast 3: These properties may experience an Eight Killing Forces if a mountain is in front of the property or a Robbery Mountain Sha formation if a jagged cliff, electrical tower, huge dead tree, lamppost, or broken mountain is in the north.

Activating the Internal Environment
Master Bedroom

To enhance wealth luck, locate your bedroom in the south, southwest, west, or north—these sectors have good mountain stars with wealth energy. For the best money luck and if the house faces Northeast 2, angle your headboard or bed toward the south (1, 3, 4, or 9 Guas only), or west or southwest (2, 6, 7, or 8 Guas only). For the best money luck and if the house faces Northeast 3, orient your headboard or bed toward the south, west, or southwest (all Guas); these directions have good mountain and facing star combinations.

Home Office
Establish your home office in the south, southwest, west, or north—these sectors have good mountain stars with wealth energy. For the best money luck, and if your home faces Northeast 2 (2, 6, 7, or 8 Guas only) or Northeast 3 (all Guas), angle your desk and body toward the south, west, or northwest.

Kitchen, Stove, Fire Mouth, and Toilets
Northwest and west are the best directions for the fire mouth; north is the worst and should be avoided to deter bankruptcy. A kitchen in the southeast or east sector will trigger bickering, fighting, and lawsuits. Stoves in the southeast area of the kitchen are even more serious.

Review the chart to find your wealth/power direction and location. Money struggles are likely if a stove or a toilet is located in your +90 sector. You can relocate a stove, but you must use another toilet if this is the case, so select a toilet in one of your negative sectors (-90, -80, -70, or -60). Also, if a toilet is in the area of your 8 facing star, wealth luck is diminished a great deal.

The Best Doors in the House (Interior and Exterior)
In homes that face Northeast 2 (2, 6, 7, or 8 Guas only) and Northeast 3 (all Guas), south, west, and northwest doors are most auspicious. These directions have good facing stars with wealth energy. Select one of these doors based on your Life Gua. If one of these directions is also your +90, you will be lucky with money! Avoid using an angled door that faces north; it will activate bankruptcy.

PERIOD 7
East 1
Chen Trigram Element: Big WOOD

East 1 (67.6° to 82.5°) Facing name: Jia

Chart: Past Luck! Up the Mountain, Down the River

Warning: Possible Eight Roads of Destruction and Robbery Mountain Sha

Level Two DEL: 67.5°

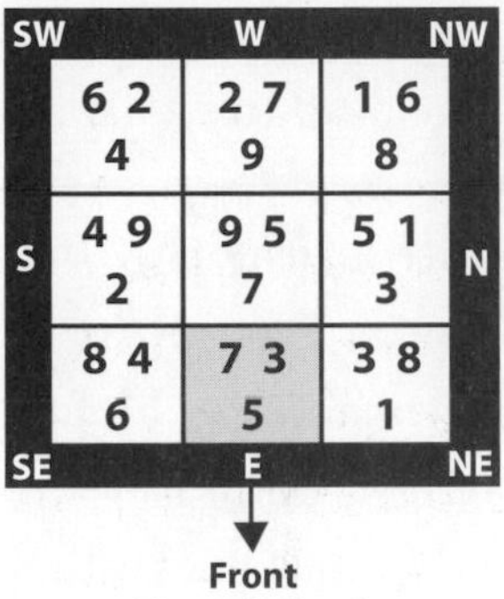
SW
W
NW
6 2
4
2 7
9
1 6
8
S
4 9
2
9 5
7
5 1
3
N
8 4
6
7 3
5
3 8
1
SE
E
NE
Front

Figure 49: East 1

Figure 49 is the natal chart for east-facing properties facing between 67.6 and 82.5 degrees. Known as East 1, this is the first fifteen degrees of east. Note: The following recommendations are specific to this chart.

Activating the External Environment

Requires Water in the Northeast, Mountain in the Southeast

Alternate Water Locations: North and South

Though not a Pearl or Parent String, this chart is known as Up the Mountain, Down the River. This home was best activated by facing a mountain or high ground. But now that Period 7 has expired, this residence could attract prevalent lawsuits. To extract prosperity luck from this chart, add a water feature—such as a small koi pond, a waterfall, or a large fountain—to the northeast section of your front yard. Additionally, simulate a mountain with high ground, landscape mounds, or boulders (no sharp or jagged edges) in the southeast of your front yard.

This site should have none of the bad landforms described in chapter 3. Remedy any negative landforms—such as T-junctures, sloping land, drains, and so forth—using the Master's Tips as guidelines. Overall, if the energies are tapped correctly and no adverse landforms are present, the house indicates good potential for wealth luck. An Eight Roads of Destruction formation is possible if your driveway or a nearby road approaches or exits from the northeast. The house may also have a Robbery Mountain Sha formation if a jagged cliff, an electrical tower, a huge dead tree, a lamppost, or a broken mountain is in the south.

Activating the Internal Environment
Master Bedroom

To enhance wealth luck, locate your bedroom in the southwest, northwest, or southeast—these sectors have good mountain stars with wealth energy. For the best money luck, angle your headboard or bed toward the northwest or south (all Guas) or southeast (1, 3, 4, or 9 Guas only); these directions have good mountain and facing star combinations.

Home Office

Establish your home office in the southwest, northwest, or southeast— these sectors have good mountain stars with wealth energy. For the best money luck, angle your desk and body toward the northwest or south (all Guas), north (1, 3, 4, or 9 Guas only), or northeast (2, 6, 7, or 8 Guas only)—these directions have good facing stars with wealth energy.

Kitchen, Stove, Fire Mouth, and Toilets

Northeast, south, and north are the best directions for the fire mouth. A stove in the north area of the kitchen can create serious bad luck.

Review the Eight Mansions chart to find your wealth/power direction and location. Money struggles are likely if a stove or a toilet is located in your +90 sector. You can relocate a stove, but you must use another toilet if this is the case, so select a toilet in one of your negative sectors (-90, -80, -70, or -60). Also, if a toilet is in the area of your 8 facing star, wealth luck is diminished a great deal.

The Best Doors in the House (Interior and Exterior)

The best doors in the house face northwest and south (all Guas), north (1, 3, 4, or 9 Guas only), or northeast (2, 6, 7, or 8 Guas only)—the continual use of these good facing stars activates wealth. Select one of these doors based on your Life Gua. If one of these directions is also your +90, you will be lucky with money!

PERIOD 7

East 2 and East 3

Chen Trigram   Element: Big Wood

East 2 (82.6° to 97.5°)

Facing name: Mao and the Rabbit

East 3 (97.6° to 112.5°) Facing name: Yi

Chart: Past Luck! Prosperous Sitting and Facing (Wang Shan Wang Shui)

Warning: Eight Roads of Destruction, Eight Killing Forces and Robbery Mountain Sha

Major DEL at 90°!

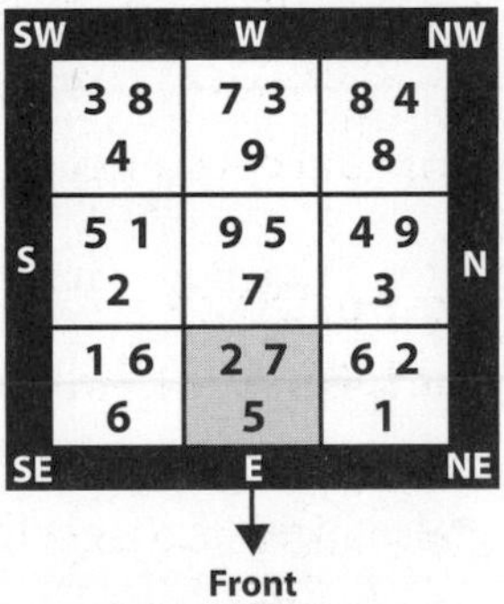

SW	W	NW
3 8 **4**	7 3 **9**	8 4 **8**
5 1 **2**	9 5 **7**	4 9 **3**
1 6 **6**	2 7 **5**	6 2 **1**
SE	E	NE

S (left side), N (right side)

Front

Figure 50: East 2 & 3

Figure 50 is the natal chart for east-facing properties facing between 82.6 and 112.5 degrees. Known as East 2 and East 3, these are the second and third fifteen degrees of east. Note: The following recommendations are specific to this chart.

Activating the External Environment
Requires Water in the Southwest, Mountain in the Northwest
Alternate Water Locations: South and North

A formation known as Prosperous Sitting and Facing (Wang Shan Wang Shui) made this chart lucky in Period 7. Currently, this home could attract prevalent lawsuits if a pool is in the back. To extract prosperity luck from this chart, add a water feature—such as a small koi pond, a waterfall, or a large fountain—to the southwest section of your front yard. Additionally, simulate a mountain with high ground, landscape mounds, or boulders (no sharp or jagged edges) in the northwest region of your backyard.

This site should have none of the bad landforms described in chapter 3. Remedy any negative landforms—such as T-junctures, sloping land, drains, and so forth—using the Master's Tips as guidelines. Overall, if the energies are tapped correctly and no adverse landforms are present, this house indicates good potential for wealth luck.

East 2: An Eight Killings formation is possible if mountain energy comes from the southwest. A Robbery Mountain Sha formation is also likely if a jagged cliff, electrical tower, a huge dead tree, lamppost, or a broken mountain is in the northeast.

East 3: You may experience an Eight Roads of Destruction if your driveway or a nearby road approaches or exits from the southeast. A Robbery Mountain Sha formation is possible if a jagged cliff, electrical tower, a huge dead tree, lamppost, or a broken mountain is in the northeast.

Activating the Internal Environment
Master Bedroom
To enhance wealth luck, locate your bedroom in the northwest, northeast, or southeast—these orientations have good mountain stars with wealth energy. For the best money luck if the house faces East 2, angle

your headboard or bed toward the northwest (2, 6, 7, or 8 Guas only), north or southeast (1, 3, 4, or 9 Guas only). For the best money luck if the house faces East 3, angle your headboard or bed toward the southeast, or northwest (all Guas), or north (1, 3, 4, or 9 Guas only); these directions have good mountain and facing star combinations.

Home Office
Establish your home office in the northwest, northeast, or southeast—these have good mountain stars with wealth energy. For the best money luck and if the house faces East 2, angle your desk and body toward the southwest (2, 6, 7, or 8 Guas only) or north, southeast, or south (1, 3, 4, or 9 Guas only)—these directions have good facing stars with wealth energy. For the best money luck and if the house faces East 3, position your desk and body toward the southwest, southeast, or south (all Guas), or north (1, 3, 4, or 9 Guas only)—these orientations have good facing stars with wealth energy.

Kitchen, Stove, Fire Mouth, and Toilets
South, north, and southwest are the best directions for the fire mouth. A stove in the south area of the kitchen can create serious bad luck. Review the Eight Mansions chart to find your wealth/power direction and location. Money struggles are likely if a stove or a toilet is located in your +90 sector. You can relocate a stove, but you must use another toilet if this is the case, so select a toilet in one of your negative sectors (-90, -80, -70, or -60). Also, if a toilet is in the area of your 8 facing star, wealth luck is diminished a great deal.

The Best Doors in the House (Interior and Exterior)
For the best money luck if the house is an East 2, use doors that face southwest (2, 6, 7, or 8 Guas only) or north, southeast, and south (1, 3, 4, or 9 Guas only)—these directions have good facing stars with wealth energy. In East 3 residences, the most auspicious doors are southwest, southeast, and south (all Guas), or north (1, 3, 4, or 9 Guas only); the

continual use of these good facing stars activates wealth energy. Select one of these doors based on your Life Gua. If one of these directions is also your +90, you will be lucky with money!

PERIOD 7
Southeast 1
Xun Trigram   Element: Small Wood

Southeast 1 (112.6° to 127.5°)
  Facing name: Chen and the Dragon

Special Chart: Past luck!
  Prosperous Sitting and Facing
  (Wang Shan Wang Shui)

Warning: Possible Eight Killing Forces
  and Robbery Mountain Sha

Level Two DEL: 112.5°

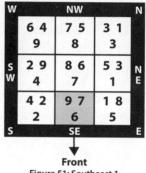

Front
Figure 51: Southeast 1

Figure 51 is the natal chart for southeast-facing properties facing between 112.6 and 127.5 degrees. Known as Southeast 1, this is the first fifteen degrees of southeast. Note: The following recommendations are specific to this chart.

Activating the External Environment
Requires Water in the East or North,
Mountain in the Southeast or East
Bankruptcy Indicated: Water in the Northwest
This house has a Prosperous Sitting and Facing (Wang Shan Wang Shui). In Period 7, it was a lucky wealth-building chart, but to extract prosperity from this chart for the current period, you must add a water feature—such

as a small koi pond, a waterfall, or a large fountain—to the east section of your front yard. If you are unable to place it there, north is the second best area for water. A pool or other large body of water in the back (northwest) indicates bankruptcy, but a pool in the north activates wealth. Also, simulate a mountain in the southeast and east sectors of your front yard with landscape mounds or boulders (no sharp or jagged edges). Do not align these features directly with the front door. Any formation taller than three feet is considered a mountain in Feng Shui.

An Eight Killings formation is possible if mountain energy comes to the house from the north. The house may also have a Robbery Mountain Sha formation if a jagged cliff, an electrical tower, a huge dead tree, a lamppost, or a broken mountain is in the northeast. Remedy any negative landforms mentioned in chapter 3—such as T-junctures, sloping land, drains, and so forth—using the Master's Tips as guidelines. This chart's facing stars in front and back can hurt money luck, so it's important to extract the good.

Activating the Internal Environment
Master Bedroom
To enhance wealth luck, locate your bedroom in the west, east, or southeast (second floor)—these sectors have good mountain stars with wealth energy. For the best money luck, angle your headboard or bed toward the east or west (all Guas); these directions have good mountain and facing star combinations.

Home Office
Establish your home office in the west, east, or southeast (second floor)—these sectors have good mountain stars with wealth energy. For the best money luck, angle your desk and body toward the east or southwest (all Guas), or north (1, 3, 4, or 9 Guas only)—these directions have good facing stars with wealth energy.

Kitchen, Stove, Fire Mouth, and Toilets

East, north, and southwest are the best directions for the fire mouth; northwest is the worst and should be avoided to deter bankruptcy. If your kitchen is in the northeast sector of the house, money loss is likely. Stoves in the northeast area of the kitchen are even more serious.

Review the Eight Mansions chart to find your wealth/power direction and location. Money struggles are likely if a stove or a toilet is located in your +90 sector. You can relocate a stove, but you must use another toilet if this is the case, so select a toilet in one of your negative sectors (-90, -80, -70, or -60). Also, if a toilet is in the area of your 8 facing star, wealth luck is diminished a great deal.

The Best Doors in the House (Interior and Exterior)

The best doors in the house face east and southwest (all Guas), or north (1, 3, 4, or 9 Guas only)—these directions have good facing stars with wealth energy. Select one of these doors based on your Life Gua. If one of these directions is also your +90, you will be lucky with money! Avoid back doors that face northwest; they will activate bankruptcy with regular use.

PERIOD 7
Southeast 2 and Southeast 3
Xun Trigram   Element: Small Wood

Southeast 2 (127.6° to 142.5°)
    Facing name: Xun

Southeast 3 (142.6° to 157.5°)
    Facing name: Su and the Snake

Special Chart: Past Luck! Pearl String
    (Lin Cu San Poon Gua)

Warning: Eight Roads of Destruction,
    Eight Killing Forces,
    and Robbery Mountain Sha

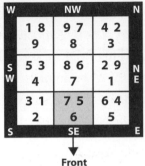

Front
Figure 52: Southeast 2 & 3

Figure 52 is the natal chart for southeast-facing properties facing between 127.6 and 157.5 degrees. Known as Southeast 2 and Southeast 3, these are the second and third fifteen degrees of southeast. Note: The following recommendations are specific to this chart.

Activating the External Environment
Requires Water in the West, Mountain in the Northwest
Alternate Water: South and Northeast
Bankruptcy Indicated: Water in the Southeast
Though this house is a Pearl String (Lin Cu San Poon Gua) formation, it is out of luck now. Even in its heydey it had to be properly activated—especially the southeast Pearl Strings—to benefit the occupants. If activated correctly in Period 7, this particular Pearl String brought powerful relationship luck. Improper activation (e.g., water in the front) attracted incredibly bad luck, such as bankruptcy, divorce, and accidents. The fortune-producing momentum of these homes has diminished since February 4, 2004, so

they are no longer timely, especially with the 5 facing star in the front of the house as part of the natal chart. You can counter-balance this negative energy with metal, but if a frequently used door is on a 5 facing star, you may still experience problems on a regular basis. Metal hurts this energy, and the constant activation by using the door does just that—activates it.

To extract wealth luck from this house, install a water feature—such as a koi pond, a pool, a waterfall, a huge fountain, or a lake—in the west section of the backyard. If this is not possible, the second best area is the south. Also, simulate a mountain in the northwest area of your backyard to activate good support and release additional wealth luck. A mountain in the west is also excellent to enhance money luck.

Southeast 2: An Eight Roads of Destruction formation is possible if your driveway or a nearby road approaches or exits from the south or east. This home may also have a Robbery Mountain Sha formation if a jagged cliff, an electrical tower, a huge dead tree, a lamppost, or a broken mountain is in the northeast.

Southeast 3: An Eight Killings formation is possible if a mountain brings energy to the house from the west. Also, watch out for a Robbery Mountain Sha formation if a jagged cliff, an electrical tower, a huge dead tree, a lamppost, or a broken mountain is in the east.

Activating the Internal Environment
Master Bedroom

To enhance wealth luck, locate your bedroom in the west, northwest, or east—these sectors have good mountain stars with wealth energy. For the best money luck if the house faces Southeast 2, angle your headboard or bed toward the west (2, 6, 7, or 8 Guas only), or east (1, 3, 4, or 9 Guas only). In homes that face Southeast 3, position your headboard or bed toward the west or east (all Guas); these directions have good mountain and facing star combinations.

Home Office

Establish your home office in the west, northwest, or east—these sectors have good mountain stars with wealth energy. For the best money luck if the house faces Southeast 2, orient your desk and body toward the west or northeast (2, 6, 7, or 8 Guas only), or south (1, 3, 4, or 9 Guas only)—these directions have good facing stars with wealth energy. In homes that face Southeast 3, angle your desk and body toward the west, northeast, or south (all Guas)—these directions have good facing stars with wealth energy.

Kitchen, Stove, Fire Mouth, and Toilets

West, northeast, and south are the best directions for the fire mouth, because fire activates the wealth energy of these powerful facing stars. To deter bankruptcy, avoid a southeast-facing fire mouth. If your kitchen is in the southwest sector of the house, money loss is likely. Stoves in the southwest area of the kitchen are even more serious.

Review the Eight Mansions chart to find your wealth/power direction and location. Money struggles are likely if a stove or a toilet is located in your +90 sector. You can relocate a stove, but you must use another toilet if this is the case, so select a toilet in one of your negative sectors (-90, -80, -70, or -60). Also, if a toilet is in the area of your 8 facing star, wealth luck is diminished a great deal.

The Best Doors in the House (Interior and Exterior)

For the best money luck if the house is a Southeast 2, use doors that face west and northeast (2, 6, 7, or 8 Guas only), or south (1, 3, 4, or 9 Guas only)—these directions have good facing stars with wealth energy. In Southeast 3 homes, west, northeast, and south (all Guas) doors are best—these directions have good facing stars with wealth energy. Using a southwest door will bring clients to high-powered lawyers, especially if this chart is properly activated by good landforms. Select one of these doors based on your Life Gua. If one of these directions is also your

+90, you will be lucky with money! Avoid accessing the front door if it faces southeast. Regular use can activate bankruptcy. Add a high-quality metal, such as bronze, copper, or brass, on or near the door and use it approximately 5 percent of the time.

Eight

....

Jewels, Pearls, and Jade: The Most Secret Wealth-Building Techniques

....

Make my home everywhere within the four seas.
The world is my home, the world is my oyster.
Xiao He to the Emperor, Han Dynasty

The hundreds of formulas, systems, and techniques of Classical Feng Shui help assess and solve almost every type of situation and problem. A solid 65 percent of these strategies are devoted to enhancing wealth, success, prosperity, and money. I decided that the first book that I wrote would discuss wealth secrets, because Classical Feng Shui itself so clearly addresses this area of life. It's also the most asked question from my clients: "How can wealth be enhanced?" Wealth is many things to many people. It certainly indicates more than just money. In fact, most people tend to discuss the overall richness of their lives: a fabulous family, powerful connections, vital health, close friends, a deep spiritual connection, education, travel, mentoring others, and so on.

The remaining formulas in Feng Shui are designed to ensure health, longevity, and relationships. It is important to understand that it is neither possible nor appropriate to incorporate *all* of the wealth-building techniques into one site. Through careful calculations, however, a Feng Shui Master or practitioner can create a cohesive blend of several strategies for maximum results.

Why so many different formulas? They allow for all possible situations and environment types—mountains, water, cities, large tracts of land, businesses, homes, castles, temples, churches, office buildings, and so forth. Also, formulas were developed to assist people in achieving their desires, including wealth, real estate, companionship, children, success, position, power, fame, influence, love, sex, nobility, health, and longevity.

The following wealth-building examples are some of the most popular and preferred techniques, which apply to residential and commercial sites.

Precious Jewel Lines, or Gold Dragons (Jin Lung)

Precious Jewel Lines (PJL), also known as Gold Dragons, are specific compass degrees that can bring great money luck and, as the name implies, precious things and "jewels" to your life. In any of the eight directions, there are six PJLs from which to choose, making a total of forty-eight. An example of a Precious Jewel Line degree is 86.5, which is part of the east direction. PJLs are appropriate for any structure and have various applications. PJLs most commonly apply to doors; generally the main door of a home or business can be set to these auspicious degrees. Driveways, sidewalks, trails, entrance gates, building foundations, important interior doors, desks, and beds can also be angled toward these special degrees.

In new-home design, I like to use PJLs for the entire foundation to bring wealth luck and harmony to my clients. To accomplish this, measurements must be taken at the staking of the foundation and prior to pouring.

Aligning doors with these special degrees is a great way to bring additional luck to a home or building already constructed. This technique is extremely common in Southeast Asia—PJLs appear in office buildings, banks, malls, and homes. It's a great way to welcome extra fortune, but it takes some work. First, you must remove the doorjamb and the threshold to change the tilt, or angle, of the opening. When these elements are shifted, the door moves too. To ensure correct geometry, a sensitive and expertly crafted Luo Pan is needed. Though I have seen a few of these degrees occur naturally or accidentally, they are rare. I found one last year while home shopping with a client. The builder inadvertently (and serendipitously) constructed a house on a PJL. What a lucky home this will be for the fortunate new owners.

In 2005, within two weeks of purchasing my home in North Scottsdale, which I have since sold, I tilted my front door to a PJL. To begin with, my house had great overall Feng Shui. It faced west (my +70), an excellent direction for relationship luck and connecting with the community. A couple months after moving in, a popular local television program—*Sonoran Living Live*—invited me to appear on the show. What a jewel of a gig for me! I was the new kid on the block and hardly knew anyone in the city. After that appearance, I was asked back to do another TV spot. They wanted to tape me conducting a live Feng Shui assessment. It was an original and different experience for the station, which had never seen anyone use a Luo Pan before.

When I decided to move and sell my home in Scottsdale, the Phoenix area ranked among the worst markets in the country. Some people had no showings for a year or more. Even though I had to reduce the price drastically, I did sell my home in less than seven months, even in that disastrous economic climate. It was the first time I didn't profit from a home, but I believe the PJL protected and helped me move forward with my plans.

Not convinced that degrees can affect you or that they are important? Try to plot a flight plan without specific degrees, longitude, and latitude.

MASTER'S TIP

You will need a Feng Shui Master to assist you in applying these incredibly lucky degrees. They can be used to set a building foundation, door degree, driveway, or roads to bring wealth luck.

Xuan Kong Da Gua, or the Big Sixty-four Hexagrams

Xuan Kong Da Gua (Mysterious Void Wind/Water School of Great Divinatory Symbols) is also known as the Big Sixty-four Hexagrams or I Ching Method of Feng Shui. It is based on the sixty-four hexagrams of the ancient text of Taoist divination, the I Ching. This particularly potent set of formulas, appropriate for residential and commercial applications, describes ideal settings for the location and the orientation of a building in relation to its surroundings. Each configuration, or formation, described in the formulas has the potential to deliver great wealth and success to the occupants under certain circumstances. The formulas are complex and contain an enormous body of information, as anyone who has read the I Ching or sought to understand the meanings of the hexagrams can appreciate.

To activate a formation, four factors must be perfectly aligned. These include the facing and the sitting directions of a building in relation to an incoming dragon (a mountain or ridge) and a body of water (or river). Naturally occurring environmental features are best and the most potent messengers of luck. The degree of success will depend on the size, proximity, and beauty of the mountain and the water relative to the building. The system is most commonly used as a means of date selection for the auspicious timing of important events, such as the opening of a business, the moving of a household, or a wedding.

MASTER'S TIP

The Xuan Kong Da Gua, considered a masterful technique, is used to bring wealth, health, power, prestige, companionship, fame, recognition, leadership, and more.

Water Dragons (Shui Lung)

The sage is like water.
Water is good, nourishes all things,
and does not compete with them.
It dwells in humble places that others disdain;
hence it is close to the Tao.
In his dwelling, the sage loves the earth.
In his mind, he loves what is profound.
In his associations, he is kind and gentle.
In his speech, he is sincere.
In his ruling, he is just.
In business, he is proficient.
In his action, he is timely.
Because he does not compete,
he does not find fault in others.
—Lao Tzu (604–517 BC)
  Tao Te Ching, VIII

In nearly every part of the world, Water Dragons are natural to the environment. They are nothing more than a river or stream winding through the landscape, resembling the undulating body of this mythical reptile; hence the name. To qualify as a natural Water Dragon, a waterway must resemble the body of a dragon. A main channel that serves as the dragon's body must be visible; it should also possess distinct side channels that act as the dragon's feet. The power of a Water Dragon is enhanced if water pools at certain points. Naturally occurring Water Dragons do not form in swift-flowing water, stagnant water, or water falling from great heights.

Over hundreds of years of observation, the Chinese designed numerous water-centric formulas to produce wealth, including but not limited to Water Dragon techniques. The ancients discovered that water was a conduit of energy and a living entity: Where there was energy, there was wealth. Filmmaker Saida Medvedeva in her 2008 documentary, *Water*, confirmed this notion and added a twist—water possesses molecular memory too.

Great waterways such as the Yellow River meander through China, so it's no surprise that Chinese scholars developed a fascination with the water's behavior and its effect on urban developments and individual homes. That's why the flow, the direction, and the egress of water from a site are important. The old masters also understood the unpredictability of water, and if they could harness its energy, they could obtain a great deal of fortune. Just look at the Three Gorges Dam on the Yangtze as humans' domination over the natural environment, specifically water.

Manmade Water Dragons are quite popular in Southeast Asia but rarely show up in the United States and other Western countries. Taiwanese masters especially find all sorts of applications for these techniques. My primary teacher, Grand Master Yap Cheng Hai, is quite famous for his applications of Water Dragons in Southeast Asia. He learned this specialized system in Taiwan from his mentor, Master Chan Chuan Huai (also spelled Tan Chuan Hui). It is said that Master Chan's clients are among Taiwan's billionaires, including the Sugar King, the Cement King, and the Plastics King. Water Dragon formulas will bring powerful things in your life, sometimes slowly, sometimes quickly.

Over time, formulas for all possible facings were devised for the purpose of creating manmade Water Dragons. A comprehensive body of knowledge came from this study, and many techniques pertaining to wealth were founded on this data. But the breadth of information is voluminous—that's why I am focusing on just one ancient text known as the *Water Dragon Classic* (Shui Lung Jing) as it appeared in Lillian Too's *Water Feng Shui for Wealth*.[16] **To create a manmade Water Dragon, certain criteria must be met. The following ideas are paramount. Keep in mind that the formulas are compass-based:**

- Water Dragons are designed in relation to the direction of the front door.

- Water Dragons require a fairly flat or level piece of land.

- Water must be seen from the door.

- Water must pass by the door, but not be too close.

- Water must flow right to left, or left to right depending on the door degree and direction.

- A portion of the Water Dragon stream should be visibly above ground; the other will be underground and invisible.

- It should be no more than twelve inches wide and nine inches deep.

- Two sumps are involved: one to swirl the water near the point of entry, the other near the exit point.

- An *exact* exit degree is paramount; one degree off could create disaster.

- A specific ring on the San He Luo Pan, known as the Heaven Plate or Water Ring, is used to measure the water entrance and exit degrees.

- A different compass is used to measure the door direction.

---

16. *Water Feng Shui for Wealth* is currently out of print. Grand Master Yap did not reveal the exact exit degrees in this book, as it was written for the masses and not for those who would practice Feng Shui. Lillian Too sought Master Yap's assistance and advice in writing two other of her earlier books.

Water Dragons are expensive, complicated to install, and require constant maintenance. Most Feng Shui Masters charge as much as $100,000 for a Water Dragon formula design, depending on the size and the application. Lillian Too offers a good primer on Water Dragons in her book *Water Feng Shui for Wealth*. She wrote it in collaboration with Grand Master Yap Cheng Hai. When it was published, it became instantly popular with Feng Shui aficionados.

Unless you have studied and practiced Feng Shui for many years, it is not advisable to attempt to create a Water Dragon; you could have extremely bad results. Some of Grand Master Yap's students tried their hand at building them on their own properties. It was a learning process, and many had to alter their design to get good results. These formulas were the last thing Grand Master Yap taught at his school, and for good reason. They are powerful, and you need skill and discretion to do them properly.

I installed a Water Dragon known as the Unity of Three Priceless Jewels for a client in Houston in the spring of 2001. The result was good wealth luck. Water dragons are a wealth formula, not necessarily designed to enhance health and relationships, although this may be one of the good results. The client still lives in the house, and has experienced excellent business opportunities all over the world, including a project in India equivalent to the Alaska pipeline. In less than two years, my client became very wealthy and continues to amass a fortune.

Besides the Unity of Three Priceless Jewels, other Water Dragons designed for extreme wealth have tantalizing names—Golden City Water, Emperor's Jade Belt, Ten Thousand Cases of Gold, Carry the Goldfish (or Treasure), Five Fortunes Coming to the Door, and the Golden Pathway.

In recent years, the validity of Water Dragons has become a hotly debated topic in Feng Shui circles. Some say they are a hoax—ineffective and impotent. This is certainly not true! They are a legitimate Classical Feng Shui discipline, and since they involve real water, they can extract good and bad results. Grand Master Yap and his teacher, Master

Chan, have both experienced their own successes with Water Dragons, serving as a wonderful testament to their potential power.

Many people grasp for this secret knowledge, mistaking Water Dragon formulas as the pinnacle of Feng Shui. Not so. Water Dragons do not and will not remedy bad Feng Shui. Install one in conjunction with poor Feng Shui, however, and you have a recipe for disaster. Just as with all wealth-producing formulas, the overall Feng Shui of a site must be excellent.

I rarely use Water Dragons for private residences because I believe this technique is better suited for large projects, such as master-planned communities, complexes of commercial buildings, and shopping centers. The power of a Water Dragon can overwhelm a smaller structure. As long as the basics are incorporated when it comes single-family dwellings—great roads, stable landforms, good Flying Stars and Eight Mansions coupled with simple wealth-building techniques—everything else should fall into place without a Water Dragon. But, if a client is lucky enough to have a natural Water Dragon, a stream or a river on their property, I love to tap this energy to support wealth by simply taking advantage of what's already there. Natural water features are auspicious and vastly superior to artificially created ones.

MASTER'S TIP

Water Dragons are a highly specialized field of Feng Shui. If implemented correctly, they can bring immense good fortune and extreme wealth. They are often referred to as "billionaire's Feng Shui."

Five Ghosts Carry Treasure (Wu Gwei Yun Cai)

Though the name of this highly guarded secret technique sounds weird and mysterious, it is a powerful wealth-producing formula that delivers, bringing immense good fortune! It is said that when this method is applied correctly, it's like having five ghosts or spirit angels carry prosperity right to your door. Many masters believe that this formula will only last about twelve years or so. However, my research indicates that the luck can extend well past twenty or thirty years. Much depends on the natural mountains surrounding the site.

The Five Ghosts Carry Treasure method is technically a water formula. Basically three things need to be in harmony: door direction, water flow, and mountain energy. Wealth is derived by tapping into the combined energy of these great forces. Of course, a real mountain and a natural body of water are best, but pools, man-made streams, waterfalls and simulated mountains are excellent substitutes.

Mountainous regions offer lots of opportunities to use this energy. In flatter areas, I default to manmade formations, such as out-structures, landscape mounds, large boulders, casitas, two-story detached garages, and pavilions. Yes, even these virtual or simulated mountains work well.

Here's an example of how a Five Ghosts could be designed for a north-facing home:

- The front door direction is North 1 (337.6 to 352.5 degrees).

- A real mountain is located in the South 1 (specifically chi from 157.5 to 172.5 degrees).

- Water is from the North 3 (7.6 to 22.5 degrees).

If you don't have a real mountain in the south, you can simulate a mountain with large boulders (no jagged or sharp edges) or landscape mounds. In either case, the man-made elevation must be three feet or higher to be considered a mountain. You could also create a tall structure in that location, which would also activate the mountain aspect of this formula. The water is fairly simple; a man-made stream could be designed to flow past and in view of your front door. In the example given above, it needs to flow from left to right as you are looking out the door. Each formula will have a different water flow depending on the door direction.

Your interior and exterior Feng Shui should be good prior to employing the Five Ghosts technique. Also, before placing water *anywhere*, the

Flying Stars must be considered. If you have a bad star in the north of your home, you cannot use the above formula. Refer to chapters 6 and 7 to see where you should place water on your property.

These formulas are complex and it takes some experience to implement them correctly to get the best possible result. Seventy-two variables encompass the eight directions in which you are able to design the perfect Five Ghost for a site. Five Ghost formulas have internal applications as well. They are used exclusively for home or commercial offices to bring wealth luck. This is how the formula works for an office using the same formula above but interpreting the direction, mountain, and water a little differently:

- The office door is the "water" (North 3 between 7.6 and 22.5 degrees).

- Where you face (North 1 between 337.6 and 352.5 degrees) while sitting at your desk is the "direction."

- Tall, heavy bookshelves; armoires; or heavy file cabinets can be used as the "mountain" (South 1 between 157.5 and 172.5 degrees).

A large piece of property can provide all kinds of interesting opportunities with which to experiment, including the chance to create two Five Ghosts Carry Treasures. I did this for a client in San Antonio, Texas, who had almost four acres of land facing the Guadalupe River—gorgeous!

The effect is even more profound when other systems of Feng Shui are factored in the mix to fine-tune or enhance other significant aspects of the site. I have experimented with this formula extensively because it's one of my favorites. If this technique is interpreted and implemented correctly, Five Ghosts Carry Treasure is one of the most powerful wealth-building tools available to a Feng Shui Master.

MASTER'S TIP

Real Mountains are the most commanding way to implement these mega-wealth producing formulas. You will need a skilled Feng Shui Master to help you place water and tap mountain energy. In the absence of real mountains, you can create virtual mountains with landscape mounds or huge boulders.

Dragon Gate Eight Formations
(Long Men Ba Da Ju)

In Taiwan this set of formulas is known as Chien Kun National Treasure (Qian Kun Guo Bao). Technically, these, too, are water formulas, but unlike the Five Ghosts technique, this method makes use of specific water exits. The following three considerations must be in harmony when designing a Dragon Gate formation: water entrance, water exit, and incoming dragon or mountain. First and foremost, the design process begins by using the sitting direction—or back—of the site or structure. Next, it is important to determine from which direction the water will enter: one direction brings wealth, while the other attracts nobility and success. The mountain direction will indicate who in the family receives the benefit, and there are six, fifteen-degree increments from which to choose.

Here's an example of how a formation might be designed if the building sits in Southeast 1, Southeast 2, or Southeast 3 (112.6 to 157.5 degrees):

- Water enters from West 1, West 2, or West 3 (247.6 to 292.5 degrees).

- Water exits from Northeast 2 (37.6 to 52.5 degrees).

- There is an incoming mountain from South 1, South 2, or South 3 (157.6 to 202.5 degrees).

This formation (a house sitting southeast and facing northwest) brings overall family wealth but will benefit the eldest child or son when he or she is of age. The following two other key considerations must be accounted for when designing a Dragon Gate: the natal Flying Star chart of the house, and the proper flow of the water.

If water flows past the front door, basic water rules must be followed. Water will flow left to right or right to left, depending on the door direction. This applies to *all* water formulas. Even though the Dragon Gate formations are not based on the door direction, if water can be seen or flows by the front door, the flow must be correct. In our example above, the house faces northwest and sits in the southeast. If water begins in the west and exits in the northeast—it will have to pass the front door. Otherwise, serious money loss is possible if the basic principles of water flow are violated.

Grand Master Yap does not consider these as potent as the Five Ghosts Carry Treasure formations. I agree, but I have had excellent results when it comes to jump-starting a career, particularly with a natural mountain or high ridge nearby. Don't hesitate to collaborate with a landscape architect: these techniques are simple to include in your landscape design. In the end, it will look like a gorgeous man-made stream incorporated into the schematic.

Dragon Gate Eight formations are also perfectly suited for large-scale projects, such as urban planning and development, shopping malls, and master-planned communities.

MASTER'S TIP

Dragon Gate Eight formations are yet another powerful wealth-producing technique available to a Feng Shui Master or practitioner. If your home has natural mountains or you want to jump-start your business or career, ask your consultant about designing one for you.

The Assistant Star Water Method
(Fu Xing Shui Fa)

This technique offers ample and comprehensive choices when it comes to bringing wealth luck to your site via roads or real water, which are used in conjunction with the door direction. A master or practitioner has twenty-four possible door directions and numerous water (virtual and real) directions and exits from which to choose.

You will get specific results, depending on the choice of water direction. For example, certain water directions bring "wealth from heaven," a high government position, riches and nobility, and good children. These formulas can determine whether lawsuits, robbery, gambling, loneliness, mishaps, or quarrels are possible based on the placement.

An example of how this technique is applied is the front door faces South 1, South 2, or South 3. A driveway approaches from Southwest 1, 2, or 3. A water exit or drain is located in the southeast. The formation in our example can indicate the acquisition of a great fortune. But water exiting from the south (e.g., a drain in the front of the house) serves as evidence that your career will be hindered, accompanied by serious money loss. I am fond of using the Assistant Star method in new-home construction and when I'm designing a good, wealth-attracting driveway.

Three Harmony Doorways

Despite the name, you don't need three doors to implement this wealth-producing formula. It involves a door direction, an incoming road, and a driveway or sidewalk. These formulas have what is known as a main harmony and a sub-harmony—when the formula is applied correctly, a brilliant mix of yin and yang energy results. This particular technique attracts lucrative, prosperous, noble, and harmonious chi to the household; it can be used for roads, driveways, or sidewalks. They are the most powerful when the road or driveway can also be placed in the actual location that the method calls for. Here is an example of how a Three Harmony Doorway can be created:

- The door direction is at Northeast 3 (52.6 to 67.5 degrees).

- A sidewalk comes from North 2 (352.6 to 7.5 degrees).

In our example, the formula becomes very effective if the sidewalk not only begins from the south direction, but also is located south of your garden. New homes under construction can easily benefit from this technique, as the driveway has not been yet staked and pored. If also combined with a Precious Jewel Line, it can bring double good luck. Three Harmony Doorways offer twelve door directions with twelve complementary road directions. Depending on which entrance you choose, these formulas are designed to attract wealth luck or relationship luck; either way it is brought to you in a most harmonious and noble manner. The entrance of the driveway, road, or sidewalk should also lure in a good facing star.

MASTER'S TIP

Three Harmony Doorways are known to bring harmony, nobility, and prosperity to a home or business. They are simple to create for homes already constructed by using a sidewalk or pathway.

Court Official Water Formations

This technique is named after the importance of the judiciary in Asian cultures. In ancient China, serving as an officer of the court was a prestigious and sought-after post, one that required high intelligence, the mastery of certain skills, and the ability to pass a battery of grueling exams. No wonder these potent formulas were patterned after a government position that brought wealth, opportunities, and status.

Court Official Water Formations are great techniques for those aspiring to take their career or business to new heights. These formulas are particularly useful for people seeking authority and status, such as high-powered lawyers or judges. Court Official formulas have several major indications or predictive results—high government positions, nobility with high status, huge fame, extreme riches, a world-famous author, and fame and wealth combined.

These formulas draw on a combination of energies from roads or real water, door directions, and nearby buildings. A building could be a towering, stately tree; a pagoda; a high-rise building (twin towers are best); or a tall mountain. A road, real water, electric gates, a curving sidewalk or pathway, or even a door represents water. In some situations, doors and gates denote virtual water—because of this, electric gates are considered auspicious.

Whether real or virtual, "sentimental water" (water that moves slowly) is the absolute best option when it comes to gaining and retaining wealth. One of my students has a huge electric gate that activates her 8 facing star and it brings her incredible money luck. The success of a gated community depends on the energy of its gates to stimulate a wealth star. These formulas are even more powerful when combined with San Yuan Flying Stars. The secret to this technique is proper building placement and an excellent water entrance. A cleverly designed Court Official Water Formation can double or triple career luck. The following configuration may attract a lofty position in government:

- Door direction in Northwest 1, Northwest 2, or Northwest 3 (292.6 to 337.5 degrees).

- An eighteen-story high-rise located in the northwest (not in direct alignment with the door).

- A waterfall that comes from North 1 (337.6 to 352.5 degrees)

For the formula to work correctly, the building must be physically located in the sector indicated by the formulas. In our example above, that means the building could be anywhere in the forty-five degrees of northwest. A word of warning: A road should not come straight toward the front of the house, or money loss will be the result. A road that comes straight toward the back of the house could indicate losing family.

MASTER'S TIP

Ask your Feng Shui Master or practitioner about designing a Court Official if you want to boost your career. If you are a lawyer, judge, or executive, the Court Official is excellent for gaining power and status.

Castle Gate Formations

Castle Gate Formations (Cheng Men Jue) offer two approaches, both of which are under the auspices of Classical Feng Shui. I learned both styles from two different teachers. These formations are highly prized and can bring prosperity and wealth to every area of your life. Technically they are water formulas designed to manipulate energy for wealth luck. Traditional Castle Gate Formations are the most sophisticated water techniques offered in the San Yuan/Xuan Kong system.

The traditional method for this technique is to surround three sides of a building with mountains—often referred to as "Land Embrace"—while leaving a gap or opening at the front of the site. The best scenario is mountains with a natural space between them, which creates a concentrated form of energy. This opening becomes the gateway of chi, and it is captured when real water is placed in the front of the site, bringing wealth to the recipients. Buildings, however, can be substituted in place of real mountains, but this becomes a little more tricky. As you may have guessed by now, natural mountains near a home site allow for numerous wealth-producing formulas. In fact, a gap between mountains may also be used in the Five Ghosts Carry Treasure and Dragon Gate Eight formations.

The other popular method is known as Castle Gate Theory, Sent Mun Kuet, or He Tu Castle Gate, and it works best with big water near or in the front of the house. With this well-known technique, it is said that one "steals chi from heaven" by manipulating the Flying Star chart of the house.

The current prosperity energy is activated by real water when a door to a natural body of water, such as a lake, pond, or ocean, is opened.

This door or gate is only good for the period in which you create it. For example, if you opened a Castle Gate in Period 7, it will offer no wealth luck now in Period 8.

Jade Belt Formations

Jade has always been sacred in the long and illustrious history of China. The ancient Chinese believed that jade was the essence of heaven and earth. At one time, rich businessmen and high-ranking officials used jade as money; wealthy Chinese families distinguished their class rank with custom-designed jade tassels.

The term "jade belt" comes from the ancient custom of storing jade in a belt and wearing it around the waist. This act represented wealth and was no doubt the reason it was adopted as a Feng Shui technique. When the Jade Belt formation is particularly lucrative, it is referred to as an Emperor's Jade Belt.

A simple yet powerful method of attracting money luck to your home or business, a Jade Belt formation is a road or driveway that wraps around a site like a belt encircles a waist. It can also show up as winding water, such as a river that embraces the front of a house—water is an emblem of influence, wealth, and power. In lieu of real water, especially for city dwellers that may not have a nearby waterway, streets and roads can also form natural Jade Belts. Though all these scenarios are auspicious for gaining wealth and recognition, a large piece of land is best to maximize the potential of a good Jade Belt.

These formations can be designed on your site if you have sufficient land to do so. But watch out for ever-popular circular driveways—these are unlucky designs.

MASTER'S TIP

Create a Jade Belt formation by having a road or driveway
wrap around your home or property like belt.

The Sky Horse Technique

The expertise and acumen of Grand Master Yang Yun Song, who lived during the Tang Dynasty and is mentioned in many ancient classics, is still legendary. These accounts describe his powerful Feng Shui skills, which were so potent that he could make a person rich in one hour. Even to this day his methods and techniques are largely a mystery. In fact, many consider these tales in the realm of myth and magic—beautiful and charming fables. But many lineages have managed to maintain and pass down the secrets that were transmitted orally from master to student. One of these mystical formulas of Grand Master Yang is called the Sky Horse Formation.

The Sky Horse strategy conjures up an image of a thoroughbred equine winning the race. This technique attracts money quickly and always implies speed, travel, or movement. The Feng Shui of the site must be excellent; it will speed things up—good or bad. In Chinese astrology the term the "Heavenly Sky Horse Star" is used, and this primarily indicates travel for a person, often opportunities abroad.

The Sky Horse can be applied to your home or business. This technique is based on the direction of an important exterior door—generally the front door—and the incorporation of a road, pathway, or driveway. For existing homes, the easiest way to design a Sky Horse is by creating a pathway. If you are building a new home, a driveway works great. For large sites and projects, a road is the best foundation for a Sky Horse.

The technique is specific to fifteen-degree increments for the door and the road in question. The Sky Horse formula includes twelve door directions with four compatible road directions, which are known as the four traveling houses or traveling Guas. They are Northeast 3 (the House of Gen), Southwest 3 (the House of Kun), Northwest 3 (the House of Chien), and Southeast 3 (the House of Xun). Here's an example of a how a Sky Horse may be created: the front door faces South 2 (172.6 to 187.5 degrees) and a road comes from Southwest 3 direction (232.6 to 247.5 degrees)

The natal Flying Star chart of the house or business should also be considered, because roads, driveways, or pathways act as virtual water. The road should bring in a good facing star with wealth energy (1, 6, 8, or 9)—placing the road on a Precious Jewel Line will attract additional money luck. In our example, this particular Sky Horse Formation is meant to bring excellent business relationships and connections. I designed one for a client in Payson, Arizona, using a simple garden pathway. It lead down to a terrace, had six steps (a heavenly number), and was elaborately lit for importance. The clients experienced excellent results. Within a short time they attracted a new investor—whom they had never met—to their development project.

MASTER'S TIP

Ask your Feng Shui Master or practitioner to use this technique "to help make your fortune faster by sitting on the horse," as Master Yap says.

Five Ghosts Carry Treasure II

Many wealth-producing formulas in Classical Feng Shui evolved and developed over time. The Five Ghosts Carry Treasure II is one of those that expanded into a completely different approach, although it shares the name of the original technique. It is a more advanced application of the first method in that it uses specific water exits. Master Yap told us the prime minister of Taiwan's Feng Shui Master gave him his notebook on this technique, which Master Yap treasures to this day.

This method is allegedly more secret than the more widely known version of Five Ghosts Carry Treasure mentioned earlier. Even the original Five Ghosts formulas have only been revealed in books over the past five years or so. This formula does not use the door direction. Rather, it relies on the sitting or back of the property, the incoming and outgoing directions of water or a road, and a mountain or a tall building. Here is an example of the formula:

- House sits in the north (337.6 to 22.5 degrees).

- Water comes from South 1 (157.6 to 172.5 degrees).

- Water exits South 3 (187.6 to 202.5 degrees).

- Mountain is in West 2 (262.6 to 277.5 degrees).

The water or road exit is optional, especially real water. But, if a driveway or road could be designed to exit in the suggested direction, great wealth luck can result. Both of the Five Ghosts techniques are designed to bring wealth luck, and a master or practitioner will design one depending on what is possible at the site before them.

Pearl String Formations (Lin Shu San Poon Gua)

Pearl Strings are also known as Continuous Bead formations. They are special wealth-producing Flying Star charts of that system. These incredible formations are said to bring great wealth and pearls, rare and expensive treasures, to the occupants of a house or building.

Pearl String Formations are based on the facing direction of a structure and always fall on one of the intercardinal points: northwest, southwest, northeast, or southeast. For the Pearl String to be effective, the structure must sit on a specific fifteen-degree increment of one of those directions. Pearl String charts for Period 7 and Period 8 are identified in chapters 6 and 7.

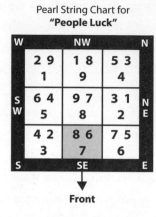

Pearl String Chart for
"People Luck"

↓
Front

This Period 8, Southeast 1 Pearl String is lucky for people and relationships. Notice how the "string" of numbers run in sequence *toward* the mountain star in all nine palaces.

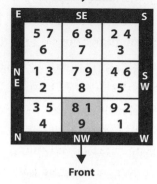

Pearl String Chart for
"Money Luck"

↓
Front

This Period 8, Northwest 1 Pearl String is lucky for money and accumulating wealth. Notice how the "string" of numbers run in sequence *toward* the facing star in all nine palaces.

....
Figure: 53: The two different Pearl String Charts

There are actually two types of Pearl String Formations—one that attracts money luck and one that fosters luck with people. Both are auspicious, but if you want to increase affluence, the Pearl String for wealth is the preferred facing. The previous illustrations demonstrate both charts. Notice in Figure 53, the chart on the left, how the numbers run in sequence toward the mountain star in all nine palaces (3, 4, 5 and 7, 8, 9). This is the Pearl String chart for wealth and prosperity. Now look at Figure 53 again, and notice the chart on the right. The numbers run in sequence toward the facing star in all nine palaces (4, 5, 6 and 1, 2, 3). This chart is for people luck—health, relationships, employees, and fertility. This is where the term "string" comes into play. The sequence of numbers form beads on a string, and because these formations attract rare and expensive things, they represent pearls.

Both Pearl String charts must be supported by a mountain in the front and water in the back. In Feng Shui, this is known as Up the Mountain, Down the River—a colorful way of describing the movement of chi. The presence of a mountain at the facing first activates energy as it travels up; then the energy is activated as it flows down to the river (water in the back).

If these formations are not activated properly, for instance the water and the mountain are switched, misfortune can ensue. Pearl String Formations are effective for twenty years and attract wealth only in the current period. After its time has passed, the Feng Shui must be adjusted. For example, all Period 7 Pearl Strings have expired. To extract wealth from these homes, the powerful 8 energy must be activated.

Meanwhile, perfectly placed water and mountains aren't always enough when it comes to extracting maximum fortune. The landforms in your immediate environment must also support this special chart. For example, if a client's residence backs to a golf course pond and faces a real mountain within two miles, the circumstances are perfect to activate the Pearl String. To truly capture the energy, however, I ask clients to place large boulders or landscape mounds about three feet high in their front yard and a beautiful swimming pool or waterfall in the backyard. This is the most effective way of capitalizing on the luck of these special charts.

The Pearl String Formation also works well for large hotels that back to a lake or an ocean. I visited such a place in Penang, Malaysia, while studying with Grand Master Yap. The hotel was wildly successful because it had a Pearl String for wealth. At approximately eighteen stories high, the building itself served as the mountain and the ocean behind it provided the perfect activation.

One of my clients, a successful mortgage broker and investor, called me for a consultation on two of her homes, a main residence and an investment property. The investment property was new and nearly complete when I saw it in Scottsdale's elite DC Ranch (a successful, exclusive master-planned community with an average price of $1 million). She bought this property in the red-hot Phoenix real estate market and planned to flip it as soon as it was finished. But it was a Pearl String for wealth, and I encouraged her to sell her current home—which was not as lucky—and move into the DC Ranch residence. This house would provide her more than money luck; she would enjoy relationship and health fortune as well. She followed my suggestions and after living in the house for about nine months, she told me she had her best year ever, topping her success in the Phoenix boom. And she continued to make money during the real estate meltdown. In fact, more money than ever!

These special charts occur four times in Period 7 (Southeast 2, Southeast 3, Northwest 2, and Northwest 3), and only twice in Period 8 (Southeast 1 and Northwest 1).

MASTER'S TIP

To capture the full luck potential the Pearl String Charts offer, you must place a mountain in the front and water in the back. Refer to chapters 6 and 7 for examples on how to simulate a mountain and where exactly to place the water.

Combination of Ten Formations *(He Shih Chu)*

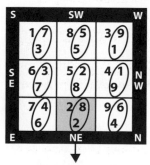

Figure 54: Combination of Ten to the Facing– A true Combination of Ten charts will add up to ten in each palace either *towards* the facing star, as in the chart above, or with and towards the mountain star. The chart can bring great wealth if activated correctly.

The Combination of Ten is a special Flying Star chart that brings wealth, opportunities, prestige, and powerful connections. To the Chinese, the number ten represents completion; ten is also considered auspicious in the Xuan Kong Flying Star system. Combination of Ten charts offer the potential to double the fortune of a house, however, just like Pearl Strings, they must be activated specifically and correctly. The Combination of Ten also offers two different types of charts—money luck and people luck.

Figure 54 is a Combination of Ten star chart that is lucky for wealth and prosperity; the focus is on the front or facing of the site.

Notice that the facing star and the time or base star add to ten—this must occur in all nine palaces to have a Combination of Ten chart, also known in this case as the Combination of Ten Facing Structure. For maximum effect, add water and make it extraordinarily beautiful and important.

In Figure 55, the focus shifts to the sitting or back of your property. Look at how the mountain star and the time or base star add to ten in all nine palaces. This is known as the Combination of Ten Sitting Structure, and it is extremely lucky for reputation, health, authority, and relationships—or, in other words, people luck. To experience optimal results with this chart, make sure you install a high, sustainable retaining wall; create land higher than the front of the property; place massive boulders; construct multi-level landscaped beds; or apply any combination thereof in the back of your property. Avoid open fences, such as wrought iron—these provide a weak backing. Water or vast, open spaces or roads will also diminish the power of this chart. Without question, if you are lucky enough to have a natural mountain, hill, or gorgeous ridge behind your home, you will receive the maximum benefit of this chart.

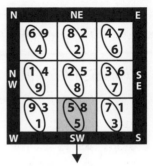

Figure 55: Combination of Ten to the Sitting– This is an example of a Combination of Ten chart that adds to ten in each and every palace *towards* the mountain or sitting star.

Some say that these special charts override any negative aspects of a house. This statement, however, is simply not true. In fact, bad landforms and the wealth-depleting scenarios described in chapter 3 can totally negate the potential of these charts.

Case in point—I had a client in Arizona whose home was a Feng Shui disaster. It did have the Combination of Ten chart indicating wealth luck. However, this house was plagued with problems. The reason the potential of this chart could not be realized was because it had two major Death and Empty Lines, an extreme drop at the back, and the house was built over a vortex. It clearly did not override these bad situations, and the client's life spiraled downward.

Before you activate your special chart with mountain and water, correct any bad road and land formations identified in chapter 3. These special charts occur four times in Period 7 (South 2, South 3, North 2, and North 3) and only twice in Period 8 (Southwest 1 and Northeast 1).

MASTER'S TIP

These lucky buildings and houses must have the proper external features to bring you money, wealth, and prestige!

Parent String Gua Formations
(Fu Mu San Poon Gua)

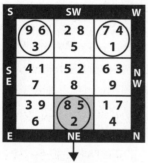

Figure 56: Parent String for Wealth– Parent String charts are very lucky for enhancing wealth, opportunities, and money. Notice in the chart above, that in every place there is a combination of three numbers–in no particular order–the combination of 1, 4, 7 or 2, 5, 8 or 3, 6, 9.

Parent Strings are also referred to as Three Combinations, and they are the third wealth-producing Xuan Kong Flying Star chart. These charts represent the cosmic trinity—heaven-earth-man or father-mother-son energies. Because of this, some Feng Shui texts hold that this prosperous chi will permeate endlessly and transcend all periods. This is actually an over-exaggeration. These charts are lucky only in their period, which last at most twenty years. For example, the luck of the Parent String charts for Period 8 will expire in Period 9, beginning February 4, 2024.

Notice Figure 56. In all nine palaces, one of these combinations will show up—in no particular order—as 1, 4, 7, or 2, 5, 8, or 3, 6, 9. In other words, it doesn't matter whether the number is the mountain, facing, or time star. The three combinations must be grouped as described above and must occur in every palace to be a Parent String chart.

The Parent String also has an Up the Mountain, Down the River flow of energy. Thus, these wealth-producing charts are activated like a Pearl String—mountain in front, water in back. They are said to bring *three* times the good fortune when extracted correctly. These rare charts deliver outstanding health, ample fame, good reputation, great fortunes, and harmony to the lucky recipients.

These charts are very rare and do not occur at all in Period 7. However, in Period 8 there are four occurrences: Southwest 2, Southwest 3, Northeast 2, and Northeast 3.

Implementing Wealth Formulas

Wealth-producing formulas are powerful, indeed. They can work to your benefit or detriment, depending on the situation. That is why it is important not to apply these methods unless the overall Feng Shui of a residence or business is stable. If any of the undesirable formations mentioned in the previous chapters are present, disastrous results can follow. Before installing water, make sure all wealth-depleting problems are corrected. Once water is introduced to a bad site, your money, health, or relationships could be in jeopardy. Remember, a Feng Shui Master or practitioner will cross-check these formulas with basic water principles, Flying Stars, and a host of other methods before designing the perfect wealth-producing feature for your home.

MASTER'S TIP

The general Feng Shui of your site—residential or commercial—should be excellent prior to installing any of the wealth-producing formulas. Ideally, your site should not have any of the negative configurations mentioned in chapter 3.

Nine

....

What Affects Wealth and What Does Not

....

Like the weather, one's fortune
may change by the evening.
Luen Meng Zheng, Song Dynasty

After nearly a thirty-year exposure to Feng Shui, it is my opinion that the general public is still confused as to what will affect their wealth and what won't. After reading the previous chapters, I hope you have a better understanding of how authentic Feng Shui works and the numerous techniques available in assisting you to build wealth.

The five categories that will *definitively* affect your wealth luck are Feng/**Wind** (direction), Shui/**Water** (energy), **Mountains** (Shan), **Fire** (Ho) and **Form and Shape** (Xing Fa). In each of these categories I have included classic Feng Shui formulas, Eight Mansions, Flying Stars, and landforms—how they can affect you—both interior and exterior of your home or building.

The Influence of Wind *(Feng)* on Wealth

Though the word *feng* translates as "wind," it actually means "direction," and it is the direction of energy that is so important in Feng Shui. The foundation of a property's assessment begins with the direction it faces; the orientation of a residence in the natural environment will determine the potential wealth luck of the occupants.

For a business, the direction of the main door is everything. While no place is perfect, Feng Shui offers solutions to ensure that precious and vital chi circulates and settles the site, thereby extending the good fortunes of those who inhabit that space. And using a direction that supports you doesn't stop there. You will benefit if your bed, desk, fire mouth, or really any place you spend a great deal of time in activates a good direction. Whenever possible, Feng Shui makes use of both location and direction, but direction is more powerful. So, if you cannot use both, choose a good direction.

The Influence of Water *(Shui)* on Wealth

Well-placed water can bring great wealth and riches, but when water is badly placed it can cause devastation. For example, water, real or virtual, should always activate a good facing star (8, 1, or 9). If water is placed in the location or direction of a 2, 5, or 3 facing star you will experience negative results, such as illness, bankruptcy, and lawsuits. Chapters 6 and 7 will give you the correct placement of water—inside and outside your home—according to your natal Flying Star chart.

The Influence of Mountains *(Shan)* on Wealth

As humans, we are awed by the beauty and humbled by the stature of mountains—they are unmoving yet emit powerful energy. Thus, undulating mountains exemplify all the best of Feng Shui. Mountains are known by many names in Classical Feng Shui: dragons, *shan*, *lung*, and *sar*. Just as fire and water have many interpretations, so do mountains. Boulders, high ground, retaining walls, landscape mounds, hills, cliffs, brick walls, ridges, detached garages, plateaus, cement or stucco walls, tall buildings, large statues, stone planters or pots, armoires, heavy bookcases, and staircases are just a few examples of mountain energy.

The Influence of Fire (Ho) on Wealth

In Feng Shui, the placement of fire in your home is vitally important. After water, it is the most powerful chi-activating element. Fire in Feng Shui represents many different things, obviously real fire, such as stoves, indoor fireplaces, ovens, grills, outdoor fireplaces, fire pits, torches, and outdoor kitchens. Modern-day fire includes televisions, computers, electrical indoor hubs, electrical towers, and power stations. Very triangular-shaped, pointy mountains are interpreted as fire. If a fire-shaped mountain is also red, it is double fire. The 9 Star (either mountain or facing) is fire in the Flying Star system; it will ignite energy.

The Influence of Form and Shape (Xing Fa) on Wealth

The study of form is the oldest aspect of Feng Shui, dating back thousands of years. Feng Shui operates on the principle that the landscape is alive with unseen forces caused by the shape, color, and size of physical structures that make up the landscape. When analyzing a home or workplace, these factors must be taken into account.

No Magic Bullet: Things Having Little or No Influence on Your Wealth

Everyone would love the magic bullet to cure a bad house, out-of-shape body, and uninspired love life. This is how Feng Shui became all the rage when it was first introduced—"place a candle in your 'fame' corner, a picture of love birds in your 'marriage' sector, and a fish tank in your 'career' corner—and all good things will come." How wonderful it would be if it worked like this, but authentic Feng Shui cannot be reduced to using trinkets. We have discussed what will actually bring you auspicious opportunities for prosperity or disaster. Things that will have little or no affect on your wealth luck are commonly featured in Feng Shui books and include as coin-choked frogs, crystals, pictures of love birds, bamboo flutes, red walls, candles, and Arowana (dragon fish).

MASTER'S TIP

The external and internal environments will affect your luck, but the most important considerations are external landforms. This is known as the macro-level in evaluating a site to determine the quality of energy around it. We cannot escape nature and its energy. As far as crystals, bamboo flutes, artwork, mirrors, and so on, this is not how ancient or modern-day masters practice Feng Shui. A skilled Feng Shui Master or practitioner will always move or alter the energy of your home without incorporating charms and trinkets.

In Conclusion

Classical Feng Shui is a gift to mankind that helps us help ourselves; even a little knowledge on the subject can tilt the scales in your favor. Unfortunately, self-knowledge, wishful thinking, positive affirmations, journaling, and other self-help techniques are not enough to elevate you above a bad situation. Good intentions and a positive attitude are powerful tools for change, but most people cannot maintain this 24/7 or long enough to outweigh the effects of a house with bad Feng Shui. Even if you could use your energy to rise above horrible Feng Shui, you would eventually exhaust yourself because the daily battle between you and that sloping land or T-juncture would simply wear you out. To create real change, you must move the energy in the physical environment, much like the case studies I've described in this book. If you can't significantly alter the energy, then the solution may be to find another home or building. I always tell my clients when I suggest relocation: "It's only a house —you are so much more important."

If your interest is to build wealth, you must have a site that is secure and stable in the environment. Avoid all bad situations discussed in chapter 3. Such formations will cause you harm, struggle, money loss, affairs, financial devastation, divorce (more money loss), and other hell-on-earth experiences that can deplete your energy and exhaust you. Think of friends, business associates, or family members who have lived with these destructive external forces; recall the outcome of their lives.

It may seem odd when you first hear the notions I talk about in this book, but much of Feng Shui is common sense and practicality at its best. Feng Shui, therefore, is simultaneously a mystery and not a mystery. Just remember that everything is energy, including us, and because of that we will automatically have a relationship or dance with the living environment. This is a given; it could be good or bad depending on the arrangement. Feng Shui is often referred to as the "art of arrangement"—this is what it really means. Where is the road, the mountain, and the water? And how are they "arranged" or placed in our personal environment and surroundings?

If you are fortunate enough to know a skilled Feng Shui Master or practitioner who can assist you in selecting and designing your projects, you are blessed indeed. And if you have one who can implement some of the wealth secrets described in chapter 8, or avoid those listed in chapter 3, you are already on your way to success. You don't have to be Donald Trump to have a Feng Shui Master in your pocket. There are many excellent Feng Shui Masters and practitioners all over the world who can help you find or design spaces that support you.

Life will always have its cycles. You're never on top all the time, but great Feng Shui can make a major difference, carry you when you're experiencing the ebb, and minimize the negative effects of a downturn.

It provides that stable foothold in your pursuits to achieve your wealth-building dreams and goals. Here's to your great success in all areas of your life!

Glossary of Terms

This book includes Feng Shui terms using both Wade-Giles and Pinyin; in several instances the glossary gives both spellings. The Chinese-to-English translations also include some in Mandarin and others in Cantonese.

24 Mountains: Nothing to do with actual mountains, simply a term used for the twenty-four possible facing directions of buildings. The 24 mountain ring/directions is the single most important ring on the Luo Pan/Chinese compass. Each of the eight directions has three divisions comprising a total of twenty four.

Age of Eight: *See* Period 8.

Almanac, Chinese: Also referred to as the *Tong Shu*. Since ancient times, this annual publication is of great importance to the people everywhere in Asia. It serves as a useful guide to everyday life, dispensing advice on good days for burials, weddings, and business transactions. Even in modern times, millions of people still consult the Chinese almanac every day.

Assistant Star Water Method: A technique used to enhance wealth, health, or relationships with an energy path, such as a road, driveway, or footpath.

Auspicious: The Chinese favor the term "auspicious," meaning something is lucky, and good events will ensue.

Ba Gua: Also spelled pa kua. An octagonal arrangement of the eight rigrams or Guas of Taoist mysticism; used as a basic tool of energy assessment in Feng Shui.

Ba Gua Mirror: This mirror (flat, concave, or convex) is surrounded by the eight Trigrams and used to deflect negative energy or something in view that is not desirable. This Ba Gua is identified as having three solid lines at the top, known as the Chien/Qian Trigram or Gua.

Bankruptcy: Inability to pay debts; insolvency; losing all your wealth or property.

Basements: Traditional basements are built at the sub-ground level and into the earth. They often have small egress windows looking out on the ground level (dirt or earth). The earth level is cold chi or cold energy.

Ba Zhai: Also spelled Pa Chai, this is the Eight Mansions system. It is also referred to as the East-West System and the Major Wandering Stars. The minor wandering stars are the Tan Lang stars; this may be covered in a future book.

Big Dipper Casting Golden Light: Known as Jin Guang Dou Lin Jing in Chinese (also Kam Kwong Dou Lam King). This style of Eight Mansions is used in this book; it is also called Golden Star Classic.

Black Hat Sect: A new school of Feng Shui created in the 1980s. It was brought to the Western world by Professor Thomas Lin Yun, a Buddhist monk of the Black Hat Order of Tibetan Buddhism. Although not considered an authentic system of Feng Shui, Black Hat is the most recognized style in the world except in Asian countries, which are most familiar with traditional schools of Feng Shui.

Black Turtle: The rear of your property, part of the celestial animals.

Book of Changes: Also known as the I Ching.

Bright Hall: This area is an open space near the front door (interior and exterior) where chi can collect; in Chinese known as the Ming Tang.

Broken mountain: This is a term used in Feng Shui to depict a mountain that has been excavated, scarred, or destroyed in any fashion. If such a mountain is in view of a home site or business, it is considered extremely inauspicious.

Canal: An artificial waterway for boats or irrigation. In Feng Shui, canals are considered rivers; they can be particularly ruinous if they run behind your home.

Cardinal directions: Points of geographic orientation—north, south, east, and west. The specific and exact points of these directions are 0/360, north; 90 degrees, east; 180 degrees, south; and 270 degrees, west.

Castle Gate: a wealth-producing formula in the San Yuan school; the Chinese term is Cheng Men Jue. There are actually two popular variations of a Castle Gate. See chapter 8 for more detail.

Chai: House, also spelled Zhai.

Chasing the Dragon: The technique of assessing the energy of a mountain from location to location, or examining the mountain's most powerful point of chi and following that vein of energy.

Chen: One of the eight Trigrams of the Ba Gua. It represents the eldest son, thunder, and spring. In the Later Heaven arrangement of the Ba Gua, the Chen Trigram is located in the east.

Chi: The vital life-force energy of the universe and everything in it; sometimes chi is referred to as cosmic breath. It is also spelled ch'i or qi and is pronounced "chee."

Chien: One of the eight Trigrams of the Ba Gua, also spelled Qian. It represents the father, the heavens, and late autumn. In the Later Heaven arrangement of the Ba Gua, the Chien Trigram is located in the northwest.

Chinese lunar calendar: A calendar based on the moon cycles.

Chinese solar calendar: A calendar based on the rotation of the earth around the sun.

Ching Dynasty: The last ruling dynasty of China; lasted between 1644 and 1912 AD.

Chueh Ming: In the Eight Mansions system, this represents total loss, divorce, and bankruptcy. According to Master Yap's numeric representation, it is -90.

Classical Feng Shui: Also known as traditional Feng Shui. It is authentic, genuine Feng Shui that has been developed and applied for hundreds, even thousands, of years in Asia. Sophisticated forms are practiced in Hong Kong, Taiwan, Malaysia, and Singapore. Classical Feng Shui is just being introduced and practiced in Western countries and has not reached mainstream status. The traditional systems of Feng Shui are the San He ("three combinations") and San Yuan ("three cycles"). All techniques, methods, and formulas are under one or the other. Feng Shui masters and practitioners use both systems as one comprehensive body of knowledge.

Cold chi: A room or home built below the earth's surface or into the ground is considered cold chi; these are yin, or dead, environments.

Combination of 10: A wealth-producing chart in the Flying Star system where the stars add to ten in all nine palaces. In Chinese it is called He Shih Chu.

Commercial spaces: Business-related property intended to generate a profit, including shopping centers, office buildings, malls, restaurants, retail shops, boutiques, salons, spas, and hotels.

Compass, Chinese: *See* Luo Pan.

Cosmic Trinity: Known in Chinese as Tien-Di-Ren. Three categories of luck, specifically heaven luck, man luck, and earth luck. The Chinese believe heaven luck is fixed, however, people have control over Feng Shui (earth luck) and personal effort (man luck).

Court Official: A technique used to bring status and power to a lawyer, judge, or high official using a building (virtual mountain) to tap the energy.

Death and Emptiness Lines (DEL): Also known as a void, or empty lines, they invite a host of negative events if doors fall on these degrees, which are on the exact cardinal points, 90°, 180°, 270°, and 360°/0°. Though other DELs exist, the consequences are less severe. Void lines are reserved for temples, churches, synagogues, and other places of worship. These degrees can attract or serve as doorways for ghosts or spirits. Also known as Kong Wang or Kun Mang.

Direct and Indirect Spirit: This theory restricts the placement of water in four directions in certain Periods. For instance in Period 6, 7, 8, and 9, it suggests that water can *only* be placed in the north, southwest, east, or southeast. Southwest would be the "optimal" position in Period 8 and considered direct spirit. In Period 7, it was the east. Master Joseph Yu and other masters refer to this theory as the Holy 1 and the Holy 0. Grand Master Yap Cheng Hai considers this theory somewhat faulty and not totally accurate; for the most part I do not consider it when placing water. Instead I focus on the overall Feng Shui and activate the wealth stars (both mountain and water), with the 8 facing star receiving the foremost consideration. My clients have enjoyed very prosperous outcomes as a result.

Direction: One of the most important aspects of determining the energy of a site or structure is taking the compass direction. Generally, the direction is read at the main door of the structure.

Diving driveway: When land or a driveway slopes to the front door, the energy is said to *dive* toward the house. This is considered sha or negative chi because it is too direct and intense to bring good luck.

Double Stars Meet at Facing: "Shuang Xing Dao Xiang" in Chinese means that two stars in the Flying Star system are in the front of the house or building.

Double Stars Meet at Sitting: "Shuang Xing Dao Zuo" in Chinese means that two stars in the Flying Star system are at the back of the house or building.

Dragon: In Feng Shui, a dragon is a mountain. "Dragon" is a term also used for something powerful or curving, recalling the legendary creature's body shape. It can apply to land and water. The Chinese so revere the dragon that it is used in multiple applications and meanings.

Dragon Gate: The gate that successful scholars pass through, metaphorically speaking, transforming themselves from a simple carp into a powerful dragon.

Dragon Gate Eight Formula: Known in Chinese as Long Men Ba Da Ju, this powerful set of formulas involves the energetic harmony of water, mountains, and designed water exits.

Dragon's vein: The dragon's vein is an area of chi accumulation, most commonly places of running water. In Feng Shui, mountains and mountain ranges are called dragons. Where the dragon meets the terrain is its lair, or the most powerful spot of a site.

Drain: An opening in the ground, usually covered with a grate, which takes water away from an area. Uncovered drains are rectangular and sometimes seen in subdivisions. In Feng Shui, these are considered water exits and can bring wealth or disaster. A drain near a main door of a home or business is always bad. Only exposed drains are important in Feng Shui; underground and invisible formations do not count.

Early Heaven Ba Gua: This is the first arrangement of the eight Trigrams; known as the Ho Tien or Fu Xi Ba Gua in Chinese. It can be easily recognized as the Chien Trigram (three solid lines) and is always placed on the top. This is the arrangement used in Ba Gua mirrors to deter sha chi.

Earth luck: One of the three categories of luck that humans can experience; your luck will increase by using Feng Shui, also known as earth luck. The Chinese word for earth is *di*.

East Life Group: In the Eight Mansions system, people are divided into the East or West group. The 1, 3, 4, and 9 Life Guas are part of the East Life Group.

Eight House: This is another name for the Eight Mansions; in Chinese it is Pa Chai or Ba Zhai.

Eight House Bright Mirror: In Chinese, Pa Chai Ming Jing is one of the eight different styles of the Eight Mansions system. This style uses the sitting direction of the house instead of the facing.

Eight Killing Forces: A formation where the door direction and the energy of a nearby mountain are out of harmony; they are serious and bring disaster to the household.

Eight Life Stations: Also known as the Eight Life Aspirations, these stations correspond to a point on the Ba Gua and an aspect of life—south, fame; southwest, marriage; southeast, wealth; north, career; and so forth. This is the work of Black Hat Sect founder Lin Yun. Eight Life Stations is not found in classic texts or part of the genuine Feng Shui of ancient practice and principles. It is neither an aspect of the Eight Mansions system nor even a derivative of that system. Some popular Feng Shui books that promote Classical Feng Shui also include the Eight Life Aspirations, which only adds to the confusion!

Eight Roads of Destruction: Also known as the Eight Roads to Hell, this formation is based on the egress of a road or driveway from a property in correlation to the front door. Even though the road or driveway is considered virtual water, the direction it exits is called a water exit. This unlucky formation can have disastrous results, so remedial measures must be taken.

Electrical towers: The high-tension towers that bring electricity to an area emit incredibly negative energy. The Swedish government has done extensive research on how these towers affect human beings: children are most vulnerable to this intense energy.

Energy: The Chinese call energy chi (also spelled qi) pronounced "chee." Our entire universe is energy; there are many types of chi—human, environmental, and heavenly (the solar system).

Esoteric: Knowledge that is available only to a narrow range of enlightened or initiated people or a specially educated group. Feng Shui is part of Chinese metaphysics and is considered esoteric.

External environment: This covers the terrain and topography, including mountains, water, and other natural formations. It also encompasses manmade features such as roads, pools, retaining walls, highways, poles, drains, washes, tall buildings, stop signs, fire hydrants, and other structures.

Facing direction: The front side of the home or building, generally where the front or main door is located and faces the street.

Facing Star: Also known as the water star, this star is located in the upper right-hand corner of a Flying Star chart in all nine palaces or sectors. The facing star is in charge of wealth luck.

Feng: The Chinese word for wind; pronounced "fung," although "foong" is a more accurate sound.

Feng Shui: Known as Kan Yu (translated as "the way of heaven and earth") until about a hundred years ago, it is the Chinese system of maximizing the accumulation of beneficial chi, which improves the quality of life and luck of the occupants of a particular building or location. The literal translation is "wind and water"; however, in Classical Feng Shui "wind" means direction and "water" refers to energy. Pronounced "fung shway" or "foong shway."

Feng Shui master: One who has mastered the skills of Classical Feng Shui and/or has been declared as such by his or her teacher, or both. It is also said that a practitioner becomes a master when his or her clients refer to them as master. Most Feng Shui Masters from classic traditions will belong to a lineage of their teachers. This is also known as a lineage carrier, meaning the master carries on the teachings and practices of his or her education. A Feng Shui Master generally oversees his or her own school and students as well.

Feng Shui schools: There are two major schools (not physical locations, rather they are systems) of Classical Feng Shui: San He and San Yuan. Hundreds of formulas, techniques, and systems are subsets of either school. If you practice Classical Feng Shui, you use the San He and the San Yuan systems as one extensive body of knowledge.

Fire Burning Heaven's Gate: The northwest location of your site is known as "heaven's gate." The 6 star also represents the heavens. When there is the real element of fire, such as a stove or kitchen, in the northwest sector of the house, it is said that fire is burning heaven's gate. This can also happened when the 9 star and the 6 star (of the Flying Star system) come together in *any* palace, but is considered seriously inauspicious when these stars are present in the northwest. Either the star combination (6, 9) or the presence of real fire in the northwest always brings bad luck to the father, the president, or the leader.

Fire mouth: The direction of the stove knobs, a concept that is important in the Eight Mansions system. It is sometimes mistakenly referred to as the oven mouth.

Five Ghosts Carry Treasure: Also referred to as Five Ghosts Carry Money. A secret formula for wealth from Taiwan and a favorite technique among Asian masters. It is powerful and uses mountains and water to support people to accumulate wealth.

Five Ghosts Carry Treasure II: An advanced form of the original formula using the sitting direction and water exits.

Flying Stars: Known as Xuan Kong Fei Xing in Chinese, meaning "mysterious void" or "the subtle mysteries of time and space." It is a popular Feng Shui system superior in addressing the time aspect of energy. Refer to chapter 5 for additional information on this vast system.

Forbidden City: This Beijing landmark served as the Chinese imperial palace for nearly five hundred years until 1912. It now houses the Palace Museum.

Fu Wei: The direction and location for stability as it applies to the Eight Mansions system. According to Master Yap's numeric representation, it is +60.

Fu Xi: A sage, king, and shaman who was responsible for discovering and arranging the Early Heaven Ba Gua.

Gateway: An opening, often a gap between mountains or buildings, where chi is concentrated and can be used to support certain wealth-producing techniques, such as Five Ghosts Carry Treasure formations.

Gen: One of the eight Trigrams of the Ba Gua, also spelled "ken." It represents the youngest son, the mountain, and early spring. In the Later Heaven arrangement of the Ba Gua, the Gen Trigram is located in the northeast.

Golden Star Classic: Translates as Kam Kwong Dou Lam King in Chinese, also spelled Jin Guang Dou Lin Jing. It is also known as the Big Dipper Casting Golden Light, the style of Eight Mansions used in this book.

Grand master of Feng Shui: Someone with this title has been practicing and teaching for many years, belongs to a respected lineage of masters, and has at least one master among his or her pupils.

Grave sites: A burial place for the dead. The first type of Feng Shui practiced in China was known as Yin Feng Shui, and it involved the selection of burial locations. This tradition is still active in Asian culture—the perfect arrangement for the deceased is big business. Living next to a cemetery will not bring good luck and is especially bad for money luck. One may also experience frequent visits from spirits.

Great Cycle: Lasts for 180 years; *see* Period Eight.

Green Dragon: A celestial animal that represents the left side of your property as you look out the front door.

Gua: Alternatively spelled "kua" and also known as a Trigram. It represents one of eight Guas of the Ba Gua, defined by a combination of three solid or broken lines.

Gua Number: Also referred to as Ming Gua (unrelated to the Ming Dynasty). To determine your personal Life Gua number, use your birthday. See chapter 4 for specific instructions.

Heaven Luck: One of the three categories of luck that humans can experience. The Chinese believe every human has a destiny and a fate determined by the heavens (*tien*). This category cannot be changed and is considered fixed. *See* Cosmic Trinity.

Heavenly Heart: The central palace of the Luo Shu (magic square of 15) and the center of the home or building.

Hexagrams: The eight Trigrams stacked one on top of another—creating sixty-four possible combinations. The hexagrams are the foundation of the I Ching.

High-rise building: In the external environment, high-rise buildings and skyscrapers function as virtual or urban mountains.

Ho: The Chinese word for fire.

Ho Hai: Also known as Wo Hai. Part of the Eight Mansions system and can bring mishaps—nothing goes smoothly. According to Master Yap's numeric representation, this is -60.

Houseboat: This type of dwelling is popular in certain parts of the country. Living on a boat creates instability—a foundation on water is precarious. Money and health will always be issues.

I Ching: A philosophical and divinatory book based on the sixty-four hexagrams of Taoist mysticism. It is also known as the *Classic of Changes* or *Book of Changes*.

I Ching Feng Shui: Also known as Xuan Kong Da Gua. A San Yuan system of Feng Shui that relies on the sixty-four hexagrams of the I Ching. Often referred to as the Big 64 Hexagrams, this method offers various techniques—the most popular is the auspicious date selection for important events.

Incoming dragon: The energy of a mountain that comes directly to your home or building. If a mountain range is nearby, the highest peak is measured with a Luo Pan because it has the most powerful energy. An entire science is based on determining the effects of mountain energy on any given site. In Feng Shui, mountains and dragons are referred to interchangeably.

Interior environment: The interior environment encompasses anything within the walls of a structure including kitchen, staircase, master bedroom, fireplaces, bathrooms, hallways, dining room, bedrooms, appliances, furniture, and so on.

Intercardinal directions: Northwest, southwest, northeast, and southeast.

Jade Belt: A road or driveway that wraps around a structure in a semi-circle; it brings incredibly good money luck.

Kan: One of the eight Trigrams. It represents the middle son, the moon and mid-winter. In the Later Heaven Arrangement of the Ba Gua, it is located in the north.

Kong Wang: Also known as Kun Mang, they are void lines or Death and Empty Line (DEL); they invite a host of negative events if doors are at these degrees. *See* DEL.

Kun: One of the eight Trigrams. It represents the mother, the earth and late summer. In the Later Heaven Ba Gua, it is located in the southwest.

Later Heaven Ba Gua: The second arrangement of the Trigrams known as the Wen Wang or Xien Tien Ba Gua. This is used extensively in the application of Classical Feng Shui.

Li: One of the eight Trigrams. It represents the middle daughter, fire and full summer. In the Later Heaven arrangement of the Ba Gua, it is located in the south.

Lineage: The line of transmission of sacred knowledge from a common ancestor who is deemed the founder.

Liu Sha: In the Eight Mansions system, it also known as the Six Killings direction and can bring backstabbing, affairs, and lawsuits. According to Master Yap's numeric representation, it is -80.

Location: A particular place or position, differing from the concept of direction. For example, your living room might be located on the south side of your home (location), but your desk faces north (direction).

Long chi: Energy that runs along an extended road or pathway.

Lunar calendar: A calendar based on the cycles of the moon.

Lung: The Chinese word for dragon.

Luo Pan: The Luo Pan is the quintessential tool of a Feng Shui practitioner. It is a compass that contains four to forty concentric rings of information. The most popular model is approximately ten inches across, square, and often constructed of fine woods. The circle part of the Luo Pan is made of brass and rotates to align with the compass itself, which is located in the center. There are three major types of Luo Pan—the San Yuan Luo Pan, the San He Luo Pan, and the Chung He Luo Pan (also known as Zong He or Zhung He), which is a combination of the first two. Though Luo Pan have similar basic components, Feng Shui Masters do customize their own with secret information for them and their students.

Luo Shu: A square that contains nine palaces or cells with a number in each; it adds to fifteen in any direction. The Luo Shu is also known as the Magic Square of 15.

Main door: This is usually the front door of the home or business. If the occupants always enter the residence from the garage, this may also be considered a main door.

Man luck: One of the three categories of luck that a human can experience. This area of fortune is mutable and defined by individual effort, such as hard work, study, education, experience, and good deeds. The Chinese word for man is *Ren*. *See* Cosmic Trinity.

Ming Dynasty: A ruling dynasty of China, which lasted from 1368 to 1644.

Mountains: Actual mountains, of course, as well as virtual mountains such as tall buildings, landscape mounds, retaining walls, huge boulders, or any object of mass in the environment. *See* Dragon.

Nien Yen: This is the incorrect form of the Yen Nien (+70) in the Eight Mansions system.

Pai: Chinese for school, faction, or group.

Pa Loo Hwang Chuen: The Chinese term for Eight Roads of Destruction.

Pa Sha Hwang Chuen: The Chinese translation of the Eight Killing Forces.

Parent String Formation: Known in Chinese as Fu Mu San Poon Gua and sometimes referred to as the Three Combinations, these are special wealth-producing Flying Star charts. This formation of energy applies to certain structures—which are activated by a mountain in the front of the property and water in the back—on intercardinal directions. They only last for twenty years and are unlucky if not activated properly.

Pearl String Formation: Known in Chinese as Lin Cu San Poon Gua and sometimes referred to as the Continuous Bead Formations, these are special wealth-producing Flying Star charts that only show up in homes that face an intercardinal direction. Though excellent energy for prosperity, this formation only lasts for twenty years and is unlucky if not activated properly.

Period: This is a twenty-year increment of time that affects the luck of humans and influences the world with its energy. These twenty-year periods were first tracked and recorded by the ancient Chinese in about 2500 BC. They observed that every 180 years the planets in our solar system line up. It was further noted that every twenty years the Milky Way shifts and influences the events of humankind. These periods run from one to nine every twenty years and then start all over again. Nine periods comprise a megacycle of 180 years.

Period 8: The current Age of Eight or Period Eight began February 4, 2004, and will end February 3, 2024. Tracking time through periods is part of the Flying Star system (Xuan Kong Fei Xing).

Praxis: An exercise or practice of an art, science, or skill.

Precious Jewel Line (PJL): Also known as Gold Dragons, these are specific degrees that brings precious assets and jewels, wealth luck, and nobility to your life. There are only forty-eight of these degrees out of 360.

Prosperous Sitting and Facing: Known in Chinese as Wang Shan Wang Shui. A Flying Star chart that means good for people, good for money. These charts have the perfect placement of the current prosperous stars—the facing star is at the facing (good for money), and the mountain star is at the sitting (good for people).

Red Phoenix: A celestial animal that represents the front edge of your property; also known as Vermilion Bird.

Retaining walls: High walls, at least three to six feet in height, which can be used to secure a site and prevent loss of energy. The more dynamic the landscape, the more walls are needed to protect sloping areas or sharp drop-offs.

Road: A route, path, or open way for vehicles. In Feng Shui, roads are *rivers* of energy, or chi, and play a huge part in analyzing a site because energy is powerful. These virtual, or urban, rivers are calculated when assessing, designing, enhancing, or implementing countermeasures or enhancements for a site.

Robbery Mountain Sha: Known in Chinese as Chor San Kibb Sart. It is a formation that takes away or robs energy from the site. See chapter 3 for more information.

San He: Also known as San Hup. One of the two major schools of study in Classical Feng Shui—the other is San Yuan. The San He system, excellent for tapping natural landforms, primarily addresses large-scale projects, land plots, urban developments, city planning, and master-planned communities. The system is extensive and has several practical techniques for new and existing residential spaces as well. When assessing and altering a site or a structure, San He and San Yuan can be blended for maximum results.

San Yuan: One of the two major schools of Classical Feng Shui. The Flying Stars is part of this system; it excels in techniques of timing.

Sector: An area inside or outside a building: south sector, north sector, and so on.

Sha chi: Also known as shar chi. Extremely negative energy, or killing chi.

Shan: The Chinese word for mountain.

Sheng Chi: Part of the Eight Mansions system. It can bring life-generating energy, wealth, and opportunities. Using Master Yap's numeric representation, this is +90.

Shui: The Chinese word for water; pronounced "shway."

Sitting: In Feng Shui this term refers to the back of the house, as if the structure is sitting in a chair on the land or property. It is the heavy part of the house, also considered a mountain.

Sitting Star: Also known as the Mountain Star in the Flying Star system. It influences people luck, such as fertility, employees, and health.

Sky Horse: A technique that speeds up the Feng Shui of a site. It uses roads or pathways as conduits of energy to activate this formula.

Solar calendar: A calendar based on the movements of the sun.

Southeast Asia: Countries south of China and east of India, including Thailand, Vietnam, Cambodia, Laos, Myanmar, the Philippines, and Singapore.

Squeezed chi: A phenomenon that happens when a building is extremely narrow and does not allow chi to flow or expand. It will deplete wealth and create debt.

Tai Chi: The black and white symbol of Taoist philosophy; a sphere with two semi-circles intertwined showing the division of yin and yang energy. An alternate spelling is taiji.

Tao: Also known as "the Way," and is the core of Taoism (pronounced with a "D" sound).

Tapping the energy or chi: A technique that invites the available energy from the external environment to support the occupants of a structure.

Three Harmony Doorways: A technique that uses door direction and a pathway or driveway to bring harmony and wealth to a house.

Three Killings: Also known as Sam Sart in Chinese. This negative energy visits a different direction annually. Digging into the earth can disturb this energy and can bring on calamity, which is why it's also referred to as calamity sha.

Tien Yi: Part of the Eight Mansion system. It can bring excellent health and wealth. In Chinese it means "heavenly doctor" or "the doctor from heaven watches over you." Using Master Yap's numeric representation, it is +80.

Tilting a door: A time-honored tradition used by Feng Shui Masters and practitioners to change the degree of a door and the energy of a space. The doorframe and threshold are re-angled toward the desired degree. When the door is re-hung, it is tilted on a different degree.

Time Star: Also known as the base star in the Flying Star system; it is the single star below the mountain and facing star of the chart.

Tipping point: The moment a product or idea spreads like wildfire. A phrase coined by Malcolm Gladwell in his book *The Tipping Point: How Little Things Can Make a Big Difference.*

T-juncture: When two roads meet perpendicularly to create a T. The formation is toxic when a home or business sits at the top and center of that T.

Traditional Feng Shui: Another term for classical Chinese Feng Shui.

Trigram: Another term used for Gua. A Trigram or Gua represents one of eight Guas of the Ba Gua, defined by a combination of three solid or broken lines.

Tui: Also spelled Dui. One of the eight Trigrams that represents the youngest daughter, the lake, and mid-fall. In the Later Heaven Ba Gua, it is located in the west.

Up the Mountain, Down the River: Also known as Shang Shan Xia Shui in Chinese. The prominent stars of the period are in reversed positions.

Virtual mountains: High-rise structures, such as apartments, office buildings, and skyscrapers, are considered virtual, or urban, mountains and will influence the energy of nearby structures accordingly.

Virtual water: Roads, sidewalks, driveways, low ground, highways, and other similar formations that are purveyors of chi.

Washes: In the external environment, these natural and man-made channels whisk away water from a site.

Water: In Feng Shui, water is the secret to enhancing wealth, prosperity, longevity, nobility, and relationships. The Chinese word is *shui*, and it represents energy and life force. Water, according to Feng Shui, is the most powerful element on the planet.

Water Dragons: Also known as billionaire's Feng Shui. These formulas create extreme wealth with specific water flows and exits. It is a highly specialized area of Feng Shui for which Grand Master Yap Cheng Hai is famous.

Water exits: The location or direction where water leaves a site. Water exits are used in Feng Shui to bring good results, but if they are not placed well, disaster can ensue.

Waterfalls: Used to enhance wealth luck; the direction of the waterfall is important.

Water Star: Also called the Facing Star in the Flying Star system; it is in charge of wealth luck.

Western Feng Shui: In addition to the Black Hat Sect, other schools cropped up that incorporated the principles, but not the rituals, associated with Lin Yun's followers. As the masters of Classical Feng Shui started to teach around the world, some of the most well-acclaimed instructors and authors of Western Feng Shui began to learn Classical Feng Shui. Unwilling to give up the Western-style Feng Shui that made them famous, they mixed the old with the new, thereby adding to the confusion over authentic Feng Shui. More than half of the Feng Shui books written about the subject include a hodgepodge of both theories.

West Life Group: In the Eight Mansions system, people are divided into the East or West group. The 2, 6, 7, and 8 Life Guas are part of the West Life Group.

White Tiger: The celestial animal that represents the right-hand side of your property as you look out your front door.

Wu Gwei: Part of the Eight Mansions system that can attract lawsuits, bad romance, and betrayals. Using Master Yap's numeric representation, it is -70. This is also known as the Five Ghosts direction.

Wu Xing: Also known as the five elements of Feng Shui: wood, fire, earth, metal, and water.

Xing Fa: Form and shape techniques in Feng Shui.

Xun: One of the eight Trigrams of the Ba Gua, also spelled as Sun. It represents the eldest daughter, the wind and early summer. In the Later Heaven arrangement of the Ba Gua, the Xun Trigram is located in the southeast.

Yang: Alive, active, and moving energy; considered the male energy of the yin-yang symbol.

Yang Feng Shui: Feng Shui was first practiced for the selection of a perfect grave site, or what is commonly known by the Chinese as Yin Feng Shui—Feng Shui for the dead. Later, techniques were developed to increase luck and opportunities for houses of the living.

Yellow Spring: A term used by the Chinese to describe hell or the underworld.

Yen Nien: Part of the Eight Mansions system that can bring longevity, good relationships, and love. Using Master Yap's numeric representation, it is +70. It is a common mistake to spell this term as Nen Yien.

Yin: Female energy, passive, and dead; the perfect complement is yang energy.

Zen: A school of Mahayana Buddhism that originated in Japan. It involves the practice of harmony and peace. For homes or buildings, a Zen design includes clean lines and austere spaces. The overall design is calming to the mind.

Bibliography

Alexander, Christopher, Sara Ishikawa, Murray Silverstein, Max Jacobson, Ingrid Fiksdahl-King, and Shlomo Angel. *A Pattern Language: Towns, Buildings, Construction.* New York: Oxford University Press, 1977.

Alexander, Christopher. *The Timeless Way of Building.* New York: Oxford University Press, 1979.

BBC News. "The People's Republic at 50: Special Report." October 6, 1999. http://news.bbc.co.uk/2/hi/special_report/1999/09/99/china_50_years_of_communism/456465.stm.

———. "Regions and territories: Macau." January, 23, 2008. http://news.bbc.co.uk/2/hi/asia-pacific/country_profiles/4080105.stm.

Biktashev, Val, Elizabeth Moran, and Joseph Yu. *The Complete Idiot's Guide to Feng Shui.* Indianapolis, IN: Alpha Books, 2002.

Byrne, Rhonda. *The Secret*. Hillsboro, OR: Beyond Words Publishing, 2006.

Dunn, Ashley. "Ancient Chinese Craft Shifts Building Designs in the U. S." *New York Times*, September 22, 1994. http://query.nytimes.com/gst/fullpage.html res=9906EED7163AF931A1575AC0A962958260.

Emoto, Masaru. *The Hidden Message in Water*. Hillsboro, OR: Beyond Words Publishing, 2004.

——. *The True Power of Water*. Hillsboro, OR: Beyond Words Publishing, 2005.

Gladwell, Malcolm. *The Tipping Point: How Little Things Can Make a Big Difference*. New York: Little, Brown and Company, 2000. Boston: First Back Bay, 2002.

Hall, Edward T. *The Hidden Dimension*. Garden City, NY: Doubleday, 1966.

Hall, Edward T., and Mildred Reed Hall. *The Fourth Dimension in Architecture: The Impact of Building on Behavior*. Santa Fe, NM: Sunstone Press, 1995.

Hicks, Esther, and Jerry Hicks. *Ask and It Is Given: Learning to Manifest Your Desires*. Carlsbad, CA: Hay House Inc., 2004.

Holson, Laura. "Disney Bows to Feng Shui." *International Herald Tribune*, April 25, 2005. http://www.iht.com/articles/2005/04/24/business/disney.php.

Huang, Alfred. *The Numerology of the I Ching: A Sourcebook of Symbols, Structures, and Traditional Wisdom*. Rochester, VT: Inner Traditions, 2000.

Jun, Cheng Jian, and Adriana Fernandes-Gonçalves. *Chinese Feng Shui Compass: Step by Step Guide*. Shenzhen, China: Donnelly Bright Sun Printing, 1998.

Kiyosaki, Robert T., and Donald. J. Trump. *Why We Want You to Be Rich: Two Men, One Message.* New York: Rich Publishing, 2006.

Los Angeles Times. "Las Vegas Sands IPO Raises $690 Million." December 15, 2004. http://articles.latimes.com/2004/dec/15 /business/fi-wrap15.

Major, John S., Sarah A. Queen, Andrew Seth Meyer, and Harold D. Roth, translators. *The Huainanzi: A Guide to the Theory and Practice of Government in Early Han China, by Liu An, King of Huainan.* New York: Columbia University Press, 2010.

McDowell, Edwin. "Threat of Crime Rises on the Main Highways." *New York Times*, October 28, 1992.

Mercado, Jonathan. "Getting Ready for More Prosperity in 2007." *Manila Standard Today*, December 12, 2006. http://www.manila standardtoday.com/?page=goodLife1_dec12_2006.

Miller, Brian. "Buddhist Wynn Gets Primeval, Big Ideas." GlobeSt .com, May 23, 2006. http://www.globest.com.

Moore, Martha. "City, Suburban Designs Could Be Bad for Your Health." *USA Today*, April 22, 2003. http://www.usatoday.com /news/health/2003-04-22-walk-cover_x.htm.

Rawe, Julie. "Exporting the Fun." *Time*, July 25, 2004. http://www.time .com/time/magazine/article/0,9171,901040802-672582,00.html.

Ray, Paul H., and Sherry Ruth Anderson. *The Cultural Creative: How 50 Million People Are Changing the World.* New York: Three Rivers Press, 2000.

Reuters. "Officials Embrace Feng Shui Amid Job Worries." May 17, 2007. http://www.reuters.com/article/oddlyEnoughNews /idUSPEK30417020070517.

———. "Macau Gambling Growth Outstrips Vegas." February 12, 2008. http://www.reuters.com/article/summitNews /idUSN1226487020080212.

Rifkin, Jeremy. *The Hydrogen Economy—The Creation of the Worldwide Energy Web and the Redistribution of Power on Earth*. New York: Jeremy P. Tarcher/Penguin Press, 2002.

Seattle Times news service. "Beijing Airport Sets Olympian Tone." March 1, 2008. http://seattletimes.nwsource.com/html/ nationworld/2004253007_airport01.html?syndication=rss.

Skinner, Stephen. *Guide to the Feng Shui Compass*. St. Paul, MN: Llewellyn Worldwide, 2008.

———. *K.I.S.S. Guide to Feng Shui*. New York: DK Publishing, Inc., 2001.

Spencer, Richard. "Beijing Abandons Mao's Dream of Workers' Paradise." *Telegraph*, July 18, 2008. http://www.telegraph.co.uk/earth/ earthnews/3347499/Beijing-abandons-Maos-dream-of-workers -paradise.html.

Stein, Joel. "Wynn's Big Bet." *Time*, June 20, 2005. http://www.time .com/ time/magazine/article/0,9171,1056262,00.html.

Todd, Aaron. "Understanding Cultural Differences." *Canadian Gaming Business*, January 2007.

Too, Lillian, and Yap Cheng Hai. *Applied Pa-Kua and Lo Shu Feng Shui*. Adelaide, South Australia: Oriental Publications, 1993.

———. *Water Feng Shui for Wealth: An Advanced Manual on Water Feng Shui Based on the Water Dragon Classic*. Kuala Lumpur, Malaysia: Konsep Books, 1996.

Wai-yin Kwok, Vivian. "Ho's Macau Gambling Empire Goes Public." *Forbes*, January 9, 2008. http://www.forbes.com/2008/01/09/ sociedade-jogos-macau-markets-equity-cx_vk_0109markets02.html.

Watson, Lyall. *The Nature of Things: The Secret Life of Inanimate Objects*. London: Hodder & Stoughton, 1990.

Weiss, Lois. "Ground Broken for Trump International Hotel & Tower." *Real Estate Weekly*, June 28, 1995. http://www.rew-online.com/.

Wong, Eva. *Feng Shui: The Ancient Wisdom of Harmonious Living for Modern Times*. Boston: Shambala Publications, Inc., 1996.

Yellow Emperor Huangdi. *The Twelve Principles of Yin and Yang*. Translated by Hua Ching Ni as *The Tao: The Subtle Universal Law and Integral Way of Life*. Los Angeles, CA: Seven Star Communications, 1998.

Worldwide Classical Feng Shui Schools and Consultants

The following is a list of Classical Feng Shui teachers around the world who, in addition to Feng Shui training, also offer consulting services, books, and other products. Prices vary for consultations depending on the scope, with large commercial projects commanding the highest fees; Masters often take a small percentage of the estimated construction cost for hotels, casinos, office buildings, spas, master-planned communities, and shopping centers. Most residential spaces are priced by the size of the home or by the hour. Generally, a Feng Shui consultation is approximately two to three hours and will cost $300 to $900 (USD). Penthouses and estate homes can be considerably higher. Most non-Asian masters will generate a written/electronic report as well; this is not the custom in Southeast Asia. Consultations are always best if done on-site, however many practitioners offer long-distance Feng Shui consulting for homes.

There are a number of excellent Feng Shui Masters around the world that offer classes on one or more of the Five Chinese Metaphysical Arts. You can receive training on Classical Feng Shui (San He and San Yuan), Face Reading (Mian Xiang), Chinese astrology (Ba Zi, also known as Four Pillars of Destiny and Zi Wei Dou Shu), and Traditional Chinese Medicine (acupuncture, herbology).

Matriculating from a respected lineage is desirable, but this alone should not determine the master you choose to study with. Select one with whom you resonate. I do not personally know every teacher/consultant I have listed, and you will need to do your own due diligence in selecting a qualified professional teacher or consultant. The list is by no means exhaustive, and I have not listed anyone who mixes Classical Feng Shui with Western. Needless to say, I have not listed anyone practicing Western styles or Tibetan Black Hat Tantric Feng Shui (TBHT) at all.

The American College of Classical Feng Shui (ACCFS) Dragon-Gate Feng Shui, LLC

Denise Liotta Dennis, Feng Shui Master

Offers consulting services (residential and commercial) books, and training classes with thirty-six different modules that constitute the Foundation series, the Professional series, and the Mastery series. Also accepts one-on-one mentored students upon approval. ACCFS offers live classes and online classes every month.

Scottsdale, Arizona and Houston, Texas USA
Phone: 480-241-5211
Phone: 480-664-9885
Email: denise@dragongatefengshui.net
Web: www.dragongatefengshui.com

Yap Cheng Hai Academy Sdn. Bhd.

Grand Master Yap Cheng Hai

Offers books, software, consulting and training on Classical Feng Shui, primarily in Kuala Lumpur

Suite 11-01, 11th Floor

Wisma Hangsam

1 Jalan Hang Lekir

50000 Kuala Lumpur, Malaysia

Phone: +(603) 2070 8009

Email: info@ychacademy.com

Web: www.ychacademy.com

Lillian Too's World of Feng Shui

Lillian Too, Feng Shui Master

Offers books, magazines, products, and live classes on Classical Feng Shui in Kuala Lumpur

Kuala Lumpur, Malaysia

Phone: +(603) 2080 3488

Email: courses@wofs.com

Web: www.lillian-too.com

Feng Shui Research Center

Grand Master Joseph Yu

Offers books, live classes worldwide, and correspondence courses on Chinese astrology and Classical Feng Shui

26 Betty Roman Blvd.

Markham, Ontario L6C 0A4

Canada

Phone: 905-604-0998

Phone: 416-721-7094

Email: josephyu@astro-fengshui.com

Web: www.astro-fengshui.com

The America Feng Shui Institute
Grand Master Larry Sang
Offers books, live classes in California, and online courses on Classical Feng Shui, Chinese astrology, and face reading
111 N. Atlantic Blvd., Ste. 352
Monterey Park, CA 91754
Phone: 626-571-2757
Email: fsinfo@amfengshui.com
Web: www.amfengshui.com

Mastery Academy of Chinese Metaphysics Sdn. Bhd.
Joey Yap, Feng Shui Master
Offers books, videos, live classes worldwide, and online training on Classical Feng Shui, Chinese astrology, and face reading
19-3, The Boulevard, Mid Valley City
59200 Kuala Lumpur, Malaysia
Phone: +603 2284 8080
Email: enquiry@masteryacademy.com
Web: www.masteryacademy.com

Raymond Lo Feng Shui Research
Grand Master Raymond Lo
Offers books and live classes worldwide on Classical Feng Shui and Chinese astrology
Rm. 1233A, Star House
Tsimshatsui, Kowloon, Hong Kong
Phone: +852 2736 9568
Phone: +852 9024 9438
Email: raymond@fengshui-lo.com
Website: www.raymond-lo.com

Feng Shui Dragon Enterprises
Master Gayle Atherton
Offers consulting services, Chinese astrology, books,
free mini–seminars on her website, and a Feng Shui kit
P. O. Box 886
Double Bay, NSW 1360
2028, Australia
Phone: +61 02 9362 8089
Email: inquiries@fengshui.com
Web: www.fengshui.com.au

The Imperial School of
Feng Shui and Chinese Horoscopes
Grand Master Chan Kun Wah
Offers correspondence and live training worldwide on
Classical Feng Shui and Chinese astrology
59 Pettycur Road
Kinghorn, Fife, KY3 9RN, Scotland
Phone: +44 (0) 159 289 1682
Email: pam@masterkwchan.com
Web: www.masterkwchan.com

Naturally Connected Feng Shui
Jennifer Bartle-Smith, Feng Shui Master
Offers live training courses on Classical Feng Shui,
in addition to consulting services, primarily in Australia
6-8 Riley Street, Rosebud 3939
Victoria, Australia
Phone: +61 3 402 321 505
Email: jennifer@naturallyconnected.com.au
Web: www.naturallyconnected.com.au

The International School of Feng Shui

Master Ken Lai

*Offers live training courses worldwide on
Classical Feng Shui and Chinese astrology*

P. O. Box 2124
Maple Grove, MN 55311
Phone: 763-218-1484
Email: kenlai93@yahoo
Web: www.kenlaifengshui.com

Healing Qi

David Twicken, Feng Shui Master

*Offers books, e-books, correspondence, and live courses internationally
on Classical Feng Shui, Qi Gong, traditional Chinese medicine,
and Chinese astrology*

Email: david@healingqi.com
Web: www.healingqi.com

Singapore Feng Shui Centre

Master Vincent Koh

*Offers books, software, and live training courses on
Feng Shui and Chinese astrology*

10 Ubi Crescent #04-66 Ubi Techpark
Singapore 408564
Phone: +65 6747 8226
Email: singfc@fengshui.com.sg
Web: www.fengshui.com.sg

Pak Hok Ming Metaphysic Institute
Master Pak Hok Ming
Offers books, products, and courses on Feng Shui and Chinese astrology
8/F, Bangkok Bangkok Bank Building,
490-492 Nathan Road, Kowloon, Hong Kong
Phone: +852 2388 6878
Email: fengshui@hongkong.com
Web: www.hokming.com

Feng Shui College
Howard Choy, AIA, Feng Shui Master
Offers books and training course internationally on Classical Feng Shui
Sydney, Australia
Phone: +49 30 2838 5855
Email: info@fengshuicollege.ac
Website: www.arqitektur.com

The School of Chinese Metaphysics (SCM)
Master Peter Leung
SCM offers books, software, live training courses on Classical Feng Shui
102 Allanford Road
Toronto, ON M1T 2N5
Phone: +416 288-9238
Email: info@fengshuisos.com
Website: www.fengshuisos.com

Central Academy Of Feng Shui (CAFS)
Master Francis Leyau
*CAFS offers books, products, and live training courses
on Feng Shui and Chinese astrology*
169-1, Jalan Sarjana, Taman Connaught, Cheras, 56000
Kuala Lumpur, Malaysia
Phone: +60 3-91320199
Email: enquiry@fengshuimastery.com
Web: www.fengshuimastery.com

Thomas Coxon Associates
Thomas Coxon, Feng Shui Master
20 Lutterworth Road, Aylestone
Leicester, England LE2 8PE
Phone: +44 116 2836777
Email: fengshui@webleicester.co.uk
Website: www.fengshui-consultants.co.uk

Feng Shui 100
Master Mas Kehardthum
*Offers live Feng Shui training classes in Thailand,
correspondence courses, books, and software*
31st Floor of the State Tower, Silom Road
Bangkok, Thailand
Phone: +668-1431-4011
Email: info@fengshui100.com
Website: www.fengshui100.com

Feng Shui That Works
Alan Stirling, Feng Shui Master
Offers live and correspondence courses on Feng Shui,
9 Star Ki (Japanese astrology), dowsing, and Chinese astrology
16 Ash Road, ME2 2JL UK
Phone: +44 (0)203 0114938
Email: alan888@btinternet.com
Web: www.fengshuithatworks.co.uk

Master Shyan Tseng (June Lao Shi) also known as Master JN or Master June Nickoff
Offers public training courses and accepts indoor students
upon approval, active in Taiwan.

These Feng Shui masters also offer consulting services:
Katherine Gould, Arizona; Jennifer Bonetto, California (*both affiliated with ACCFS*); Maria Santilario, Spain; Bridgette O'Sullivan, Ireland; Cynthia Murray, Colorado; Jayne Goodrick; England; Di Grobler and Christine McNair, South Africa; Angle de Para, Florida; Scheherazade "Sherry" Merchant, India; Nathalie Mourier and Helen Weber, France; and Birgit Fischer, Petra Coll-Exposito, Nicole Zoremba, and Eva-Maria Spöetta, Germany.

Feng Shui masters who teach through books but may also consult with clients:
Eva Wong
(*As of this writing, Master Wong has entered the spiritual life as a Taoist nun*)
www.shambhala.com/fengshui

Stephen Skinner
www.sskinner.com

Master Val Biktashev and Elizabeth Moran
www.aafengshui.com

Index

Guide to the Feng Shui Compass

A Compendium of Classical Feng Shui

Stephen Skinner

Guide to the Feng Shui Compass
A Compendium of Classical Feng Shui
STEPHEN SKINNER

With the lo p'an, the art of feng shui becomes a true science. The result of over thirty years of research and practice, *The Guide to the Feng Shui Compass* is the first book in English to explain what the lo p'an is, how it works, and how to read and use it for luck, happiness, and an improved life. It includes a history of feng shui and a detailed description of the seventy-five rings of the lo p'an. Featuring clear explanations and instructions, this groundbreaking guide will turn anyone into an expert with any lo p'an, ancient or modern.

978-0-7387-2349-5, 448 pp., 7 x 10 $65.00

101 Feng Shui Tips for Your Home
Richard Webster

For thousand of years, people in the Far East have used feng shui to improve their home and family lives and live in harmony with the earth. Certainly, people who practice feng shui achieve a deep contentment that is denied most others. They usually do well romantically and financially. Architects around the world are beginning to incorporate the concepts of feng shui into their designs. Even people like Donald Trump freely admit to using feng shui.

Now you can make subtle and inexpensive changes to your home that can literally transform your life. If you're in the market for a house, learn what to look for in room design, single level vs. split level, staircases, front door location, and more. If you want to improve upon your existing home, find out how its current design may be creating negative energy, and discover simple ways to remedy the situation without the cost of major renovations or remodeling.

978-1-56718-809-7, 192 pp., 5¼ x 8 $11.95

Cosmic Energy
How to Harness the Invisible Power
Around You to Transform Your Life
ANNE JIRSCH

Some people seem to lead a charmed life—they get what they want, they're in the right place at the right time, and even when they experience setbacks, they land on their feet. They're not just lucky—they're attuned to their cosmic energy.

Renowned psychic Anne Jirsch teaches readers how to connect with the flow of the universe to dramatically improve their lives. Using current studies, client examples, and personal stories, she explains a variety of highly effective techniques, from visualization and manifesting to working with etheric energy and thought field therapy.

Once the reader understands the basics of cosmic energy, Jirsch reveals how they can use the knowledge to improve their relationships, health, career, and finances.

978-0-7387-2125-5, 264 pp., 6 x 9   **$16.95**

Blissology
The Art & Science of Happiness
ANDY BAGGOTT

Become the master of your own life and destiny with a simple four-step process that combines powerful law-of-attraction techniques, cutting-edge science, and the wisdom of some of the world's oldest spiritual traditions. According to author Andy Baggott, we have more control over our life and our feelings than we realize. In *Blissology*, he shows how to reclaim this control and, in doing so, reclaim your power to create the life of your dreams.

This is a real, hands-on approach—you don't need to take great leaps of faith or radically change your beliefs in order to achieve a better life. Simply by using the tools and techniques within these pages, you can immediately begin to understand, practice, live, and share happiness, creating a life that is truly fulfilling and successful.

978-0-7387-2004-3, 216 pp., 5 x 7   **$14.95**

Feng Shui for Beginners
Successful Living by Design
Richard Webster

Not advancing fast enough in your career? Maybe your desk is located in a "negative position." Wish you had a more peaceful family life? Hang a mirror in your dining room and watch what happens. Is money flowing out of your life rather than into it? You may want to look to the construction of your staircase!

For thousands of years, the ancient art of feng shui has helped people harness universal forces and lead lives rich in good health, wealth, and happiness. The basic techniques in *Feng Shui for Beginners* are very simple, and you can put them into place immediately in your home and work environments. Gain peace of mind, a quiet confidence, and turn adversity to your advantage with feng shui remedies.

978-1-56718-803-5, 224 pp., 5¼ x 8   **$13.95**